MW00852646

Commercial Society

Economy, Polity, and Society

Series Editors:

Virgil H. Storr, Research Associate Professor of Economics and Senior Fellow, F. A. Hayek Program for Advanced Study in Philosophy, Politics and Economics, George Mason University

Jayme S. Lemke, Senior Research Fellow, Mercatus Center, George Mason University

The foundations of political economy—from Adam Smith to the Austrian school of economics, to contemporary research in public choice and institutional analysis—are sturdy and well established, but far from calcified. On the contrary, the boundaries of the research built on this foundation are ever expanding. One approach to political economy that has gained considerable traction in recent years combines the insights and methods of three distinct, but related, subfields within economics and political science: the Austrian, Virginia, and Bloomington schools of political economy. The vision of this book series is to capitalize on the intellectual gains from the interactions between these approaches in order to both feed the growing interest in this approach and advance social scientists' understanding of economy, polity, and society. This series seeks to publish works that combine the Austrian school's insights on knowledge, the Virginia school's insights into incentives in non-market contexts, and the Bloomington school's multiple methods, real-world approach to institutional design as a powerful tool for understanding social behavior in a diversity of contexts.

Titles in the Series:

Interdisciplinary Studies of the Market Order: New Applications of Market Process Theory
Edited by Peter J. Boettke, Christopher J. Coyne, and Virgil Henry Storr

Knowledge and Incentives in Policy: Using Public Choice and Market Process Theory to Analyze Public Policy Issues
Edited by Stefanie Haeffele

Exploring the Political Economy and Social Philosophy of James M. Buchanan
Edited by Paul Dragos Aligica, Christopher J. Coyne, and Stefanie Haeffele

Exploring the Political Economy and Social Philosophy of F.A. Hayek
Edited by Peter J. Boettke, Jayme S. Lemke, and Virgil Henry Storr

Commercial Society

A Primer on Ethics
and Economics

Cathleen Johnson, Robert Lusch,
and David Schmidtz

ROWMAN & LITTLEFIELD
INTERNATIONAL

London • New York

Published by Rowman & Littlefield International Ltd
6 Tinworth Street, London, SE11 5AL
www.rowmaninternational.com

Rowman & Littlefield International Ltd. is an affiliate of Rowman & Littlefield
4501 Forbes Boulevard, Suite 200, Lanham, Maryland 20706, USA
With additional offices in Boulder, New York, Toronto (Canada), and Plymouth (UK)
www.rowman.com

Selection and editorial matter © 2020, Cathleen Johnson
and David Schmidtz

Copyright in individual chapters is held by the respective chapter authors.

All rights reserved. No part of this book may be reproduced in any form or by any
electronic or mechanical means, including information storage and retrieval systems,
without written permission from the publisher, except by a reviewer who may quote
passages in a review.

British Library Cataloguing in Publication Data
A catalogue record for this book is available from the British Library

ISBN: HB 978-1-78661-355-4
           PB 978-1-78661-356-1

Library of Congress Cataloging-in-Publication Data

978-1-78661-355-4 (cloth)
978-1-78661-356-1 (paperback)
978-1-78661-357-8 (electronic)

∞™ The paper used in this publication meets the minimum requirements of
American National Standard for Information Sciences—Permanence of Paper
for Printed Library Materials, ANSI/NISO Z39.48–1992.

Contents

Acknowledgments

In 2014, Bob Lusch began sitting in on Dave Schmidtz's graduate course on ethical entrepreneurship. A few weeks, later, Bob and Virginia Lusch invited Schmidtz and Cate Johnson to spend a weekend with them at their ranch south of Tucson. It was there, among the four of us, that the idea of a course and eventually a book on this topic was hatched. In 2015, Bob, Cate, and Dave taught the course at Arizona State University to a group of sixteen high school teachers from South Sudan and Rwanda. We thank Ed Eisele for the financial, logistical, and intellectual support that made that course possible.

The three of us then ran a workshop in Tucson in the summer of 2015 to a group of fourteen high school teachers from school districts around the state of Arizona. The workshop was supported by a grant from the John Templeton Foundation. Of course, the opinions expressed here are those of the respective authors and do not necessarily reflect the views of the Templeton Foundation. We are grateful also for support for this project from the Social Philosophy & Policy Foundation, the Bradley Foundation, the Thomas W. Smith Foundation, and the Sarah Scaife Foundation.

Johnson and Schmidtz were part of a reading group of PPE majors at King's College London. We thank the members of that reading group for their insight and enthusiasm: Alexandra Bacon, Zane Chee Yong Wei, Daphne Friedrich, Roberto Fumagalli, Sukirti Lohani, Piet Ruig, and Merlin Wehrs.

We have many colleagues to thank for encouragement and input (with apologies to those whose names we neglect to mention): Richard Abbott, David Ahumada, Robert Armstrong, Lisa Bender, Cynthia Berens, Peter Boettke, Monty Brown, Rick Bryson, Frank Byers, Mariano Chavez, Nicole Cochran, Sarah Corker, Carolyn and Garland Cox, Dan Dhaliwahl, Courtney Dunn, Susan Elliott, Tahia Farooque, Tawni Ferrarini, Hannah Fournier,

Shauna Garland, Esteban Gonzalez, Daniel Green, Ingrid Gregg, Ted Guillory, Steve Haessler, Jonathan Haidt, Josh Hall, James Harrigan, Scott Harris, William Hasselberger III, Carmen Ortiz Henley, Mandi Hering, Roberta Herzberg, Angeles Herrara, Charles Holt, Carrie Houston, Richard Hutchison, Peter Lipsey, Max Irving, and Mario Juarez, Ken and Randy Kendrick, Sandra Kimball, Tiffany Kiramidjian, Heidi Kirkland, Travis Klein, Sheila Martinez, Jim McDowell, Fred Miller, Dave Montano, Brian Moreno, John and Kathy Morton, Rodrigo Mungula, Clint Nelson, Jim Otteson, Robin Palmer, Jeff Paul, Patrick Peatrowsky, Scott Piper, Vann Prime, Amy Proulx, Tauhidur Rahman, Matt Rahr, Stacia Reeves, Charles Rosett, Dan Shahar, Tamara Sharp, Mark Shug, Candace Smith, Thomas W. Smith, Doreen Sorce, Virgil Storr, Shawn Tierney, John Tomasi, Toby Torrey, Amy Tucker, Doug den Uyl, Steve Vargo, Alberto Vidana, Trevor Wagner, Lawrence White, James Whiting, and Ken Zarda. Long though this list may be, we have nonetheless limited it to people whose influence has been pivotal. We and this text are profoundly in their debt.

But to single out two people in particular, Patrick Harless has authored a teacher's companion to this book that is a revelation of gentle, thorough clarity. And Kerry Montano has been our program director almost since the program's inception, bringing together a succession of scholars like Patrick, and inspiring us all with her wisdom, experience, and determination. She is the glue that kept us together.

Vernon Smith was a supervisor of Schmidtz's Master's Degree in Economics and also hired Schmidtz as a Research Assistant in the Economic Science Laboratory during the heady period when it was becoming clear that Smith's work in that field would someday earn him a Nobel Prize. Vernon also supervised Cate Johnson's post-doctoral fellowship in experimental economics, which helped to launch her career in that field. It was Vernon and Candace Smith who introduced Johnson to Schmidtz in 2006, and for which our gratitude will be eternal.

Finally, we want to acknowledge the passing of one of our dearest friends, a driving force behind this venture, and one of the finest and most-acclaimed scholars ever to emerge from the field of Marketing, namely our co-author Robert Lusch. We will never forget the magic that he brought to our classroom and to our lives.

Cathleen Johnson and David Schmidtz, 2019

Chapter 1

Ethics, Economy, and Entrepreneurship

It takes skill to drive a car or to be a quarterback. It likewise takes skill to be a successful, responsible citizen and to assemble the ingredients of a great life. Skills cannot simply be handed to you. In science fiction, characters can download programs that make them instantly and effortlessly able to play a piano, fly a helicopter, or speak Russian, but in real life, developing a skill takes work.

The human condition is that we each arrive as newborn babies to a world that does not need us (at least not yet). One of the most joyful challenges of adult life is to develop skills that make the people around you better off with you than without you. It is within your power to show up at the marketplace with something to offer that will make others glad to know you.

There is almost nothing you do in a day that doesn't give you a reason to be grateful to millions of people you will never meet. Imagine waking up tomorrow morning and deciding that you want to do something entirely by yourself, without help from anyone, something simple like making a pizza. What would that mean? You would probably begin by making the dough. How would you do that? You might think you should go to the supermarket to buy some flour, but you want to make this pizza by yourself, so you want to grow the grain and mill the flour on your own. How do you do that? You may think about buying a plough, but to really make the pizza from scratch, you decide that you need to make your own plough, too. And of course, if the plough is going to be made of metal, you don't want any help digging up the ore (with your bare hands, because you would also need metal to make a shovel) and building a smelter.

So you give up on making a pizza without help. But there is, of course, another way to get pizza. You can work for wages for an hour. Then you use your wages to reward thousands of strangers around the world for doing thousands of jobs that culminate in the delivery of a pizza that no one who ever lived could have made alone.

This book is about that world, the world to which you want to contribute when you leave school. You did not invent that world. Realistically, neither did anyone else. A lot of it just happened. It didn't happen according to anyone's plan. The question for you is, what next?

How will you handle the opportunity to live a life? We can't answer that question. That's up to you. But we can say that you will need some luck. You will find that you need courage, too: courage to believe in yourself at crunch time, and before that, courage to put in years of hard work to develop skills that will give you good reason to believe in yourself at crunch time.

We like your chances.

WHAT IS TRADE?

Homo sapiens became the wisest of primates perhaps forty thousand years ago when we learned to make deals with strangers.[1] Many of the steps in our evolution as social animals involved expanding our potential for mutually advantageous cooperation. Inventing ways to be of service to each other, and even to distant strangers, is our distinctively human survival mechanism. That's humanity's superpower: not wings, fins, or fangs but our ability to cooperate even with strangers. The superpower is an astounding thing. With it, you can make a pizza in an hour that you otherwise would not be able to make in ten thousand years.

Human beings have many striking characteristics. We have opposable thumbs, which make us better at building tools. We also have vocal chords that make us able to make a range of sounds that enable us to communicate subtle ideas. (We can offer to pay a partner back next Tuesday for services rendered now—an incredibly complex idea when you think about it.) We have the intelligence to pick up ideas from people older and wiser than us. We also have the intelligence to notice when someone in our group has a new idea. Moreover, when we travel, we observe other groups solving problems in different ways. To see how other people do things is to see new, sometimes better, ways of doing things. This simple idea that a better

---

1. Anthropologists currently date the emergence of the earliest recognizably modern human species, "Cro-Magnon Man," to around this time. Sculpture, engraving, painting, and music are likewise thought to have emerged around forty thousand years ago, along with tools and ornaments that imply that there were trading networks extending beyond the immediate area. However, this is a rapidly developing field of inquiry, so many aspects of our current understanding are likely to change as we unearth new information. Check our online resources for references to the most recent scholarship.

idea might be just around the corner may have been the most inspiring idea of all. If human beings had been hermits rather than social animals, none of these special characteristics would be all that special. Our distinctive features are far more valuable by virtue of our being social animals, willing and able to cooperate.

Adam Smith noticed that our ability to communicate is a precondition for voluntary exchange. As human society grew, cooperation became a matter of working with strangers. The capacity and the need for gossip evolved together, and led to people inventing the possibility of developing a reputation. Human beings need to send and receive information about whether particular partners play fair.

As the possibility of reputation evolved, so did the possibility of extended trading networks. Twentieth-century philosopher John Rawls described society as a cooperative venture for mutual benefit. Of course, this is not a simple description. Rawls was inviting us to think about society at its best: People at their best cooperate for mutual benefit. They are happy to be of service to each other. Indeed, in society at its best, people are so eager to be of service to each other that they literally *compete* to be of service.

ARE THERE GAINS FROM TRADE?

We have various ways of getting what we want, which we can divide into two categories. First, we can get what we want in ways that make others worse off—by stealing, for example. Second, we can get what we want in ways that make others better off. For example, we can trade. In other words, we can bring services to market that other people want, and offer those services at a price they can afford. In that way, we aim to make our customers better off, and to be better off ourselves as a result. We can aspire to be part of a community that is a cooperative venture for mutual benefit.

Market society is sometimes described as a tide that lifts all boats. The metaphor is a nice reminder that the standard path to prosperity in market society is to produce what other people value. People get rich when they market the light bulb, telephone, or computer not because such inventions make customers worse off, but because such inventions make customers better off.

You will hear people say, "The rich get richer, and the poor get poorer." To believe this is to believe that if we aim to get richer, the trick is to find a way to make our neighbors poorer. But "the rich get richer, and the poor get poorer" is a cliché. Is there any reason to believe it? Where is the evidence? (A bit of advice: a **criminal** is someone who loses sight of the difference between stealing and trading. Watch out for people who talk as if they don't see any difference.)

A constructive attitude here would be to treat the cliché as a testable hypothesis. There are places where it appears to be true, but in many places it clearly is false. What would it be like to have evidence that the cliché is false in a particular time and place? Max Roser, an Oxford University economist and founder of *Our World in Data*, wrote an essay entitled "The short history of global living conditions and why it matters that we know it." Roser concluded that on virtually every dimension of material well-being—poverty, literacy, health, freedom, and education—the world in general is a vastly better place than it was just a couple of centuries ago.[2]

In places where everyone's life expectancy is rising, everyone is getting richer along the most important dimension of measurable welfare there is. (Why focus on life expectancy? Because it connects to almost everything that matters to people. Think about anyone you know. If the people you know are like people we know, then what makes life better in their eyes also makes life safer and healthier for them and for their loved ones.) In those places, the cliché is false. By contrast, if there are exceptions to the general

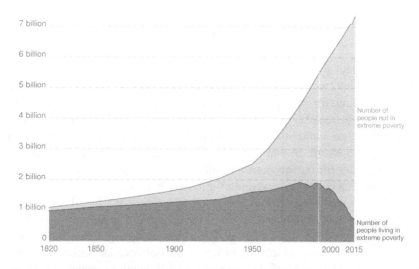

Figure 1.1. World population living in extreme poverty,[3] 1820–2015

---

2. See Figure 1.1; https://ourworldindata.org/a-history-of-global-living-conditions-in-5-charts
3. Extreme poverty is defined as living on less than $1.90 international per day. International dollars are adjusted for price differences between countries and for prices changes over time (inflation). Source: OWID based on World Bank (2019) and Bourguignon and Morrison (2002). www.Our WorldInData.org/extreme-poverty/

rule, that is, if there are places where rich people's life expectancy rose while that of poor people fell, then the cliché is true in those places: in those places, the rich really are getting richer even while poor people are indeed getting poorer. And we would want to know why. What did they lose and how did they lose it?

Of course, there is no guarantee that a society will be the proverbial rising tide that lifts all boats. Trade is cooperation for mutual benefit, and there are gains from trade, but there is no guarantee that every member of society will be involved in mutually beneficial trade. Both ethically and economically, it pays for a community to do what it reasonably can to make sure that nearly everyone has a decent chance to realize whatever potential they have to contribute to cooperative ventures. Geniuses are born into poor families every day, and no one wants to see their gifts go to waste. Everyone wants to live in a land of real opportunity—a land where we can be poor at age twenty yet reasonably anticipate not being poor when we are forty.

WHAT IS THE ECONOMIC QUESTION?

In medieval times, scholars thought the phenomenon of motion needed explanation. They asked, "Why do objects like planets keep moving when no force keeps them in motion?" The scientific revolution was launched, and what we call the Enlightenment began, when Galileo and Newton realized that medieval scholars were asking the wrong question. In developing the concept of inertia, Galileo, then Newton, concluded that things tend to remain in their current state of motion unless acted on by an external force. It is when we notice things changing that we should ask why, not when we notice things going on in the same way.

The same point applies to the social sciences, including economics. To say "no man is an island" is to say that without cooperation, we would live and die like any other large mammal. Prosperity is not natural. For tens of thousands of years, humanity lived in caves. Then something changed. The economic question is not why some people still live in caves, but rather, why doesn't everyone? What changed? Why did it change? Why is there such a thing as material progress in the first place? Progress needs explaining.

What explains the explosion of wealth since Adam Smith's time? The main answer is that there has been an explosion of trade. Trade is positive-sum. Everyone can win, and in some places, everyone does win. Some communities are indeed cooperative ventures for mutual benefit.

As recently as a century ago, staggering numbers of children (i.e., staggering to us) died before reaching the age of five. Yet, at any time, everyone has better life prospects than if they had been born a century earlier. Moreover, it is not only a privileged class whose life expectancy nearly doubled over the course of the twentieth century. For example, no group has been more shamefully mistreated than African-Americans. But it will not do to ignore the facts and pretend that no progress has been made. Between 1900 and 2010, African-American life expectancy went from thirty-three to seventy-five years.[4] Obviously, life expectancy is not everything, but let's not lose sight of the fact that people care whether their loved ones will live to a healthy old age or be cut down before the age of five.

DISCUSSION AND EXERCISES

1. In what ways is cooperation like, and in what ways is it unlike, trade? Can people cooperate without trading? Can they trade without cooperating?
2. Have humans tended to become wealthier or poorer over time? Why is this the case?
3. Can it be the case that trade makes everyone better off? Is it possible that everyone can win when people and societies trade?

---

4. See http://www.cdc.gov/nchs/data/hus/2012/018.pdf

Chapter 2

Why Ethics?

What kind of life do you want to live? What kind of society do you want to live in? These are fundamental moral questions, and they suggest further moral questions that are also fundamental economic questions.

- What's the point of business at all?
- Is trade a good thing? Under what conditions?
- Is cooperation a good thing? What exactly makes it a good thing?

WHAT DOES IT MATTER WHETHER YOU KNOW ANYTHING ABOUT ETHICS?

You probably have seen courtroom dramas on TV where the judge says to a defendant, "Ignorance of the law is no excuse." You would think everyone knows that, but people under pressure can forget the obvious. When one of us (Schmidtz) served on a grand jury a few years ago, he saw foolish people every day being arrested and charged with trafficking in illegal drugs. Often, people defended themselves by saying someone gave them $1000 to transport a package to Tucson. They did not know what was in the package. They did not want to know.

The court never showed much sympathy. The defendant should have stopped to think, obviously, but $1000 seemed to be enough to turn their brains off for a moment. And moments of stupidity ruin lives.

You might ask: If you don't know you are trafficking illegal drugs, what can they convict you of? Answer: trafficking illegal drugs. If a defendant should have known better, ignorance of the facts, just like ignorance of the law, is no excuse. If a reasonably cautious citizen would have known better, the defendant will be convicted.

Ignorance of ethics is no excuse either. Ethics involves taking responsibility for knowing the facts. If you don't know the facts and your grandmother says, "You should have known better," she is saying that you had a responsibility to be more aware of the situation you were in. Ethics involves knowing the law, within reasonable limits, but it is more than that. At a minimum, being ethical involves wanting your partners, business, or otherwise, to be glad they trusted you.

Studying ethics, economy, and entrepreneurship together gives us a chance to ask what kind of life you want to live and what kind of society you want to be a part of. Answering these seemingly simple questions requires us to ask and answer other questions, too, none of them easy. What is the point of business at all? Is trade a good thing? Always, or only under certain conditions? Is cooperation a good thing? Why, exactly?

Integrity

If you are reading this, you are probably a citizen of a commercial society. That is what we are assuming when we talk about the challenge you face in figuring out how to live a good life. More specifically, what we have in mind is the challenge of living a good life in a commercial society. Therefore, the first thing to keep in mind, as you go about your business in a commercial society, is this: every business decision is also an ethical decision. Business decisions can get a person in trouble. Ignoring the ethics of the situation may well come back to haunt us.

Integrity is an interesting word. There is a saying, "Be true to yourself." What does it mean? Part of the idea is that you have to figure out for yourself what that old saying is telling you. Another part of the idea is that you have to be honest with yourself. Being honest with yourself is one dimension of integrity. Integrity is about "getting your act together" and knowing what you want. The most important part of knowing what you want, in the long term, is knowing what it will take for you to become—and to remain—genuinely proud of who you are.

Integrity also has a social dimension. People with integrity have nothing to hide. Knowing you have nothing to hide is the essence of honest pride. By contrast, false pride is the kind of pride that makes people lie to themselves and pretend to be something they aren't. So that kind of pride, *false* pride, is almost the opposite of integrity.

Philosophers sometimes say integrity is its own reward. Looking in the mirror, knowing you have nothing to hide, is one of life's great joys. But integrity has more tangible rewards too. Having integrity does not interfere with making money. In fact, integrity can help people make better business decisions because people who have nothing to hide are not afraid of the truth. Entrepreneurs who don't fool themselves are not afraid to see reality as it is. Being unafraid of reality makes them better at responding to reality. They admit their mistakes, learn fast, and adapt. They are the ones who will correct their mistakes and give themselves a chance to come up with better ideas.

Obviously, lots of people get rich who seem to have no integrity at all, but it also seems that people who live without integrity are living on the edge of a cliff, about to take a big fall. (Check today's news to find out which star is the latest to throw his or her life away, and you will see what we mean.) They may not be murdered, or even sent to jail, but they will know they do not deserve their success, and they will live in fear of losing everything. Even from their own dishonest and distorted perspectives, they won't be living a great life. They will not be respected by others, not even by their children. They won't even respect themselves.

Here is a key to ethical and economic success: find a way to make the world a better place. Find a way to succeed. Find a way to *deserve* to succeed. Never settle for less.

Imagine you are lying in bed, seventy years from now, and you have done just about everything you are going to do in this life. You will spend whatever time you have left wondering what your life was all about. You will know then, as you already know right now, that you want to be part of something you can be proud of. You want the world to be better off with you than without you. You want the world to be glad you were here. You will know, as you already know right now, that you do not want to have to fake being proud of the fact that you cheated and did not get caught.

You know this. But you also know that, from time to time, the life ahead of you will tempt you to forget. Whether you are smart or stupid in those moments of temptation will determine how you judge the meaning of your life later on.

If you can say, "I made a pile of money," that is good. Don't let anyone tell you otherwise. But you already know that there is something better than making a pile of money. Better is being able to say, "I made the world a better place. It is good that I was here. I believed in something. When crunch time came and the world needed me after all, when it needed the best I had to give, I showed up. I stood for something."

Here is an observation. We (the authors) have each met forty-year-olds applying for graduate school. That is, we have met people who aimed for success as lawyers or doctors or some other thing, and the problem is, they got everything they ever wanted. As they got older, they came to realize they did not want enough. Later in life, they find themselves wanting to go back to school, start over, and this time do something really satisfying. Hollywood makes movies about greed and other forms of the vice of wanting too much, but we do not say enough about what a terrible mistake it can be to want too little. You do not want to wake up when you are forty to discover that your life plan is a teenager's guess about the nature of a good life. Right now, you already know you are better than that. Never let anyone tell you otherwise.

Obedience, Authority, Responsibility

Watch the Stanley Milgram film *Obedience*.[1]

After watching the Milgram film, think about how social pressure fools people into doing things they will be ashamed of later. We are not suggesting that you should believe everything that you read about the Milgram experiment. However, there are issues worth considering. What is wrong with being the kind of person who (like subjects in the Milgram experiments) did not stop, but continued to carry out the experimenter's instructions even when fellow subjects seemed to be dying as a result? No one wants to be that sort of person. Everyone wants to be a hero. So why would anyone settle for less? *What makes people afraid to stand for something?*

What makes people stop to think about what they are doing? What does it take to make sure you never wake up one day and realize that you have been following orders, or going along with the crowd—looking the other way— and that you no longer remember what it would be like to believe in yourself? It really is up to you.

We all learn sooner or later that ethics is not just a matter of opinion, just as drug runners learn sooner or later that ignorance of the law is no excuse.

Ethics is hard. In some ways, it is shockingly hard. We can't simply know how to be ethical any more than we can simply know how to fly a helicopter. Being ethical is, in many ways, a skill. It takes work. It takes practice. Still, although ethics is hard, it does not ask too much.

Ethics is about cause and effect. **Ethics is the subject of how people have to live in order for the world to be a better place with them than without them.**

Every subject in the Milgram experiment knew that the most basic rule of human civilization is "Thou shalt not kill." There may be horrible situations where people have to reasons to kill, or at least excuses. But everyone knows that "I was just following orders" is not one of them. One of the most interesting findings of the Milgram experiments seems to have been that subjects who violated this most basic rule of human civilization did not want to break

---

1. http://www.simplypsychology.org/milgram.html#video

it. Indeed, it was agonizing for them. Many were hysterical. But they lacked whatever strength a person needs to be able to stand up to social pressure. They knew that what they were being ordered to do was wrong, but somehow that knowledge was not enough in the face of "authority." If it had been one of us, we are sure we would not have obeyed. Then again, everyone says that. Everyone imagines that they are rebels.

So, think about a situation closer to home. What if your best friend is working in construction and his boss instructs him to cut corners, use substandard materials, and build a house that will fall apart a few years after a trusting customer paid good money for it? You might ask your friend what he is planning to tell the judge when he gets caught. Is your friend planning to say he didn't know? Will he say everyone does it? Will he say he was just following orders?

What would you advise him to do? Here is one bit of advice you can give that friend, and also remember for yourself at crunch time. When the crisis comes, as it will, you may find yourself gripped by fear. You may notice your heart pounding. You may try to fool yourself into thinking you have to obey an authority figure because you can't afford to lose your job. You have children to feed. If you disobey, your family will starve.

Our advice is, take a breath. Fear is tempting you to exaggerate the stakes. Don't be fooled. It's just a job. If you need to find another job, your family will not starve. Your children will grow up knowing that you are someone to be proud of. And in the end, that's what will matter to you (and your family).

The *Challenger* Space Shuttle

These are not hypothetical concerns. On January 28, 1986, one of NASA's space shuttles blew up. It turned out that a seal on the shuttle's booster rocket was safe only at temperatures above 40 degrees Fahrenheit, and the temperature at the time of launch was 18 degrees. The NASA managers knew this, but something stopped them from sounding the alarm and aborting the launch. As a result, seven people died that day. They had families.

When we imagine ourselves in that NASA managers' position, prior to launch, what do we know? Part of what we know is that if we take a stand, refuse to back down, and succeed in aborting the launch, no one including us will ever know for sure whether we did the right thing. The faulty seals may never be tested under full operation at low temperature. We may be fired without anyone (including us) ever knowing whether we were right. Would we be brave enough to sound the alarm anyway? You live in a world of uncertainty. Sometimes ethics is about being cool under pressure. Being cool under pressure is a skill. What would you have done, when you know what *could* happen, but not what *will* happen?

What Is on the Final Exam?

What your teachers can do now is warn you that there will be a test. Life will be a test. The test may come when you are not expecting it. You may not be prepared.

But we want to help you make needed preparations now, while you have time. You'll find that wealthy people, late in life, are not content merely with being rich. They have other questions. They ask whether they believed in something, whether they took a stand when their integrity demanded it. They want to know, as one day you will want to know, whether it was good, whether it mattered, that they were here on this earth. Questions like these will make up the most final of your final exams.

Final exams often come relatively early in life. There was a point-shaving scandal involving Arizona State University's (ASU) basketball team. ASU players accepted money to miss enough shots to make sure their team did not win by a margin that beat the point spread. Some people don't see the problem, so long as you aren't "hurting the team." What does it take to see the problem? How could anyone *fail* to see the problem?

Is this a case of selling what is not yours to sell? What would lead anyone to have a view that they aren't hurting anyone when they turn a sport into a scripted fraud rather than let it be the honest all-out competition that fans think they are paying to watch?

Stevin Smith was the ASU basketball player who first took the money. Smith seems to have been a normal, decent man who got caught up in a temptation for which he was not prepared. No one warned him, apparently. Even at the time, it should have been obvious that he was ruining his life and throwing away a brilliant career that would have made him a millionaire. To judge from what we have read, it seems that the people around Smith did not care enough about him to talk some sense into him. Worse, Smith did not care enough about himself. He was a fish who went for the bait, even though the hook was plain to see. In Smith's case, he was basically obeying an order to commit suicide rather than obeying an order to commit murder (as seemed to be the case in the Milgram experiments), but the fact that Smith obeyed still makes you wonder.

As teachers, there is only so much we can do. But we can say this: *Don't say you weren't warned.*

What can you do to make sure that in the heat of the moment you won't be gripped by an inexperienced teenager's fantasy: the fantasy that either you won't get caught, or if you do get caught, you'll be able to save yourself by begging for mercy? Can you make sure you won't be lured into something by some shady boss to whom you are nothing but a tool? What would it be like to be so clever that you will know how to outfox prosecutors who have been spotting inexperienced fools and putting them in jail since before you were born? Is it worth betting your life that you are that clever, or that your shady boss will come to the rescue? Think about it. Some day, the boss will put the pressure on, and the boss will be wrong. If you think about it now, in preparation for that day, you are more likely to be able to find the courage to say no and walk away.

DISCUSSION AND EXERCISES

1. What was the problem with the point-shaving scandal? What should Smith have done?
2. What can you do to make sure nothing like this ever happens to you?
3. How can you know when not to follow the orders of someone in a position of authority?

Chapter 3

Why Economy?

To make intelligent life decisions, you have to think about how you can be of service to others. That is what it means to make money: you develop the ability to be of service to others in particular ways, while others learn that what you are offering is worth giving you something in return.

WHAT DOES IT MATTER WHETHER YOU KNOW ANYTHING ABOUT THE ECONOMY?

To start with the most obvious part of the answer, humans are social animals. Our survival tool is our ability to cooperate. There are other social animals, but humans not only cooperate; we form societies, sometimes large ones. **Economy** is the name for our framework of cooperation. Functioning economies enable even complete strangers to cooperate by exchanging services.

When you learn about your economy, you are learning about various ways of being of service and about which of those services you could afford to provide. Profit tells you that what you are doing is worth doing. Profit is your signal that it is both feasible and desirable for you to stay in business.

Success in life revolves around that goal: making your services as valuable as possible to the people around you. You need to understand that the people you encounter in the marketplace are there for a reason. Like you, they came to the marketplace hoping to trade. Perhaps they showed up hoping to buy or sell a cup of coffee, or a tube of toothpaste, or a Porsche. If all goes well, buyers find something to buy at a price they can afford, sellers find something to sell at a price they can afford, and people go home having gotten what they wanted. Not everyone succeeds in making a trade, but those who do are better off.

Or at least that's the theory. Is the theory correct? To get to the answer to that question, we will have to understand why people trade in the first place, what they hope to accomplish when they trade, and whether those hopes can ever be realized.

Key Economic Questions

Adam Smith helped to invent the field we now call economics. He observed the society around him and he had questions. What is the division of labor? Why is there such a thing as the division of labor? Why doesn't everyone save money by doing everything for themselves? What does it mean to specialize? Why do people specialize? Interestingly, Adam Smith also asked *where* people specialize, and why. Why do we find specialists in large cities rather than in small villages? Why does an ounce of diamonds cost more than an ounce of water? Diamonds are just trinkets, after all, while water is essential for survival.

Economy and Law

We will talk about institutions in a forthcoming section, but for now, consider that some institutions help us to know what to expect from each other. If you go to a grocery store, for example, you probably have developed the habit of lining up at the cashier. The cashier serves the next person in line, and everyone seems to know who is next. You don't even need to talk about it; everyone just seems to know. Everyone expects the same thing. That is to say, we have a cultural, legal, and ethical framework for managing commercial traffic.

There is a reason for describing commercial activity as commercial traffic, because the challenge of managing commercial traffic is not unlike the challenge of managing traffic on our roadways. In North America, we drive on the right side of the road and stop at red lights. We understand, and expect other drivers to understand, that we have a system of stop signs, traffic lights, and settled rules of driving. Institutions like these are not miracles, but they can help us understand what to expect from each other.

Contract law is like a traffic management system in this way. Contract law helps us to coordinate and to cooperate. In fact, as an example of an institution that helps us to know what to expect from each other, contract law goes beyond managing traffic. Beyond helping us stay out of each other's way, contract law helps us work toward having a common destination. Contract law makes it safer for us to trust each other and work together.

Morality and Economy

Cooperation is one of the central moral concepts around which the lives of social animals revolve. Is anything more important than cooperation? Here is one answer. In a commercial society, there is something that comes before cooperation. Before people can cooperate, they have to come to the table with something to offer. Think about it. Think about your potential. Think about how to develop your potential into a valuable skill and a marketable service. Perhaps you learn that sort of thing in school. Perhaps not. But you have to learn it somewhere.

Economics analyzes how some societies give people reasons and opportunities to use their talents in a way that is good for others as well as for themselves. Needless to say, this is not the same thing as Ethics, but it is closer than you might have thought.

You want to have a lot to offer. You want people to respect what you bring to the table. You want them to think that what you bring to the table is excellent. Obviously, you want your trading partners to have a lot to offer as well. A society makes progress when its members put time and effort into win-win games, and have better things to do than to try to gain at other people's expense. You want to live in a society that gives people reason to be peaceful and productive.

The previous section identified an individual ethical challenge of making sure that your world is a better place with you than without you. This section identifies a society's economic challenge of making sure that people have reasons and opportunities to make their world a better place. Obviously, those two challenges can be closely related, but when a society fails to meet the economic challenge, then what is good for you and what is good for your customers can come apart. There are few guarantees here, but good institutions minimize the tradeoff between ethical and economic success. A society that respects morality does what it can to bring moral and material success together, and does what it can to avoid pulling them apart.

DISCUSSION AND EXERCISES

1. What is an economy? How is an economy organized?
2. What does a society's legal structure include? How does it support the economy?

3. If contracts and traffic rules are both institutions, what might some other institutions be?
4. Compare and contrast the terms "profitable" and "sustainable." When are conditions that make it profitable to keep delivering the service also the conditions that make delivering the service sustainable?

Chapter 4

Why Entrepreneurship?

Overnight success is rare. Some people built their fortunes steadily. For others, it was a roller coaster.[1] There is no denying that when we talk about the world of business, we are talking about a world full of risks. Everyone makes mistakes, and not everyone recovers from his or her mistakes. A business is not something to rush into blindly, but it is worth thinking about how you would recognize an excellent opportunity.

WHAT DOES IT MATTER WHETHER YOU KNOW ANYTHING ABOUT ENTREPRENEURSHIP?

To be an entrepreneur is to have a special kind of alertness. An entrepreneur sees an opportunity that other people have not seen, then decides to take the risk of running with that opportunity and seeing what can be made of it. That may involve starting a business. Entrepreneurs tend to drive progress, but there is more than one kind of entrepreneur, and some of them are bad. Some invent new forms of vandalism, or new forms of piracy. (Consider cyber-terrorism.)

But the purpose of this book is to reflect on how life might go for you, so the relevant point here is that someday you may see an opportunity to be in business for yourself, or an opportunity to make a life working for someone else's business. Either way, you need to know some basics if you want to make money. For that matter, you need to know some basics even to stay out of jail, and more fundamentally, to avoid deserving to be in jail.

---

1. For an instructive biography about how well and how badly a business deal can go, see Karl Eller, *Integrity Is All You've Got* (New York: McGraw-Hill, 2005).

18

You want your partners to trust you. It is crucial that you can deliver accurate information about what you are selling. You also need to develop the habits that make for a life of integrity, because you want your partners to trust you enough to be there for you over the long run. You need to build a reputation for having a product in which you rightly take pride. You never want to have to pretend to be proud of fooling people into thinking you had a good product. *Do you want to love what you do?* It starts with making sure you have nothing to hide.

You also need to think about the advantages and disadvantages of working for someone else. Most people work for an employer and are not directly paid by their customers. This is normal. There is nothing wrong with working for a construction company or a landscaping company or a restaurant or a cleaning service. You may spend your whole career working for someone else, living a perfectly happy life. There is no shame in playing it safe and avoiding the risk of going into business for yourself. You can work regular hours, and probably work fewer hours than the boss works. Working for wages is relatively safe and predictable, and for most of us, it is how we build up investment capital when we are young. It also is a way of getting experience in a particular business so that you develop your own idea about how you would run such a business and make it work.

There are also basic things you might need to know, such as how to take out a business license. We do not want you to be stopped by sheer lack of information. We believe this: if you are smart enough and tough enough to show up every day and do excellent work for a cleaning service or a landscaping company, then you are smart enough and tough enough to own the company yourself, and build your own network of loyal customers. Our job is to make sure you have information and to encourage you not to be afraid. Never think the world of business is just for the rich kids.

This book will not even come close to telling you everything you need to know to be successful in running your own business. But it will give you some clues. It will tell you that you need work experience. It will tell you that you need education. You need to be literate enough to deal with suppliers, lawyers, accountants, and the people at City Hall who work with you to get you a proper license. Of course, you need to be able to work with customers, and you need to know how to get your facts right and your numbers right.

It sounds like a challenge, and it is, but it can be a great life too. Are you honest enough? Do you care enough about other people to take joy in inventing services that make them better off? Do you want to give your customers good reason to do further business with you? Do you want them to recommend you to their friends? If so, then you can make a lot of money, and you can be proud of every dollar.

Business and Entrepreneurship

An entrepreneur needs to understand several elements of a successful business.

It helps to have a sense of the challenge of **marketing**. You need to know how to market your product. Simply bringing a valuable service to market is not enough. Your potential customers have to be aware of what you have to offer. So, you will need communication skills. How will you convey information about the value of the service you are trying to sell?

You want the truth to be the best marketing tool that you have. If you find that the truth is not the best advertisement for your product, then the world is telling you something overwhelmingly important: namely, your product is not good enough. It takes courage to hear that message. But when you do hear it, and then process that information honestly, you are learning something that will open a door to greater success in business and in life.

It helps to have a sense of the challenges of **accounting**. One thing you need to know about accounting is that every accounting decision is a moral decision. Good accounting is a way of telling the truth. But the real art in accounting is not simply adding up numbers. Neither is it simply telling the truth. Instead, the challenge is to tell the *relevant* truth. You have to know how to present the truth that enables your clients to see whether their business is healthy. Proper accounting involves making sure you are not fooling yourself, and making sure you are not fooling anyone else either. Not fooling yourself is an achievement. It takes wisdom, and it takes some training too.

What kind of cash flow is your client's business generating? Knowing that there will be income is not enough. Your client needs to know *when* there will be income, and whether the income stream will be timely enough to cover costs as costs arise.

You need to have a sense of all the potential costs of doing business, and which costs you have a plan for being able to afford. Which risks will you be able to handle? Which ones will ruin you if they materialize? Do you have a line of credit? Do you have the proper licenses? Do you have an exit strategy? What will you do if you wake up a year from now and realize that your business is in the wrong location, or that you failed to anticipate how much work it would be? Will you be able to admit that you made a mistake? Will you be able to correct mistakes and get your business onto a better path?

You do not need to be a genius. You do not need a plan for everything, but you do need to be honest when the time comes to admit that things are not going according to plan.

Most restaurants go out of business within a couple of years of opening. Often, people who launch these businesses have not made a big mistake. They simply realized that they had better options and that it would be a mistake to keep trying. They liquidate and reinvest not because they are bankrupt, but because experience has taught them valuable lessons. They now have better ideas about how to invest their time and money and how to provide a service for which there is greater demand. It happens. There is no shame in having doubts or learning from experience or changing your mind.

DISCUSSION AND EXERCISES

1. What is entrepreneurship?
2. Who can become an entrepreneur?
3. What are some benefits and costs associated with entrepreneurship?
4. What are the differences between being an entrepreneur and working for someone else? What are the similarities?

Part I

KEY CONCEPTS

In this part of the book, you will study powerful tools for understanding economic phenomena. Some of the most central economic concepts are also ethical concepts. You also will study ethical and entrepreneurial aspects of the challenge of building a good life as a productive member of an economy.

Chapter 5

Trade

Human beings thrive by learning how to cooperate with strangers.

Human beings are social beings. Their unique human survival mechanism is their ability to work together. The most fundamental relationship in the marketplace is cooperative rather than competitive. The fundamental market relationship is a trading relationship: people exchanging services on mutually agreeable terms.

Cooperation and trade are almost the same thing. One name comes from ethics and the other name comes from economics, but the important point is that whatever name we use, that activity—cooperating with other human beings—is our best hope for a better life in the long run. When we study trade and cooperation, we are studying the logic that delivers on that promise of a better life.

MYTH: TRADE IS ZERO-SUM

A **zero-sum game** is a game where no one gains unless someone else loses. People sometimes interpret trade as zero-sum—just like most of the recreational games that we grew up with—where the only way to win is to make another player lose. Playing those childhood games taught us a lesson that we can carry into our understanding of trade; namely, that if two people trade and one comes out a winner, the other must come out a loser. That lesson is a mistake, but it is a natural mistake and it takes work to unlearn it.[1] Think

---

1. See Paul Rubin, "Folk Economics," *Southern Economic Journal* 70, 1 (2003), pp. 157–171. As an example of the zero-sum mistake, Rubin offers the false idea that "if one person gets a job someone else must lose a job."

about being thirsty, and walking into a convenience store to buy a bottle of water. Who wins? Who loses? Is this transaction a zero-sum game, or is there a more realistic way to look at it?

THE PREHISTORY OF COMMERCE

As mentioned earlier, modern humans appeared at least 40,000 years ago. As we spread, it seems that our closest cousins, the Neanderthals, disappeared. Why? Extinction is normal, so perhaps the real question is not "why did the Neanderthals disappear?" so much as "whatever drove the Neanderthals to extinction, why didn't it take out *Homo sapiens* at the same time?" Around 500,000 years ago, the Neanderthals were hierarchical hunter-gatherer groups of two dozen. 40,000 years ago, the Neanderthals were still isolated groups of two dozen hunter-gatherers. It is hard to imagine any human society remaining so static for 460 years, let alone 460,000.

So far as scholars can see from currently available evidence, the Neanderthals weren't entrepreneurs. Cultural cross-fertilization did not occur. They did not make social progress. By contrast, modern humans evidently practiced division of labor almost from the start, engaging in trade within and between groups. Modern humans were innovators.[2]

MODERN HUMANS HAD MODERN LANGUAGE

Why did the Neanderthals not learn as humans learned, expanding their networks of cooperation as humans did? One reason: Neanderthals did not have the kind of vocal chords that would enable them to develop the capacity for speech that would emerge in human populations. To be able to speak is to be able to make one's intentions known. To be able to make one's intentions known is to be able to make promises, negotiate deals, and execute sophisticated joint plans in environments where effective cooperation increasingly came to require communicating with strangers.

---

2. Our understanding of these events is rapidly expanding! Please check our online resources for the latest news. There is evidence of the Neanderthals losing ground to various Ice Ages long before they had any contact with *Homo sapiens*. There is evidence of humanity surviving Ice Ages by domesticating dogs that made them far better hunters. There is evidence of *Homo sapiens* developing pastoral relations to livestock that made food supplies far more reliable in times when those who relied on being hunter-gatherers just couldn't find enough to eat.

THE PREHISTORY OF TECHNOLOGY

Many advances began with experimentation, spread by traders and other travelers who knew a successful experiment and an idea worth imitating when they saw one. To move trade goods over long distances, though, people had to be able to count on potential trading partners being willing to deal. People needed a basic rule of law, and property rights in particular. They had to be smart enough to remember who brought what to the table, or trade would never get off the ground.

Trade takes off when we feel so secure in our possessions that a change occurs: instead of thinking of ourselves as surrounded by thieves and pirates, we begin to think of ourselves as surrounded by trading partners: people with whom we can cooperate. We begin to feel like we can afford to trust people. We feel less vulnerable and more secure. That is to say, we are beginning to count on having **a right to say no**. As a result, instead of spending most of our time defending what we have produced, we can spend more time on producing. As we make progress, people stop seeing themselves as needing to conceal any valuables they possess. Instead, people cart their product to the market and literally advertise, displaying their valuables for all the world to see. Indeed, there comes a time when, far from needing to conceal possessions so as to avoid being a target for thieves, laws are needed to curb people's incentive to exaggerate the value of their possessions. In short, as society evolves, people begin to offer their goods in trade, provided they feel secure in their right to decline offers they do not welcome. The phenomenon of people advertising the fruit of their productivity is a clear sign that society is becoming more peaceful.

Economist Paul Seabright reflects on how astounding your life would seem to your distant ancestors:

> Citizens of the industrialized market economies have lost their sense of wonder at the fact that they can decide spontaneously to go out in search of food, clothing, furniture, and thousands of other useful, attractive, frivolous, or life-saving items, and that when they do, somebody will have anticipated their actions and thoughtfully made such items available for them to buy. For our ancestors who wandered the plains in search of game, or scratched the earth to grow grain under a capricious sky, such a future would have seemed truly miraculous, and the possibility that it might come about without the intervention of any overall controlling intelligence would have seemed incredible. Even when adventurous travelers opened up the first trade routes and the citizens of Europe and Asia first had the chance to sample each other's luxuries, their safe arrival was still so

much subject to chance and nature as to make it a source of drama and excitement as late as Shakespeare's day.[3]

WRITTEN LANGUAGE

Anthropologists currently believe trade emerged at least 40,000 years ago, farming at least 10,000 years ago. Closer to our own time, new possibilities emerged along with written languages. Any language, written or spoken, is an elaborate, rapidly evolving form of cooperation, and usually is spontaneous. What does it mean to say languages are spontaneous? It means that languages are law-like: there are rules of grammar and so on. Yet, those rules themselves were not invented by anyone; neither did they emerge as a result of any sort of legislative action. People who use the internet today would understand. We sometimes say an internet story has "gone viral." What do we mean when we say that? Notice that no government had to pass a law specifying what those words mean. Instead, someone somewhere, just a few years ago, tried to convey a certain meaning by using those words. Other people understood what the writer meant, and the writer's way of using the words rapidly spread. In other words, the meaning of the words "going viral" is itself an excellent example of a meaning that went viral. That's what languages are: sets of tools for conveying meanings that went viral.

BRONZE AND IRON

The Bronze Age was one in which metal was widely available only to the ruling class owing to the scarcity of basic ingredients, namely copper and tin. Ordinary peasants continued to use tools made of stone. The Iron Age began in twelfth century B.C., and it was revolutionary. Although copper and tin are scarce, iron is common. The trouble with iron is that a smith needs higher temperatures and more expertise to smelt iron. However, once people developed a workable process, iron tools became inexpensive. Part of what drove advances in iron smelting was that tin became more scarce, so bronze became more expensive. Tin was more scarce not because the *ore* was becoming more scarce but because trading networks that supplied tin to cities like Athens were collapsing.

An interesting aspect of this bit of history is that rich people were switching to iron from bronze tools, but poor people never could afford bronze, so poor people were switching to iron from *stone* tools. Thus, iron was an

---

3. Paul Seabright, *The Company of Strangers*. (Princeton: Princeton University Press, 2004), p. 15.

equalizer and a liberator. For people who had been unable to afford bronze, iron was literally their ticket out of the Stone Age.

BEYOND BARTER, FOR BETTER AND FOR WORSE

Coinage seems to have emerged in seventh century B.C. in Lydia, and the possibilities for production and trade expanded again. The Greeks, who most fully exploited the alphabet, were also quick to exploit the invention of coinage at about 600 B.C. Replacing bars of metal, standardized coins facilitated trade and encouraged industry, but the more revolutionary innovation was small change. Early coins, of silver and gold, had been in denominations too high for daily transactions among the poor. With small change, ordinary people could buy and sell things in small quantities.

Population growth over the next couple of centuries meant increasing demand for lumber, land, and agricultural products. In turn, this created pressure not to become agriculturally self-sufficient, but precisely the opposite. The puzzle is that as Greece began to need more food, Greece realized that it could not afford to use its land to grow food. Does that make sense? In fact, it does, and there is a crucial economic lesson here.

The lesson is that when people began to run out of food, they began to use the land to produce whatever crop could be used to purchase the greatest quantity of food. Growing wheat, for example, could not solve the problem. Producing enough wheat domestically to feed the entire Greek population was no longer possible. Increasingly, Greeks had to import food, which meant Greece needed to have something to sell. The more Greek products could command in exchange for foreign agricultural products, the better. The increasing need to import food led Greece to turn its agricultural land over to producing grapes and olives for export. Why? Because Greece's trading partners were paying a higher price for grapes and olives than they were paying for wheat. Greece did the math, started growing grapes and olives, and as a result had more food than they would have had if they had used their land to grow food.

DISCUSSION AND EXERCISES

1. Explain that last idea in your own words. How could Greece possibly think the best response to grain shortages would involve growing *less* grain?
2. What contributed to the Neanderthals going extinct?
3. In order to trade over long distances, what institutions needed to be in place?

4. Why did people eventually start advertising their valuables instead of concealing them?
5. How did iron get people out of the Stone Age?
6. How did coinage advance trade?
7. Why did the Greeks specialize?
8. Why is trade NOT a zero-sum game?
9. Here is a hard question. We ourselves do not know the answer. We tend to imagine human history as a matter of nomadic hunter-gatherer tribes gradually settling down as they began to develop crops, then coalescing into villages and finally into cities. But there is a puzzle here. According to journalist and author Jane Jacobs, cities must have come first, for "agriculture is not even tolerably productive unless it incorporates many goods and services produced in cities or transplanted from cities. The most thoroughly rural countries exhibit the most unproductive agriculture. The most thoroughly urbanized countries, on the other hand, are precisely those that produce food most abundantly."[4] Does Jacobs have a point? Which came first? Large concentrated populations, or large-scale agriculture to feed those large populations? What kind of information would we need in order to answer a question like this?

Source: This material is adapted from David Schmidtz and Jason Brennan, *A Brief History of Liberty*, Wiley Blackwell 2011. Chapter 1.

---

4. Jacobs (1970, p. 7).

Chapter 6

Resources

A resource is anything that can be put to use.

Resources are a function of human appraisal. Things become resources when people invent ways of making use of them. *"Resources are not; they become."*

—Erich Zimmerman[1]

WHAT IS A RESOURCE?

We tend to see resources as things that lie around waiting to be used, and of course that is one way of looking at it. Here is another way. Nothing is truly a resource until we see a way of putting it to use. In other words, whether anything is a resource for humans depends on human appraisal. If resources are a function of human appraisal, then resources are not fixed or static. Think about it. Imagine a high school student with free time during the summer who has access to a lawnmower, a small truck, a few friends looking for summer jobs, and who is able to launch a small landscaping business.

Once the business is launched, one of the new employees, also a high school student, wishes he had launched this business himself because, like his friend, he has access to a small truck and a lawnmower that mostly sits idle in his parents' garage. He too has friends looking for summer jobs. So here we have two people (each with a lawnmower, truck, and friends with idle time)

---

1. Erich Zimmermann, *World Resources and Industries: A Functional Appraisal of the Availability of Agricultural and Industrial Resources* (New York: Harper & Brothers, 1933), p. 3; 1951, pp. 14–15.

seeing things differently. One saw things cluttering up the garage. The other saw the business that could be built out of them.

Things are not resources. Things may have potential, but a thing becomes a resource only when it becomes useful. Things that you now take for granted as resources were not always resources. Someone had to realize that fire could be used to cook and provide warmth, that wind could power ships, that the stars could be used to guide those ships, and that horses could be domesticated to perform jobs for humans.

LAND, LABOR, AND CAPITAL

In economic theory, three types of resources are often discussed: land, labor, and capital. **Land** refers to natural resources that the earth provides, such as oceans, rivers, lakes, forests, mineral deposits, and wildlife (non-domesticated animals). **Labor** refers to human skills and capabilities. Historically we thought of labor in terms of physical skills and capabilities, but increasingly labor also refers to mental skills and capabilities. Finally, **capital** refers to the built environment or artificial environment, such as machines, buildings, and infrastructure (highways, railways, etc.).

Although land, labor, and capital are often defined as resources, they become resources for us only when we have a use for them. For thousands of years, humans inhabited a planet with fertile soils and rivers with rapidly flowing water. However, these soils and rivers became resources only when humans figured out that running water can be used to generate hydroelectricity, that some plants are worth domesticating and raising as crops, and so on. Resources are always a function of human appraisal, and human creativity determines what becomes a resource instead of remaining simply a thing.

TYPES OF RESOURCES

As you can see, our definition of resources is broad. There is more than one way to look at it, but as we use the term, a resource is anything that has a use. Resources can be **tangible** such as land or minerals. They can also be **intangible**. Consider the loyalty and honesty of employees. Consider neighbors who are in the habit of looking after one another. Consider the patent that we have registered. If we can count on it standing up in court, then we can appraise it as a valuable resource indeed. Finally, we can distinguish resources that entrepreneurs bring with them (their skills, knowledge, and personal assets under their control) from resources that entrepreneurs discover, such as the uses to which waterways or airports can be put, which crops the local climate is suitable for growing, and so on.

RESOURCE INTEGRATION AND CREATION

Because resources are a result of human appraisal, human beings in effect create resources, and such creation is always an act of discovery. This can be as profound as realizing that we can turn sand into glass, or oil into gasoline. Sometimes the appraising is a matter of seeing how to integrate seemingly separate aspects of a potential resource. The young entrepreneur who started a landscaping business was able to connect tangible resources like the truck and the lawnmower to intangibles like the skills and knowledge of the people he hired. There were other intangibles he drew upon too, like the trust of his parents. That trust gave him access to their truck and lawn mower in the first place. He also had the trust of the friends who agreed to work for him. They trusted him to treat them fairly. Trust, although intangible, is a resource.

All people continuously integrate resources to create new resources to provide service for themselves or others. This integration of resources can, and often does, include tangible and intangible things. Often, when one resource is integrated with others, ever more useful things are created. And as resources become more integrated and valued over time, society improves, at times dramatically.

OWNING THINGS

Over 700 years ago, Marco Polo came upon black goo gushing from the ground. Was this material a resource? He noticed indigenous people using it as an ointment for skin wounds. So, to the indigenous people, yes, it had a use and counted as a resource. Later on, it became far more valuable as an energy source, but not until people learned how to put it to that particular use. Keep this saying in mind: "resources are not, they become."

You might think that owning things makes you rich. You might reasonably guess that rich nations are those with mineral deposits, vast amounts of fertile soil, plenty of rivers and, ideally, access to the oceans. This premise might lead you to expect that Nigeria would be rich, since Nigeria has vast deposits of minerals and petroleum, while Hong Kong and Singapore would be poor, since these countries have nothing, compared to Nigeria, when it comes to stocks of minerals and petroleum, agricultural land, and so on. Yet, somehow, the truth is the opposite. Somehow, whatever is truly crucial is something more intangible. Whatever it is, Hong Kong has it. Singapore has it. But not Nigeria.

It is not easy to see what is really going on, but consider that the task of building a great city requires all kinds of minerals. One way of acting on that appraisal is to start looking for those minerals on your own land. If the minerals are not underneath your own land at hand, another way to access them is to secure trade agreements, a regulatory environment, and a financial industry: rare and precious intangibles. It turns out that such intangibles can be key ingredients of business propositions out of which great economies ultimately are built.

DISCUSSION AND EXERCISES

1. What is the difference between an unused item and a resource?
2. Define and give an example of land, labor, and capital.
3. Explain how intangible resources can be as important as tangible resources.
4. What is a resource integrator?
5. What does it mean to say "resources are not, they become"? Give an example of a resource that illustrates this idea.

Chapter 7

Cost

We have different ways of thinking about cost.

Whenever we act, our actions have a cost. Actions take time. They tend to consume other scarce resources as well. The most familiar way to think about the cost of buying a soda is to think that if you paid one dollar for it, then that soda cost you one dollar. We equate the cost with the price tag.

But economists have another way of thinking about cost, and the difference is important. Consider that you also spent time stopping at the convenience store. The one dollar sticker price is not the only cost that matters when you are deciding whether stopping to pick up that soda on your way to a baseball game is worth the cost. If you consider only the sticker price, you may miss something. For example, you also spend *time*. What else could you have done with that time? What if the time you spend buying the soda is time that you could have used to get to the game in time to enjoy watching the first inning?

OPPORTUNITY COST

Your **opportunity cost** is whatever you would otherwise have done with your time and money. You may not mind spending a dollar on a soda, but if it costs you the chance to see the first inning, you may well think that missing part of the game is too much to pay for a soda. When you think about missing part of the game, you are thinking about the soda's opportunity cost.

The soda's **opportunity cost** is not simply the sticker price. The opportunity cost is what you would have done with the resources you spent on it. In this case, what you spent on the soda includes time that you would have spent watching the game. University of Virginia economist Charlie Holt uses the expression "what you lose when you choose." Economists tend to think that it is worth your time to train yourself to think in terms of opportunity cost. Opportunity cost is part of what you need to think about in order to make good decisions. The opportunity cost of taking one path is the value of the path not taken.

Think about the choices you made last weekend. Say you go to bed early on Friday so you could get up early on Saturday to go on a hike. Your opportunity cost of going to bed early was, let's say, the movie you would have watched, or the party you would have gone to.

This opportunity cost is often hidden, and sometimes almost impossible to quantify. Yet, often it is the main thing to take into account when we are trying to make sound decisions about how to invest our scarce time. We say a resource is **scarce** whenever there is not enough for everyone to have as much as they want. To wish we had more time is to acknowledge that time is scarce.

Say you win a 3D printer in a drawing, but just as you pick up the printer someone in the crowd offers you $500 for it. Now you have a choice: keep the printer or sell it. If $500 is your best alternative to keeping the printer, then keeping the printer now costs you $500. But accepting the $500 also has an opportunity cost. The opportunity cost of taking the $500 in this case is that you are giving up the option of keeping the printer. If you choose the option with the highest value, the opportunity cost of that choice will be the value of your next best option.

Opportunity costs often are ignored because we are not usually presented with a bill for them, but opportunity cost is a good way of thinking about what matters most when we make choices.

TRANSACTION COST

The cost associated with actually *making* an item, that is, its production cost, is only one part of the cost of getting that item to a customer.

A **transaction cost** is the cost of whatever it takes to deliver a service from a seller to a buyer. The cost of the transaction can include the cost of advertising, renting retail space, hiring security people to monitor the retail operation, bargaining, contracting, transporting, loading and unloading, packaging, storing, tracking the item during transit, insuring, legally documenting the nature of the item to be delivered, producing and storing a record of completed delivery, and a seemingly endless list of other things. Transaction costs typically are a significant part of the cost of doing business. We will return to the topic of transaction cost in part II, but for now, we simply want to note that transaction cost is a distinct and fundamental concept.

COST IS IMPLIED BY SCARCITY

Opportunity cost is an implication of scarcity. So is transaction cost. We create routines and technologies that shave a few minutes off the time needed to complete a transaction because time is scarce. You could say we economize on the cost of time. To minimize transaction cost is to minimize the cost of time and other scarce resources (such as the cost of packaging, trucking, and advertising) that go into transacting.

Opportunity cost and transaction cost are different things, but of course they do connect. After all, the reason why time is scarce in the first place is that we have other things to do. In other words, time is scarce because time has an opportunity cost. If we can reduce the time we spend on one transaction, that gives us more time for other things.

We all operate under a time constraint. Time is scarce for all of us. Suppose you were so incredibly rich that prices *seemed* close to zero *for you*. You could buy as much of anything as you wanted. Would scarcity impact you? Think about what you would buy. Now think about using, tasting, wearing, or driving all those things you accumulated. Of course, you wouldn't be able to consume everything and enjoy everything at the same time. You may be able to consume multiple things at once (e.g., an exquisite dinner while cruising the Mediterranean). But you could not enjoy a cruise on your yacht at the same time you enjoyed your ski villa in Aspen. Your time is limited. Consumption takes time, and time is scarce. The scarcity of time constrains us all, at least for the foreseeable future. Rich and poor alike have only twenty-four hours a day. Time is so scarce that entire industries exist to save people time. As individuals and societies get better at utilizing resources, resources become relatively less scarce. But even the richest people in the world have to decide how to spend their time. So, even for the richest people in the world, scarcity is unavoidable, which is another way of saying that choice is unavoidable, and cost is unavoidable.

Comparing what is free to what we pay for is helpful in thinking about scarcity, but we need to be careful when we think about what is free. Clean air and clean water may seem free, but often someone is paying for them. The costs are just harder to see. As a community, we police polluters so we can enjoy cleaner air and water. Regulations we establish to facilitate this are not free. Taxpayers and consumers finance regulation with money that would have served some other purpose. That opportunity cost is real. Access to well-built roadways and sidewalks likewise seems free to us. Sure, we need to pay for the use of a car, but typically we don't have to pay a fee to use a specific roadway. We use most roads as much as we want. But those roads require scarce resources—like engineering design, heavy machinery, labor, and raw materials—that local, state, and federal governments pay for with tax money that could have otherwise been spent on schools or hospitals. That tax money could have also been left in the hands of taxpayers, who could have used it to buy something else.

Think about things that seem free and unlimited. Clean air might not be scarce on a deserted island. Sand might not be scarce in the middle of a desert. Water might not be scarce at a river. How about garbage in New York City? Not scarce. There is more than enough garbage in New York City for everyone to have as much as they want for free.

All of these things, though, clean air, sand, drinking water, and even piles of garbage are potentially scarce. Currently, clean air is scarce in Beijing, Shanghai, and elsewhere. Clean sand fetches a price in glass production. Drinking water in Saudi Arabia has to be created by desalination plants. As for garbage, think about aluminum cans. At one time, cans were simply thrown away. Now they are collected, recycled, and turned into new products. Sometimes, even garbage becomes a resource. As we said before, such things depend on human appraisal.

HUMANS LIVE IN A DYNAMIC CONTEXT

Besides scarcity, there is another factor that makes choice unavoidable. The world is not static. Every day we wake up to a world that has moved on from the world we woke up to the day before. Think about yourself a year, or even five years ago. Think about how you have grown and changed. Think about how much you have learned, given and received, refined your tastes, strengthened friendships, and developed skills. Think about changes in your environment that you had to respond to. Now think about how you will change in the next year. Or the next five. It's hard even to predict.

We learn, exchange, give, receive, invent, invest, or divest. In short, we respond to a continuously changing environment. What we spend now will affect what we will be able to do in the future. This is such a constant fact of life that social scientists sometimes speak of a changing *opportunity set*. Not only does our environment change through no action of our own; it is shaped by choices we have made in the past. Choice is unavoidable. Even deciding not to respond, deciding to hold off until we have more information or until we can gather more resources is still a choice (and sometimes a wise choice).

DISCUSSION AND EXERCISES

1. When it comes to resources being scarce, what about personal qualities, like integrity, or relationship qualities, like trust? A reputation for being trustworthy might be a trader's most precious asset. If that reputation is ever lost, it won't be something that can be restored overnight. What is the cost of a tarnished reputation?

2. See whether these statements make sense to you. We wrote them in the negative. Try rewriting them in your own words.

   - In a world without scarcity, everything would be possible.
   - In a world without change, alternatives would remain static.
   - In a world without scarcity and change, choice would not be necessary, and cost would not exist.

3. It might seem that we want to minimize opportunity cost. But is that true? Explain what your life might look like with very high opportunity costs and why, in some ways, that would be a good thing.

4. Compare and contrast the idea that we prefer lower opportunity cost with the idea that we prefer lower transaction cost.

5. Think about this statement: anything that lowers transactions costs would contribute to human flourishing.

   - Has the Internet lowered transaction costs? Give examples.
   - Look up the term "intermodal freight container." How did ships get loaded or unloaded before the invention of the intermodal freight container? Have they lowered transaction costs? How would your life be different without them?

Chapter 8

Institutions

An institution is a framework for interacting. Norms, laws, and customs evolve to help people know what to expect from each other. Institutions are relatively long-lived social mechanisms for establishing mutual expectations.

People often use the word "institution" as if it were a way of referring to a building. But that is misleading. Marriage, for example, is an institution, but it is not a building. It isn't something we look for in a building either, at least not in the way that we might go to a courthouse because that is where we expect to find the court. Again, when we go to a bank, we go to a building, but the bank itself is not the building. The bank is the business that operates inside the building. If the business shuts down, the building left vacant after the business is gone would not be a bank. It's just a building.

We don't want to focus too much on definitions here. The point is to have a sense of what institutions are like. Think, then, about this general idea: Institutions are durable frameworks for interaction and mutual expectation. Institutions include shared rules, customs, beliefs, and meanings that enable us to live together because they help to make us more predictable to each other. In short, institutions enable citizens to know what to expect from each other, and in that way, they help us to learn how to interact in beneficial ways.

EXPECTATIONS

Mutual expectations are shared expectations. Thus, in a way, effective institutions are shared institutions. If I am the only one who believes that customers should line up and wait their turn at the cash register, then my belief won't help us to stay out of each other's way. If I think I should drive on the right, and act on that belief in London, where everyone else is driving on the left, then my belief is a menace. So, it isn't enough for me to have a belief about which side of the street I should drive on. I need to care what other people believe, see the street from their perspective, and act in the way that they expect me to act. If I fail to see what they expect from me, then I am a menace to myself as well as to them. To know what to expect from others, we have to see how they see the situation and the rules that apply to it.

INCENTIVES

When we try to understand why people do one thing rather than another, we sometimes talk about their **incentives**. To speak of incentives is to speak of rewards that go with acting one way rather than another. We raise the topic of incentives here for this reason: an institution is a structure that creates opportunities and incentives. An **incentive structure** is a whole set of risks and rewards that lead people to do one thing rather than another. If you are playing a game of baseball, why would you ever throw the ball to first base? Answer: the rules of the game are an incentive structure that will, in particular situations, give you a reason to throw the ball to one base rather than another. The whole set of incentives is a structure that adds up to the game of baseball.

When a system of law increases the benefit of being cooperative, you might predict that there will be more cooperation. When a system raises the price of being a thief, you might expect less theft. In other words, a system of law is an incentive structure, and it gives people incentives to act in one way rather than another.

We described contract law as an institution that helps us to know what to expect from each other, and puts us in a position where we can afford to trust each other. We spoke earlier about scarcity and about *economizing*. So, in a way, we could say that a system of contract law economizes on trust. It lowers the risk associated with trust.

WHY DO INSTITUTIONS EMERGE?

Trading involves transaction costs, but institutions can lower transaction costs. For example, we learn in some cultures to line up for service, which makes transacting easier both for customers and store employees. We learn in some cultures to take turns at traffic intersections, stopping when we face a red light and proceeding on green. We learn to drive on the same side of the road as everyone else.

Importantly, institutions also enable us to know what to expect from strangers. When you buy a soda at a sporting event, you pass the money across several people to the vendor and your drink is passed along to you without anyone stealing your money or your drink. When you buy a house or automobile, you get a legal title to that asset. When you get paid at work, you assume the economic currency will be accepted as legal tender around the country. When you visit a retail store, you do not shoplift, and if you are like most people, the possibility does not even cross your mind.

The ultimate institution, and the ultimate triumph of human social coordination, might be language. We can share a language with complete strangers. Language along with many other institutions can help us solve a key problem: the problem of limited cognitive abilities. We have only so much ability to gather, process, store, and retrieve information. Written language, in particular, vastly increases our ability to retain crucial information.

More generally, one reason why we develop routines is to economize on our scarce mental capacity. Routines allow us to do various things without much thought so that we can focus on other aspects of the situation that are less familiar. You don't think about which side of the street to drive on. You just follow other drivers. Sometimes you don't really decide which merchant to trust either. You trust one bank even though the only thing you know about the bank is that other people trust it. Incredibly, that usually works out well enough. Imagine how much harder it would be to figure out what to do if you had no idea who to trust or what to expect from the people around you.

Economists theorize about rational actors. Things become interesting when we start theorizing about how to handle the simple fact that we are limited. We have limited processing power. In any case, institutions can help us to know what to expect and how to coordinate and, at their best, they can help to make some aspects of the situation so familiar that we hardly need to think about them at all. That frees us to focus more effectively on other aspects of the situation that are novel. As philosopher Alfred North Whitehead observed,

> It is a profoundly erroneous truism, repeated by all copy-books and by eminent people when they are making speeches, that we should cultivate the habit of thinking of what we are doing. The precise opposite is the case. Civilization advances by extending the number of important operations which we can perform without thinking about them.[1]

Institutions tend to be **networks** held together by mutual expectations. Assume you have a network of 100 friends or acquaintances. Suppose

---

1. Alfred North Whitehead, *Introduction to Mathematics* (New York: Henry Holt, 1911) p. 61.

each possible pair of friends consists of two people who treat each other with respect, fairness, and reciprocity (when I do something for you, the favor is returned). This is a network of shared expectations. Great things can be built on trust. But trust can break down. If we are ever betrayed, we can learn in a hurry to become suspicious. When bad experience starts teaching us to be more cautious about trusting others, our networks are at risk of breaking down. And of course, getting into a habit of knowing what to expect from each other is not always a good thing. Not all institutions are good. For example, suppose we all expect women to be paid less than men for the same work. That shared expectation is not fair and it is not right, yet it can be highly stable. If every one of us is in the grip of that shared expectation, then we may not even be able to see that there is a problem.

We are not going to pretend there is an easy solution. There are times when being ethical requires us to reflect on what is expected, and times when being ethical requires us to stand up to social pressure, and acknowledge that "business as usual" is not right. Think about it, and talk it over with people you trust.

DISCUSSION AND EXERCISES

1. Explain how trust can be considered a resource. What are some similar examples?
2. Whitehead says that civilization advances when we can do more things without thinking them. How do institutions help us do this?
3. Describe some of the institutions you encounter every day. Are these institutions beneficial or harmful?

Chapter 9

Value

Our values are what we aim at, and judge to be worth aiming at. Economics, entrepreneurship, and ethics are different ways of approaching the study of value.

Economics studies what people aim at, which ways of pursuing aims are more successful than others, and which institutions are more conducive to people getting what they want and need.

Entrepreneurs are alert to new opportunities, but what is an opportunity? An **opportunity** is a chance to act in a way that has value. A successful entrepreneur, then, is a student of value in a way. An entrepreneur is alert to novel ways to be of service. An entrepreneur pays attention to what people value, and why, and speculates about new ways, better ways, cheaper ways, and sometimes previously unimagined ways of delivering a service that people will value.

Ethics studies what is worth aiming for. As we said, Ethics is hard, so hard that we are tempted to retreat from it. We are tempted to call it a matter of opinion and avoid thinking about it. If there seem to be different opinions, and if we can't tell which opinions are more educated than others, then we are tempted to retreat to the view that Ethics is merely opinion, and nothing more.

Some people try so hard to avoid being judgmental that they end up recoiling from the very idea that we can have good reason to value one thing rather than another. So, one question is, "How far should you go to avoid taking the risk of having to admit you were wrong?" You might think that retreating from Ethics is the only way to be safe. You might think you are safe if you have no view about whether one product is better than another. You might think you are safe if you have no opinion about whether it is a good thing or a bad thing that your product causes cancer. You might think you are safe if you have no opinion about whether lying about the quality of your product is okay. Summing up, you might think that so long as you do not think, then your thoughts cannot be wrong either. The problem is, you have responsibilities, and some of them cannot be avoided.

What do you think? Should you retreat that far to avoid ever having to learn from a mistake? If you make too many excuses, and go too far to avoid responsibility, that in itself can become a fatal mistake. Perhaps the lesson is simply: don't kid yourself; ethics is really hard. We all have a lot to learn.

Here are some ideas, hard ideas, that you need to know.

OBJECTIVE VALUE

Consider something that you know is true: vitamin C is good for you. There are different opinions about this. But even though there are different opinions, there is a fundamental fact: either your body needs small doses of vitamin C to remain healthy or it doesn't. We know there is a fact of the matter, even if we do not know for sure what that fact is. A few centuries ago, before scientists discovered vitamin C, we had no idea that the human body needs it. But we still needed it. If the human body needs dietary sources of vitamin C, then small amounts of vitamin C are good for us. That is a matter of biology, not a matter of opinion. Vitamin C's importance to human health is an objective fact, and such facts are not particularly rare.

The more general bottom line is this. You decide whether you prefer to be healthy, but you do not *decide* whether your preferences are healthy. They either are or they aren't. Choices have consequences. The quality of your life will reflect the quality of your choices. Obviously, it is up to you to decide whether you care about that. Our point is simply that what you choose will have consequences.

MARKET VALUE

What is the connection between market value and objective value?

Paintings by Picasso are beautiful to some. To others, Picasso's paintings are so disturbing that looking at them is almost painful. People say beauty is in the eye of the beholder. What they mean is that aesthetic value is subjective, indeed a matter of opinion.

But now suppose three friends are at a museum looking at a Picasso painting, and the first friend says, "You know that this painting is worth 14 million dollars, right?" The second person says, "I understand, but personally, I wouldn't pay 14 cents for it." The third person says, "I hear you, but I love this painting. I'd pay twenty million for it if I had that kind of money." One strange thing about this conversation is that the three friends understand each other, and they aren't even really disagreeing. What is going on?

Part of what is going on is that all three friends understand that they are talking about two kinds of value. All three agree on what the market value is, but all three also understand that there is another kind of value—the value of being able simply to enjoy that painting for what it is—where they don't feel the same way about the painting, and there is no reason why they should. The conversation makes sense, but only because everyone involved in it understands that the painting has more than one kind of value.

One kind of value is subjective preference, while the other is objective fact. The second person understands perfectly well that the objective market value of the painting is the equivalent of a claim on $14 million worth of services. So, obviously he would pay a lot more than $14 for that. But what he would not pay a lot of money for is the right to hang the painting on the wall and simply admire its beauty. The market value is an objective fact. If an appraiser says the painting will sell for fourteen million, then the appraiser is either right or wrong and *we can find out* by actually putting the painting up for sale. That is how people find out facts when there are facts to be known.

The Picasso's market value depends on supply and demand, but if the market value is, in fact, $14 million, then that fact is, after all, a fact. I may think my house is worth a million dollars, and a real estate agent might tell me that, as a matter of fact, it will not sell for that much. One of us is wrong. We can find out who is right by putting the house up for sale. Or, perhaps we are both right but we are talking about different things. If the house truly is worth a million to me, while my agent is right to say its market value is less than that, this is crucial information. It tells me that now is a bad time for me to be trying to sell my house.

A good time to sell an item is when the community values the item more than you do. In that case, there is opportunity for mutual benefit. You have reason to sell things to people who want what you have more than you do, just as you have reason to buy things from people who want those things less than you do. Everyone has reason to move goods and services from people who value them less to people who value them more. Is that reason an ethical reason? An economic reason? Could it be both?

There are, of course, complications. Even if someone on the other side of the world values an item more than you do, that doesn't mean the difference is worth the cost of shipping. There are transaction costs. When willing buyers and sellers successfully execute a trade—money for a painting—and both sides of the trade consider themselves better off, we describe that fact as the creation of *surplus value*. Of course, the trade did not create the painting; it merely moved the painting from one person to another. And yet, the value of the painting to the person now holding it has risen. The painting did not change, yet its value rose. Both seller and the buyer cooperated in a way that made the world a better place.

What Is Money?

Money is a form of cooperation; it helps people to be useful to each other.

Suppose you go to the market to buy nails. Someone else shows up wanting to buy corn. Without money, it would be hard to predict what would happen. Things could work out pretty well. You might say, "I can spare some corn, but I am looking for someone who can spare some nails" to which someone might respond "Fantastic! I have spare nails, and corn is exactly what I'm looking for!" In that case, you can trade, and both of you would go home happy. This is a **barter** economy.

But how likely are you to find someone trying to sell exactly what you want to buy, who is also at the same time trying to buy exactly that you want to sell? It could happen, but it would take luck. If you never find the perfect trading partner, you may never complete a trade, and your surplus corn would rot. Because of the threat of spoilage, you might choose to give your surplus corn away. If you give your corn away, someone might say, "Thanks! I owe you one." This is the beginning of what we call money.

Suppose someone wants your corn and wants to give you doorknobs in return. If you don't want doorknobs, you might think you have no interest in accepting the offer. But when you think about it, you realize something. If you take the doorknobs anyway, even though you don't want them, then that will leave you with two things to sell: corn and doorknobs. That increases your chances of finding someone willing to take what you have and, in return, give you what you really want: nails.

It is a short step from here to money. A bag of doorknobs is heavy and cumbersome, and if you don't want doorknobs, you don't want to carry around a bagful of them either. You would accept an IOU for them instead. Now you have a piece of paper in your pocket that can be redeemed for door knobs. So, now you can walk up to the person selling nails and you can say, "You may not want doorknobs. I did not want them either, but I still accepted them. And you have the same reason to accept them as I did. You should be willing to give me some nails in return for this IOU because this IOU is worth something regardless of whether you want doorknobs."

Perhaps the idea of a currency backed by doorknobs is a bit silly, but the story of how money gets invented can be a lot like this. Even if no one ever wants the tangible asset for which the pieces of paper can be redeemed, a different kind of economy emerges when those IOUs begin to circulate and make transactions easier. Pretty soon, everyone is bringing goods and services to the market, and they no longer even need to collect real goods and services in return for what they are selling. Instead, amazingly, they aim to collect a pocketful of IOUs. They quickly learn that those IOUs are claims on particular services that can be redeemed whenever doing so is convenient, and IOUs are a lot easier to store and to transport.

The next step in this process is a kind of standardization. Some IOUs are for doorknobs while others are for bottle openers, but trading everything for a common unit of currency, whatever it happens to be, makes everything far easier. Markets determine how much of that currency things cost, and we are off to the races. You can sell anything for the currency, whether it is backed by gold or by doorknobs, and you can buy anything with it. You can even hire people with it, which opens up a world of possibilities. Money may be the best device ever invented for lowering **transaction costs**. Money does this by making it easier for people to find people with whom to exchange services. If someone has money, then that is a sign that they brought something to the community that someone was willing to pay for. You don't need to want what they brought. You don't even need to know what they brought. All you need to know is whether they like what you brought and whether you like what they are offering in return.

In the above story, money has emerged in your economy as a medium of exchange and a unit of accounting. You can think of your pocketful of IOUs as a measure of the services that you gave to your community but which your community has not yet returned to you.

Money comes to represent the promises we make to each other when we trade. It is also a way we can store value over time. We never have to worry about corn spoiling or doorknobs piling up everywhere. But even that is not the whole of the story. As you accumulate money, what you have accumulated is a store of wealth you can draw from when you buy the things you need to live. The money sitting in your bank account is, in essence, a pile of IOUs—services you have provided to your community without having yet asked for anything in return. If you really earned that money, then you should be proud of it.

MARGINAL VALUE

If you walked into a convenience store to buy a bottle of water, you would not be surprised to find a cooler filled with a hundred bottles of water selling for a dollar each. If you willingly hand over a dollar for a bottle, then evidently the water is worth a dollar to you, and probably more. Would you have paid $2? Maybe. But would you willingly pay a hundred dollars for a hundred bottles? Probably not.

Why? Why do you buy one bottle? If one bottle is worth a dollar, why not buy a hundred of them? The answer is that, to you, the water has a **marginal value**. The value you attach to drinking one bottle might be very high, but that value declines with each bottle you drink. That is what we mean when we say the value declines **at the margin**. The value of the total amount consumed is one question. However, when we are deciding whether to drink one more bottle, the relevant value question is a different kind of question. The question is not whether it is good to drink water but how good it would be to drink one more bottle, here and now. When economists speak of value at the margin, what they mean is the value of what comes next. In this case, they mean the value of drinking a second bottle on top of the first.

In the real world, prices can diminish at the margin too, in the sense that we can get a discount if we buy more. But if the price of a bottle in the convenience store is a constant $1, then the only thing that changes at the margin is the value you attach to having another bottle. At some point, you stop drinking. You stop even though the price you just paid, and paid gladly, has not gone up. You stop because the value of having the first bottle was high, but the value of having a second bottle, on top of the first, is not.

MARGINAL COST

If you are thinking about whether you should walk to school or take the bus, you are considering a tradeoff. There are pros and cons to each option, and they have to weigh against each other. If you walk, you will get some exercise and you will enjoy being outside. If you take the bus, you may save time and get to hang out with friends.

But your tradeoffs don't end there. You will also have to consider the cost of the bus ride, and what you think the bus ride is worth in the first place. Have you already purchased a bus pass for the month? Suppose you have already paid $20 for a monthly bus pass. In that case, the **total cost** of riding the bus this month is $12, but the **marginal cost** of riding the bus on this particular day is zero. You paid $20 for the month, but you don't pay any more for riding the bus on this particular day.

DISCUSSION AND EXERCISES

1. How is value determined? Does anything have inherent value, or is everything worth only what someone will exchange for it?
2. How are IOUs and money alike? How are they different?
3. What are the benefits of an economy featuring money over a barter economy?
4. What does "marginal" mean?

Part II

PROGRESS

How would you know whether you are making progress? You could start by deciding what to count as progress. One obvious question is what you really want out of life. Once you have an answer, then you can proceed. You can measure your progress by asking whether you are getting closer to achieving your goals.

One problem with this way of proceeding is that when we are really making progress, we are not simply making progress toward achieving goals that we had when we were in high school. Rather, in any real human life, our goals themselves are a moving target. As we get older, we develop more mature ideas about which goals are worth wanting. That means we need to keep an open mind about whether the time has come to revise our goals. It is your life. You have the right and the responsibility to reconsider the value of your goals. That is what a satisfying life is like.

This is one way to understand your personal progress, and to begin to think about how to measure it. What about social progress? How would you decide whether your whole society is making progress? Economists devise measures of economic growth. What exactly is the point?

One point is that we cannot simply ask whether society is making progress toward achieving its life goals. A society does not have a life and it does not have a life goal in the way that an individual person does. Even so, we have ways to think about how whole societies make progress. We can ask whether members of society are in a better position to achieve their goals than they were in the past. That is a sensible question, but how would we answer? One meaningful and partly measurable way to answer the question would be to investigate changes in a society over the course of a century and ask questions like: Has life expectancy gone up or down? Has infant mortality gone up or down? Have we cured one crippling disease after another? How many hours of work per week does it take on average for a worker to feed a family of four? If the number of hours needed to feed a family has fallen, that is a measurable kind of progress that almost everyone cares about. Are children getting more years of education than their parents or grandparents got? If so, that is a measurable kind of progress that almost everyone cares about.

In general, we can ask what the members of society can afford. What benefits are available to people, and at what cost? If most people can afford services unheard of in their grandparents' time, where does that leave us? It does not prove that people are happier now. No one can prove that your life will be happier if you live for eighty years than if you live for only forty. Still, what we want to see here is not proof but possibility. If people in your community can expect to have eighty healthy years rather than only forty, then people in your community have a higher ceiling of possibility.

Chapter 10

Adam Smith on Progress

Adam Smith is remembered today as a founder of modern economics. He was also one of the greatest philosophers who ever lived, and he had important things to say about progress. First, he pointed out, market society frees us from starvation; second, market society frees us from servility; third, however, the liberating impact of markets is not guaranteed because markets can be corrupted by crony capitalism (i.e., by monarchs, the politically well-connected, and merchants buying and selling political privilege).

FIRST, FREEDOM FROM STARVATION

Smith saw how commercial society liberated poor people from desperate need, most directly as a result of the division of labor and specialization. It was so important to him that it was the first thing he addressed in his *Wealth of Nations*. In a village, a poor man's son might grow up to become a doctor, but it is certain that no one will be pushing the frontier of oral surgery, for in a village there are not enough customers to sustain specialized trades. To see specialized trades, we go to a commercial hub such as London. In London, someone who otherwise would have been the village carpenter can specialize in making violins. When trade goes global, enabling trade with customers by the millions, a person can make a living, or even a fortune, by inventing something as simple as an envelope that has a clear little window so that you can see the address typed on the letter inside the envelope. It might not seem like much, but it saves businesses a few seconds (per customer, every month) retyping addresses. The profit from selling one envelope to a single customer is a fraction of a penny, but if you sell hundreds of millions of them, it adds up. Similarly, Walmart can become stunningly profitable not by making millions from each customer, but by netting a few pennies each from untold millions of transactions per day. The volume of trade is so massive that Walmart can net billions even if nearly all of the surplus value created by transactions involving Walmart is captured by its customers.

How would we ensure that when London needs more carpenters, more people go into carpentry? Smith's answer is one of his signature insights. Given price signals, we check whether there is a problem (and in the process acquire a reason to help solve the problem) by checking the price of a carpenter's wage. This simple, elegant mechanism, intuitively grasped by everyone who buys and sells, coordinates the productive efforts of people who may share neither a religion nor even a language, and who are indeed only dimly aware of each other's existence. A spike in the wages of carpenters, more reliably than anything else, alerts consumers to a need to be more economical in their use of carpentry services, simultaneously alerting prospective suppliers to a community's rising need for carpentry services. Falling prices, more reliably than anything else, signal would-be suppliers that a community already has more than it needs. From such economic coordination, made possible by free-floating price signals, the wealth of nations is made. What comes to be classified as poverty will be what previous generations would have called opulence, such that even the poorest members of market societies will have, for example, life expectancies exceeding fifty years.

Where Plato supposed the wealth of nations must ultimately depend on a guardian class assigning to each worker tasks appropriate to that worker's nature, Smith realized that no guardian class could ever know enough (or reliably care enough) to handle such a task. Only a price mechanism can track the incomprehensibly vast flood of daily feedback from buyers and sellers regarding whether X is worth producing and if so where X needs to be shipped so as to reach consumers to whom X is worth what it costs to get it to them.

The massive advances made possible by the division of labor, coupled with trade, allowed humanity to emerge from its natural condition: poverty. But that was only the first part of the story.

SECOND, FREEDOM FROM SERVILITY

One freedom that had transformed Europe's economy by Smith's time was the freedom of ordinary people to contract with persons other than their lords. In the feudal systems of previous eras, if you were born a serf, you were entitled to your lord's protection, but you lacked many rights that we now take for granted. In a feudal system, you lived where your lord told you to live. You grew what your lord told you to grow. You sold your harvest to your lord, at a price of his choosing. You could not negotiate any of it. If you wanted to leave, you needed your lord's permission. When you met your lord, you would greet him by bowing. Your lord most certainly did not see you as his equal, and neither did you.

As this system was replaced by market society, the effect was liberating for everyone, above all for the poor. Dependence on a particular lord's mercy was replaced by interdependence in a loose-knit but highly functional community of customers and suppliers. If you choose to work for an employer instead of launching a business of your own, then you are leaving it to your employer to make key decisions, and you are letting your employer bear the risk that comes with those decisions. You remain a free agent in the pivotal sense that when you conclude that you are better off quitting, you won't need permission to leave. Even as an employee, you are in crucial ways a partner, not a mere possession. To be clear, you won't necessarily prefer being a partner to being a serf. You may not feel as secure as you would like. But you will be free.

In a nutshell, freedom in commercial society involves *depending* on many but being at the *mercy* of none.

THIRD, THERE ARE NO GUARANTEES

Smith is not only a founding father of commercial society, but also the author of a critique of it that would dominate European political thought to this day.[1] He worried that the entire market system could become corrupted for two reasons: First, people tend to be too intent on running other people's lives. Second, people are insufficiently intent on properly running their own. One problem corrupts politics; the other corrupts the soul.

Smith was concerned about how stable a market could be when there was nothing to stop it from deteriorating into what we now call "crony capitalism." Adam Smith was a champion of free trade, but not of "big business." He saw big business as favoring subsidies and protections, not free trade. Partnerships between big business and big government lead to big subsidies, monopoly licensing practices, and tariffs. These ways of compromising freedom have been and always will be presented as protection for the middle class, but their true purpose is (and almost always will be) to transfer wealth and power from ordinary citizens to well-connected elites. As a result, an ordinary citizen's pivotal relationships are not with free and equal trading partners but with bureaucratic rulers: people whose grip on our community is so complete that we cannot walk away from such terms of engagement as they unilaterally propose. Thus, we reinvent feudalism. Once again, we are at the mercy of lords.

---

1. See Ryan Patrick Hanley, *Adam Smith and the Character of Virtue* (New York: Cambridge, 2009), p. 24.

Seldom do businessmen assemble—Smith observed—without someone raising the topic of how to fix prices. He thought that tradesmen are also constantly trying to form unions in order to petition for government monopoly licensing or otherwise to collude so as to raise their wages far above competitive levels. Smith judged that it rarely did much good to create government power to prevent collusion because that very power tends to become the prize that would-be monopolists seek. So, above all, Smith warned, government should avoid making it easier for would-be monopolists to collude.

As concerned as he was with political corruption, though, Smith's more pressing concern was with how capitalism can corrupt the soul, and thus fail to be as liberating as it could otherwise be. Smith saw earning esteem as bound up with earning a living. A merchant or producer of goods learns how to bring a service to the community that makes the community a better place for anyone who has anything to do with him. Our natural drive to, in Smith's words, "truck, barter, and exchange" is a drive not only to make money but to be part of a community of free and responsible reciprocators who bring something good to the table. These are people who warrant esteem, and whose esteem is worth something in return. This esteem for Smith is the ultimate coin of the realm.

The core of a virtuous relationship in a market society is this: your customer walks in the door and you offer a product partly because you envision that product making your customer better off. Your customer pays a price agreeable to you partly because your customer wants you to be happy to see her come through your door, each of you knowing that her business is helping you to feed your family. The moral point of appealing to each other's self-interest is to show each other basic respect. That is what it is like to care about other people. You care about what is in their best interest.

But Adam Smith had specific worries about how people can and do hurt themselves in market society. Specialization is the source of the greatest benefits of civilization, but when it takes the form of filling a worker's day with dreary repetitive tasks, we get bored and we lose interest. This is one of the issues that Marx had in mind in his discussions of worker alienation. Other problems can be even worse. Everyone wants recognition, but if our desire for recognition is not disciplined, it can ruin us in three ways. First, workers keep working long after they have acquired enough to meet their needs. Why? One reason is that people want to amass enough wealth to impress others. We like to keep up with the Joneses. Smith was glad that people work as hard as they do for their customers, but lamented that workers come to care so little for themselves. It takes maturity and true self-respect to transcend this drive. Not everyone knows when to quit.

Second, Smith anticipated that this alienation would not be restricted to the factory floor but would come to infect even well-paid, white-collar workers. Alienation does not require dismal working conditions on the factory floor. It can happen in the posh offices of executives who no longer see a connection between their labors and the possibility of satisfaction from a job well done. It can happen to creators who work only through intermediaries, and thus lose contact both with their product and their customers. It can happen to investors who see investing as little more than a form of gambling rather than as an honorable opportunity to invest in helping producers to achieve excellence.

Finally, here is a problem that is not unique to a commercial society, but is in fact a real problem for every society. The problem is that we tend not to notice our tendency to adjust our attitudes to conform to those of people around us, a drive that makes us far more vulnerable to social pressure. If we noticed ourselves "going along to get along," we could resist, or at least go along in a self-respecting way. But if we don't even notice this happening, our ability to avoid it is compromised. It all stems from too little self-love, not too much.

Yet, none of this is out of our control. We have what it takes to distinguish between being esteemed and deserving esteem, and to preserve our psychological independence by reminding ourselves every day that we aren't seeking to win sympathy for the false image we project. It is our real core selves for which we want to achieve a sense of belonging. Earl Warren, former Chief Justice of the U.S. Supreme Court, supposedly said, "Everything I did in my life that was worthwhile, I caught hell for." That is one way of expressing the difference between being esteemed and deserving esteem. Of course, this does not stop the worry about ending up a fraud. That worry remains. There is no such thing as addressing it "once and for all."

Is there anything unique about alienation in a commercial society? If there is something unique, perhaps it is this. Commercial society raises the frontier of human possibility. Outside of the networks of cooperation that we find in commercial societies, we might be glad to be able to gather enough food to avoid starvation. In a commercial society, it becomes possible to specialize in oral surgery, or in being a concert violinist, or any number of things. When commercial society makes such things possible, it raises our expectations. In a commercial society, you might be able to gather enough to eat with hours to spare at the end of the day, and in that spare time, you can think about all the people who are achieving greater success in life. You can imagine being so much more than you are, and you can lament falling short of what may after all have been a reasonable aspiration. If you spend your time thinking about such things, you won't be happy. It's your choice. Smith saw alienation in its full context; no matter how much we achieve, we are reminded every time we see an expensive car drive by that we could have achieved more.

Indeed, market society even makes it possible for people to have enough free time to complain! The compliment Smith wanted to pay to commercial society was to say that even in failing to be all that they could be, members of commercial society could still be in an excellent position to make life better for each other. Even laborers who work overtime to make trinkets make our world a better place, or so Smith believed. And this they accomplish even if they squander opportunities to spend their earnings in more thoughtful, creative, and self-fulfilling ways.

Smith's discussion of this possible multidimensional failure to hit the rising ceiling of our potential was not a simple critique of capitalism as much as a reflection on how much commercial society makes possible, and how little it guarantees. A precondition of free society is that people accept that they inhabit a world thick both with possibilities and responsibilities, and just as importantly, they understand that not all possibilities will be realized.

CONCLUSION

Smith told a story about the wealth of nations and how wealth grows, liberating us in the process. He also told a story about how we systematically fail to take full advantage of opportunities for the liberation that wealth creates. Smith saw commercial society emerging, liberating people economically from the shackles of destitution and culturally from shackles of feudalism. He saw commercial society potentially liberating people psychologically, too, in opening a door to a flood of human possibility. Yet, Smith also wondered, "Who will have what it takes to stride into that limitless future? Would enough people be sufficiently educated? Would the general population be a reservoir of talent, from whose ranks children would emerge who would go on to lift the ceiling of human progress?" These, for Smith, were always open questions.

DISCUSSION AND EXERCISES

1. Do human beings have a natural urge to "truck, barter, and exchange" as Smith believed?
2. What is servility? Does a market economy tend to promote or reduce servility? Explain how.
3. Why did Smith worry about the corruption of individuals' souls in a market society? Is there a remedy?

4. We described subsidies, monopoly licenses, and tariffs as "ways of compromising freedom." In what ways might this be true? Whose freedom (if anyone's) is compromised by licensed monopolies? What about subsidies? What about tariffs? See the next section for more on the topic of tariffs.

Chapter 11

Transaction Cost and Progress

Read Frederic Bastiat's short essays "A Negative Railroad" and "An Immense Discovery." We reproduce the full text of those essays here.

A NEGATIVE RAILROAD

I have said that as long as one has regard, as unfortunately happens, only to the interest of the producer, it is impossible to avoid running counter to the general interest, since the producer, as such, demands nothing but the multiplication of obstacles, wants, and efforts.

I find a remarkable illustration of this in a Bordeaux newspaper.

M. Simiot raises the following question:

Should there be a break in the tracks at Bordeaux on the railroad from Paris to Spain?

He answers the question in the affirmative and offers a number of reasons, of which I propose to examine only this:

There should be a break in the railroad from Paris to Bayonne at Bordeaux; for, if goods and passengers are forced to stop at that city, this will be profitable for boatmen, porters, owners of hotels, etc.

Here again we see clearly how the interests of those who perform services are given priority over the interests of the consumers.

But if Bordeaux has a right to profit from a break in the tracks, and if this profit is consistent with the public interest, then Angoulême, Poitiers, Tours, Orléans, and, in fact, all the intermediate points, including Ruffec, Châtellerault, etc., etc., ought also to demand breaks in the tracks, on the ground of the general interest—in the interest, that is, of domestic industry—for the more there are of these breaks in the line, the greater will be the amount paid for storage, porters, and cartage at every point along the way. By this means, we shall end by having a railroad composed of a whole series of breaks in the tracks, i.e., a negative railroad.

Whatever the protectionists may say, it is no less certain that the basic principle of restriction is the same as the basic principle of breaks in the tracks: the sacrifice of the consumer to the producer, of the end to the means.

One lesson of "Negative Railroad" is that leaps in human prosperity so often stem from innovations that lower transaction cost: container ships, FEDEX, written language, rail, auto, and air transport. This is the theme to which Bastiat's editorials returned most often. Here is another example:

AN IMMENSE DISCOVERY!

At a time when everyone is trying to find a way of reducing the costs of transportation . . .

Although the daydreams of inventors have been proverbially optimistic, I feel positively certain that I have discovered an infallible means of bringing to France the products of the whole world, and vice versa, at a considerable reduction in cost.

But it being infallible is only one of the advantages of my astounding discovery. It requires neither plans nor estimates nor preparatory studies nor engineers nor mechanics nor contractors nor capital nor stockholders nor government aid! It presents no danger of shipwreck, explosion, collision, fire, or derailment! It can be put into effect in a single day!

Finally, and this will doubtless recommend it to the public, it will not add a centime to the budget; quite the contrary. It will not increase the staff of government officials or the requirements of the bureaucracy; quite the contrary. It will cost no one his freedom; quite the contrary.

It was not chance, but observation, that put me in possession of my discovery. Let me tell you how I was led to make it.

I had this question to resolve: "Why should a thing made in Brussels, for example, cost more when it reaches Paris?"

Now, it did not take me long to perceive that the rise in price results from the existence of obstacles of several kinds between Paris and Brussels. First of all, there is the distance; we cannot traverse it without effort or loss of time, and we must either submit to this ourselves or pay someone else to submit to it. Then come rivers, marshes, irregularities of terrain, and mud; these are just so many more impediments to overcome. We succeed in doing so by raising causeways, by building bridges, by laying and paving roads, by laying steel rails, etc. But all this costs money, and the commodity transported must bear its share of the expenses. There are, besides, highway robbers, necessitating a constabulary, a police force, etc.

Now, among these obstacles between Brussels and Paris there is one that we ourselves have set up, and at great cost. There are men lying in wait along the whole length of the frontier, armed to the teeth and charged with the task of putting difficulties in the way of transporting goods from one country to the other. They are called customs officials. They act in exactly the same way as the mud and the ruts. They delay and impede commerce; they contribute to the difference that we have noted between the price paid by the consumer and the price received by the producer, a difference that it is our problem to reduce as much as possible.

And herein lies the solution of the problem. Cut the tariff.

LOWERING TRANSACTION COST

Bastiat's "immense discovery" is a lesson about transaction costs. Transaction costs are costs incurred in making a trade in a market. As mentioned in part I, they include advertising, product research, commissions, time and money spent transporting goods to and from market, equipment and space rentals, time spent waiting in line, and a seemingly limitless list of other things. And just as the division of labor propelled human progress, so did limiting transaction costs.

There are many ways to lower transaction costs. Lowering transportation cost is the most obvious. The easier we can make it to move goods and services by water, air, rail, or road, the lower these costs become. Another basic and crucial category involves making it easier and less expensive to communicate. As email, text messages, and video calls have replaced physical mail and phone calls, costs have declined dramatically. More abstractly, the ease with which we can now make exchanges by using money, credit, and even more fundamentally, language, has lowered costs significantly. To lower transaction costs is to lower the cost of trade itself. What this all really accomplishes is to lower the cost of cooperation, and this enables people to invent new ways of being good for each other.

You likely don't think about transaction costs all that much, but they once made it impossible to live what you now think of as an ordinary life. Believe it or not, the British industrial revolution came close to not happening because the Royal Mint failed to provide enough small coinage for workers, and small bank notes were illegal. The mint focused on gold coins, but these were too large for daily transactions, and there were problems at the time with silver coinage. Button makers solved the problem by issuing high-quality private coinage. "Tradesmen's tokens" were heavily used for small transactions until 1821, when the government finally got its act together. Without this reduction in transaction costs, though, history would have unfolded differently. And today, what's normal? Credit cards, debit cards, PayPal, Venmo, and a host of other things that make buying, selling, and settling debts easier every year. Imagine if none of them existed, and imagine that the smallest unit of currency were a bill of $50.

It's hard to imagine now, but it was once the case that in order to do business, people had to travel and carry physical money, sometimes a lot of it, with them. Now, weeks become seconds as we can skip getting on a boat to sail to a far-flung place in favor of a video call on a computer or phone. We can send money to each other, in any currency, with the press of a button. And these things are not reserved for the rich and the powerful. People buy the things they want every day from people in other countries, paying in currencies they have never held in their hands. The costs of transacting these deals have declined consistently for hundreds of years now. As they have, the potential for human flourishing has steadily increased.

PROPERTY RIGHTS

Division of labor and the reduction of transaction costs don't tell the whole story of human progress, not by a long shot. As a matter of fact, without property rights underlying the entire system, we would likely not have much progress at all to consider. Property rights have existed in one form or another for thousands of years. The 8th Commandment, "Thou shalt not steal" doesn't make much sense unless people can own things, after all. We find similar sorts of things in the texts of Plato, Sun Tzu, and just about every other author in the ancient world. What we do not see in the ancient world is a systematic attempt to work out *why* people have property rights. For that we had to wait until John Locke wrote the *Second Treatise of Government*, which was originally published in 1689.

In that book, Locke became one of the first authors to take issue with the feudal reality nearly everyone had lived with in one form or another for as long as anyone could remember. People were not, according to Locke, born owing allegiance to their betters. People were, he asserted, equal. And because they were equal no one could rule over anyone else or own anyone else, at least not legitimately. Because these equal people owned their own bodies, Locke continued, they also had a right to the things they produced with those bodies. And that, Locke said, is where property rights originate. Property rights flow from our basic human equality.

That all seems clear enough, but what do property rights do? How do they set the stage for human progress? At heart, property rights allow people to choose what to do with potential resources. And when that happens, we see entrepreneurial creativity.

Few stories illustrate the point nearly as well as what happened in the Chinese village of Xiaogang in 1978. Farms at the time had been collectivized, confiscated by the communist government in the name of the "People." Yen Jingchang, a farmer in Xiaogang at the time, recalls in a

National Public Radio interview, that, "No one owned anything." Jingchang remembered a meeting where a farmer half-jokingly asked communist party officials whether he owned his toothbrush. The answer was chilling, "No. Your *teeth* belong to the collective." The government assigned people to work on the farms and gave each of them a production quota. No one had much incentive to produce food because in this system no one was rewarded for producing more than necessary to satisfy the quota.

The farmers themselves secretly changed the rules, risking their lives and changing Chinese history in the process. There was nothing they could do about the government quota, so they accepted that as the cost of doing business. Each would continue, they secretly agreed, to produce and submit to the collective the amount specified in the quota. Anything they produced beyond that, they agreed, would be their individual property.

The result? Productivity increased immediately. More food was produced because the farmers finally had an incentive to produce more, to work harder. Prior to the agreement, work was simply a chore that the farmers had no choice but to undertake. After the agreement, after property rights were introduced, work became a sort of contest to see who could earn the most by his own sweat and creativity. Yen Jingchang was one of the farmers who signed the original deal.[1]

As the 18th century philosopher and historian David Hume observed, property conventions would seem magical to an outside observer. But the progress they foster is not magic; it's simply work—in response to settled rules that enable everyone to know that it pays to work.

However, settling on rules is a challenge, because in actual practice, the rules are an evolving response to a problem that is itself evolving. For example, if a person can own a patch of land, does that person own the air space above the house? If so, how high does that ownership go? A few feet? A few miles?

This was exactly what was at issue in *Hinman v. Pacific Air Transport*, a case heard by the 9th Circuit Court of Appeals in 1936. In that case a landowner sued an airline for trespassing, asserting a right to stop airlines from crossing above his property. The Court's predicament was that on the one hand, the right to say no is the backbone in a system of private property, which in turn is the backbone of cooperation among self-owners. On the other hand, much of the point of property is to facilitate commercial traffic. In the 1930s, one of the most important developments in human history was

---

1. https://marginalrevolution.com/marginalrevolution/2012/02/the-secret-agreement-that-revolution ized-china.html

unfolding—in the sky. For a court to rule that landowners could effectively veto air traffic would in effect be treating property rights as a license to stop progress. As the case turned out, the Court ruled that the right to say no extends only as high as a landowner can actually use his land. Higher altitudes were subject to navigation easements, which were held by the public and administered by the federal government.

We can explain the *Hinman* verdict in terms of property rights, but it is also a story of transaction costs. Forcing airlines to transact with untold thousands of landowners for permission to pass over each one's land would be prohibitively expensive. It would effectively ground airline travel across the country. You can see how complicated these simple questions can become. There is no magic to answering them, just better and worse attempts, which yield better and worse outcomes.

DISCUSSION AND EXERCISES

1. Think about the idea that the consumer is the end and the producer is the means. What does that mean? What is Bastiat's point?
2. Are property rights implied by ownership? If so, why did a theory of property rights not emerge until Locke wrote in the seventeenth century?
3. How far can (or should) property rights extend? Was the 9th Circuit Court of Appeals correct in its approach in the *Hinman* case?

Chapter 12

Commerce and Progress[1]

with Jason Brennan

FREEDOM FROM POVERTY

It was a complete surprise to nearly everyone when, on July 24, 1959, Vice President Richard Nixon showed Soviet Premier Nikita Khrushchev a model of a six-room American house. Khrushchev and the Soviet press scoffed, saying the model house was no more representative of typical American living standards than the Taj Mahal was of life in India. Western journalists, stunned, realized that Khrushchev was not kidding. Khrushchev was the leader, not some naïve pawn, of a Soviet machine. Yet, somehow, even he had been fooled by the propaganda. American scholars and journalists had insisted that the USSR was extending the frontiers of human productivity and prosperity.

But in that moment, everyone realized that the Soviet Union was so incredibly far behind that even the Soviet leader, Khrushchev, had no clue that the lifestyle of typical Americans was even possible. The model house that Khrushchev believed impossible was selling for $14,000. It was built to be within the price range of typical steelworkers at the time. Later that day, Nixon remarked that America's 44 million families owned 56 million cars, 50 million television sets, and 143 million radios. Some thirty-one million families owned their own homes. Nixon concluded: "What these statistics demonstrate is this: the United States, the world's largest capitalist country, has from the standpoint of the distribution of wealth come closest to the ideal of prosperity for all in a classless society."

In a command economy such as the Soviet Union, a central planner cannot know whether to order a factory to produce plastic or metal shovels, gold

---

1. This section is a chapter from *Brief History of Liberty*, by David Schmidtz and Jason Brennan.

or aluminum wire, or leather or canvas shoes. Planners must guess what to produce and where to send it. People line up for hours to receive whatever is being doled out that day. Perhaps they go home with a plastic shovel. If it is useful, they may be able to exchange it (on the black market) for canvas shoes, doled out to someone else on some other day; the fundamental fact remains that a factory producing plastic shovels won't know and won't care whether they are producing anything useful. There won't be any reason to care, since there are no paying customers anyway, except on the black market. The Soviet GDP per man-hour in 1987 was less than a third of that of the United States.

In 1800, when 95 percent of workers were farmers, many countries could not feed all of their citizens. Today, some of those countries, employing under 2 percent of their workforce in agriculture, produce excess food. Most people now living in these countries are liberated so completely from the shackles of hunger that they need not concern themselves with food production at all. Some aim to make lasting contributions to literature, art, or technology. The result, across history, is that commercially advanced societies produce not only the widgets and the food but also the artists, poets, and inventors. It is no accident that, historically, cultural hubs have also been commercial hubs: Athens in ancient Greece, Venice and Florence in Renaissance Italy, or New York today.

Greg Easterbrook observes that even as recently as "four generations ago, the poor were lean as fence posts, their arms bony and faces gaunt. To our recent ancestors, the idea that even the poor eat too much might be harder to fathom than a jetliner rising from the runway." The wealth we enjoy in the twenty-first century did not exist anywhere in the world a thousand years ago—or even fifty. In constant dollars, the United States today has, by itself, an economic output that is (even by conservative estimates) about 50 percent greater than the entire world's output in 1950.

We have come a long way. How did it happen?

When we speak of the rule of law as a framework for commerce, we do not simply mean a framework for garden-variety trucking and bartering, but also for the most far-reaching consequence of trucking and bartering, namely the rising tide of innovation. In other words, when the rule of law is working, it constitutes a twofold liberation of human ingenuity and of human society. It frees us both to form expectations (about what people around us are likely to want and need) and to exceed expectations (by inventing new ways to make our neighbors better off).

Somehow we accomplished what Francis Bacon (and his one-time secretary Thomas Hobbes) said we needed to accomplish in order to avoid the prospect of vanity degenerating into a war of all against all. Western powers figured out how to turn people away from war and toward trucking and bartering. The West turned other people's talents into a boon rather than a threat.

In a nutshell, society's most liberating achievement lies in how enabling us to trust each other turns us away from war and toward peaceful, voluntary, and mutually advantageous cooperation. To be sure, the peace of which Bacon dreamt still eludes much of the world. However, Western powers are no longer embroiled in century-long wars with each other. Bacon's vision of what science could achieve turned out to be right.

FREEDOM FROM ABSOLUTE POVERTY

The work of a scientist such as Marie Curie is one paradigm of Francis Bacon's noblest ambition for humanity. Adam Smith, in a less obvious way, was another paradigm. Indeed, Smith followed in Bacon's footsteps insofar as both, like Hobbes, pondered how to channel natural human propensities in directions that would make the rest of humanity better off rather than worse off. An exemplar of Bacon's noblest ambition would be technological innovation. For the 1700s, consider Smith's fellow Scots, the steam engine pioneers James Watt and Matthew Boulton. For the 1800s, consider the American steamship operator Cornelius Vanderbilt and the steam-powered locomotives of the Canadian railroad builder James J. Hill. Meanwhile, the "Suez Canal, completed in 1869, and the Panama Canal, completed in 1914, dramatically cut international shipping times, as did the progressive development of faster and larger steamships from the 1840s."[2]

By the 1840s, we find sentiments such as this:

> The bourgeoisie, during its rule of scarce one hundred years, has created more massive and more colossal productive forces than have all preceding generations together. Subjection of Nature's forces to man, machinery, application of chemistry to industry and agriculture, steam-navigation, railways, electric telegraphs, clearing of whole continents for cultivation, canalisation of rivers, whole populations conjured out of the ground—what earlier century had even a presentiment that such productive forces slumbered in the lap of social labour?[3]

As Marx and Engels were recording this thought, the technological revolution we see all around us today was just picking up steam (so to speak). Automobiles would replace horses—and cities would be much cleaner because of it: Imagine walking through the manure of a hundred thousand horses in

---

2. Jeffrey D. Sachs and Xiaokai Yang, *Economic Development and the Division of Labor*, (Malden: MA: Blackwell, 2003), p. 5.
3. Karl Marx and Friedrich Engels, The Communist Manifesto, (London: Verso, 2012) p. 40–41.

London in the mid-1800s. The Scrantons would pioneer innovations in heavy industry and would be superseded by Charles Schwab and Andrew Carnegie. (Schwab would develop the H-beam steel girder. A refinement of the concept, the I-beam, was light enough, strong enough, and flexible enough to permit the building of skyscrapers.) Abraham Gesner invented kerosene in 1854. By the 1870s, John D. Rockefeller pushed oil drilling and refining technology to a point where the price of oil would fall from 58 to 8 cents per gallon. People could light their homes with kerosene for about one cent per hour, reducing the demand for whale oil.

Friendly societies would spring up in America, England, Australia, and all over the world to provide health insurance and other social services to immigrants, migrant workers, and urban populations in general. In France, Louis Pasteur and Claude Bernard invented a technique called pasteurization, which slowed microbial growth. Pasteur also continued Edward Jenner's work on developing a vaccine for smallpox, rabies, and many other diseases. In England, James Tyndall and (in the twentieth century) Alexander Fleming were discovering antibiotics. (Precursors to both vaccines and antibiotics were known in China at least 2500 years ago.) Technology drove heavy industry, which drove urbanization, and the need for better medicine and better sanitation was being met at the same time. Alexander Graham Bell patented the telephone in 1876, and the Hungarian engineer Tivadar Puskas, with help from his collaborator Thomas Edison, invented the telephone exchange and, later on, the multiple switchboard. The cost of transportation and the cost of communication were falling drastically, driving a new age of commercial and technological progress. As recently as two hundred years ago, an average person lived on about a dollar a day—extreme poverty as the World Bank defines it today. According to one estimate, worldwide gross domestic product per capita between 5000 B.C. and A.D. 1800 did not even double. Since then, it has risen more than thirtyfold.

Wealth was created, not merely captured.

Many of us think that life was simpler for our ancestors, and in one way this has to be true: our ancestors had a smaller and less intimidating menu of life choices. Yet, average life expectancies in the West rose several decades over the past century, translating directly into staggering gains in terms of what average people can do with their lives. We are not saying that this explosion of wealth made people more free by definition. Indeed, we all know people whose rising wealth did not set them free. Still, as a matter of fact, average people can, and generally do, live richer, freer, and longer lives than average people led in 1800. What average workers can buy with a day's earnings has risen explosively, and rising wealth tends to translate into being able to accomplish more. For example, buying a bicycle in 1895 would cost an average American 36 times as many hours of labor as a vastly more useful bicycle would cost by 1997. Buying *Encyclopedia Britannica* would have cost thirty-five times as many hours in 1895. Today about two-thirds of Americans attend some college after high school; about a third end up with college degrees. A hundred years ago, the question would have been what percentage finish high school. Hundreds of years ago, few families could afford books. Today, most families can access millions of books for free, without leaving their homes, if (as most do) they have a computer with Internet access.

FREEDOM TO CRITICIZE

Jean-Jacques Rousseau criticized commercial society for teaching people to be vain, stupid, manipulative, and preoccupied with trinkets. Economist of culture Tyler Cowen would say: yes, the market produces artists who do not impress you. There will always be musicians such as the Clash (and there will always be people like our friend Tyler to Rock the Casbah). Their art may be a bigger commercial success than any of Rousseau's writings. And yet, despite the passing of centuries, a child born to working-class parents is more likely to read Rousseau in our day than in Rousseau's.

We observed earlier that a civilization's commercial hubs will also be its cultural hubs. Suppose you find market society repulsive, and you are seeking the most devastating critique of markets you can find. Where would you go? The places to shop for top-quality criticism are London, New York, or Boston—not Pyongyang, Havana, or even Moscow. Only in commercial society were critics such as Marx and Rousseau free to speak their minds. Critics, needless to say, come from the right as well as from the left. Conservatives, fundamentalists, and evangelicals today, who lament the moral decay of commercial society, never dream of leaving it, because their ancestors risked their lives migrating to commercial societies for good reason. Only in a commercial society were they secure in the right to choose their faith. In other words, alternatives to materialistic lifestyles tend to be secure in commercial societies and less so elsewhere, since commercial societies tend also to be tolerant societies.

INGREDIENTS OF COMMERCIAL PROGRESS

Our daily dealings with each other are an evolving web of mutual understandings: these come into play every time we stop at a traffic light, leave a tip at a restaurant, leave our weapons at home, or enter a voting booth. We pretty much know what to expect from each other, and knowing what to expect enables us to live well together. This is why we can live as close together as we do, while at the same time having as much room to breathe as we do. Knowing what to expect enables us to adapt to each other.

Not being obliged to conform to expectations is, likewise, an enormous benefit. The two benefits seem mutually exclusive, yet freedom of contract lets us reap both at once. We can rely on being able to go to market and find someone selling cauliflower at an affordable price. We can also rely on being able to go to market and find someone rendering obsolete what a few years ago had been cutting-edge technology. We make progress by testing what has not previously been tested. We experiment.

There is, however, a problem with experiments: many of them don't work. Rather, the ideas they test turn out to be bad ideas. Thus, long-term social progress involves encouraging people not only to experiment but also to shut down experiments when the ideas behind them prove unsound.

What kind of framework encourages experimentation without at the same time preserving bad ideas? Here is one hypothesis: in societies that work and sustain progress over long periods, people tend to be free from the burden of paying for other people's mistaken experiments and tend to be free to try (and pay for) their own. We considered one crucial ingredient of commercial progress: intellectuals tend to be free to invent and to push the frontier of technological progress. If some intellectuals choose to become social critics or philosophers instead of inventors, so be it. Critics and philosophers serve us well in their own way. They make us pause to reflect on the point of technological progress—and occasionally remind us that there has, after all, been progress. Society was not always the way it is today, nor will it always be as it is today.

THE RIGHT TO SAY NO

In medieval Europe, the church set prices. The laws had a noble purpose: to prevent exploitation, to increase fairness, and to serve the needs of the poor. But the laws did not deliver the intended result. Instead, they reinforced the medieval guilds—which had monopolies on the trade of certain goods and services—and prevented goods from being produced at a level that might have reflected the relative scarcity of, and demand for, those goods. The laws kept Europe economically stagnant and made sure that the poor stayed poor. Eliminating price controls helped Europe and its poor classes to become rich.

Philosophers have written much about the idea that the consent of the governed is a prerequisite of legitimate government but little about the parallel idea that consent is a prerequisite of legitimate trade. In a free society, you can vote. But in a really free society, you can vote with your feet. The fundamental thing about commerce in a market is that you have a right to walk away from any proposed terms of trade in search of something better.

This was a right that farmers in Limoges lacked when Adam Smith was composing his *Wealth of Nations*. So, in 1774, when Anne Robert Jacques Turgot became controller-general of France, he tried to do something about it. Turgot had been a tax collector for the province of Limousin since 1761. There he found half a million peasants living in mud huts and using plows that were no better than those of ancient Rome. Between taxes and church tithes, the peasants managed to keep about a fifth of their meager incomes. Turgot saw that, as long as peasants were not allowed to sell their products to the highest bidder but were legally required instead to sell their produce to a particular aristocrat at prices of that aristocrat's choosing, they would live on the edge of starvation. In 1776, as controller-general, Turgot issued the Six Edicts, which included removing controls on grain production, reducing tariffs, and ending the corvée. (The corvée, defended by Rousseau, was a vestige of feudalism, requiring peasants to spend up to fourteen days per year without pay, building and maintaining the king's roads.) Turgot also eliminated the craft guilds' monopoly privileges on grounds that people should not need permission to choose an occupation. Turgot sought and temporarily won for his constituents the right to choose their own occupation—under feudalism, peasants had no such right. Turgot also increased taxes on higher estates, which made him unpopular with the nobility and landed gentry. He was dismissed after refusing to grant favors to friends of Marie-Antoinette. His reforms were reversed. The corvée continued until the French Revolution in 1789.

In sum, Turgot found rural France in tatters, with peasants lacking the most rudimentary freedoms: the freedom to choose an occupation, to choose their customers, to choose their prices, and so on. Under such circumstances, it was inevitable that peasants would be on the edge of starvation. Turgot knew what the workers needed. He saw that basic liberty was the key to releasing the ingenuity and perseverance by which peasants could and would liberate themselves from material deprivation. Turgot did all he could to give the peasants the freedom they needed. The corrupt monarchy that opposed him thereby sealed its own fate.

Turgot was a force in intellectual as well as political circles. He was an influential acquaintance of Benjamin Franklin and Voltaire. He met Adam Smith in 1765 and gave Smith several books pertaining to Smith's research on the wealth of nations. In 1750, Turgot predicted the American Revolution and foresaw that this new country, America, would suffer from the legacy of slavery and from civil war far more than it would ever suffer at the hands of a foreign invader. He also predicted a bloody revolution in France that would culminate in the king's execution. He warned that switching to paper currency could and would result in hyper-inflation.

Turgot also spoke as if the land itself, rather than human ingenuity, is the ultimate producer of the explosion of wealth we see all around us. If he were around today, he would see that he had been mistaken. No one stays home nowadays hoping to inherit the family farm; a person's fortune is constituted mainly by her job skills, as long as people are free to move where their job skills are most valued. The price of land within cities rises relatively quickly, in part because people are willing to pay a premium to live in close proximity to increasingly productive concentrations of job skills.

THE AGE OF ROBBER BARONS

Charles Comte, writing in 1817, saw government power as producing "a kind of subordination that subjected the laboring men to the idle and devouring men, and which gave to the latter the means of existing without producing."[4] Karl Marx, speaking about something that we might today call the "military—industrial complex," lamented: "All revolutions perfected this machine instead of smashing it. The parties that contended in turn for domination regarded the possession of this huge state edifice as the principal spoils of the victor." In a later work, *The Civil War in France*, Marx writes of "the State parasite feeding upon, and clogging, the free movement of society."[5]

In 1846, England finally repealed its Corn Laws, which had protected English landowners by limiting the importation of corn since 1689. An era of relatively free trade ensued. Meanwhile, every transcontinental railroad subsidized in the nineteenth century by the U.S. government went bankrupt, while the sole unsubsidized transcontinental railroad, Great Northern, prospered. Subsidies divert effort into what generates them rather than into what attracts customers. For example, if you subsidize a railroad by granting it money or land for every mile of track laid, then the subsidy gives them an incentive to lay as many miles of track as possible. Without the subsidy, their incentive is to get from point A to point B in the most efficient way. This is how some railroads came to deserve the nickname of "robber barons."

---

4. Comte, Charles (1817) "De l'organisation sociale considérée dans ses rapports avec les moyens de subsistance des peuples," *La Censeur Européen* 2: 1–66, at 22.
5. For the first quotation, see Karl Marx and Friedrich Engels, *Selected Works in Three Volumes*, Moscow: Progress Publishers (1983), Volume 1, p. 477. For the second quotation, see Karl Marx, and Friedrich Engels (1983b) *Selected Works in Three Volumes*, Moscow: Progress Publishers (1983). Volume 2, p. 222.

Ill-served customers turned to the unsubsidized Great Northern Railroad—the one transcontinental railroad that labored to keep transportation costs to a minimum, the one whose mission was to provide valuable service at an affordable price, and thus the one transcontinental railroad that never went bankrupt.

Each of the railroads was run by people who were in some sense entrepreneurs, but whether entrepreneurs are productive or destructive depends on circumstances. William Baumol concluded that there are more entrepreneurs in some societies than in others, but that the number of entrepreneurs does not explain why some societies grow rich while others stay poor. The key variable is whether a society's entrepreneurs are productive, unproductive, or downright destructive. Citing evidence from ancient Rome, early China, and Medieval and Renaissance Europe, Baumol found enormous variation between societies in terms of how entrepreneurs allocate their time and resources. Simply put, entrepreneurs are entrepreneurial. They go where the opportunity is. If there is money to be made at other people's expense—organized crime, rent-seeking (including campaigning for subsidies), and so on—then we'll find entrepreneurs in those roles, doing what entrepreneurs do. If fortunes can be made by inventing new ways of making customers better off, then there, too, we will find entrepreneurs. And when philosophers and moral leaders are careful to distinguish between the two—honoring entrepreneurs who create wealth while damning entrepreneurs who merely capture it—they help to tip entrepreneurial energy in a positive direction.

SMITH'S LEGACY

We have discussed the institutional background that encourages technological innovation, division of labor, and expanding markets. A society's infrastructure must also secure people in their possessions so that people feel comfortable showing up at the market with goods for sale, feel secure enough to invest in the future, and so on. Some ways of allocating property rights are conducive to the creation of wealth; others are not. Property rights are allocated in one way in Zimbabwe (President Mugabe takes whatever he wants), and the result is devastating poverty. By contrast, stable, private ownership of the means of production robustly translates into nearly all of us being wealthier than our grandparents were.

It is a general feature of prosperous countries that they take formal property rights seriously. To Marx, however, this correlation made no sense. Put yourself in Marx's shoes. Looking around Paris or London in the nineteenth-century, Marx saw a stark material contrast between the rich and the poor.

Both the rich gentleman and the poor laborer were recognized as having a right to own property, but the formal freedom that liberal society aims to provide – freedom from interference – is not enough. For example, there is no law that prevents you from buying a house, but the Marxist point is that if you can't afford to pay full price for a house with cash up front, and if you could not begin to borrow money if interest rates are as high as 60 percent, then your formal freedom to buy a house—the fact that the law is not stopping you—is a cruel joke. Real freedom, Marxists say, is a matter of what workers actually are able to do. So, where in the world is this "real" freedom found? As a matter of historical record, commercial societies have evolved to become more free in precisely the way that really matters according to Marxists: that is, formal freedoms seemingly go hand in hand with people of all classes becoming wealthy enough to do more with their lives than would otherwise be possible. We see this happening, but how? To Marx, the problem is that the poor have formal rights but they have no actual property. Is it possible that Marx was missing something? Yes, according to Peruvian economist Hernando De Soto. From what De Soto could see, Marx got it backwards; the actual problem is the exact opposite in developing countries. In countries like Peru, De Soto observed, the poor possess plenty of real assets. What they lack is formal rights. De Soto estimated that the poorest of the poor in the developing world possess $9.3 trillion worth of land. This was roughly the size of the U.S. GDP at the time, and perhaps a thousand times the size of the entire world's foreign aid budget (leaving aside military aid). But then why is there such a contrast between the West, where we find pockets of misery in an ocean of comfort, and the rest of the world, where we find pockets of comfort in an ocean of misery? If workers in developing countries own trillions of dollars' worth of land, why do they still have almost nothing compared to what their counterparts have in the West?

The key is that there is a difference between possessing land and owning it. A person who might start a chain of Mexican restaurants in Tucson puts that same energy into selling homemade food by the side of the road in rural Mexico. There is no public record of him incorporating. He has no documents. As far as the government is concerned, his business does not exist. Having no legal property, he cannot sell shares or franchises, so he cannot raise investment capital. He cannot even take out a loan because legally he has no collateral to secure the loan. He will never raise enough money for a proper building with a kitchen and a flush toilet.

On De Soto's analysis, Western entrepreneurs operate within an infrastructure of formal law that enables them to expand their businesses. It is relatively easy for them to get a business license, and therefore relatively easy for them to access lines of low-cost credit. De Soto argues that low-cost credit has empowered human ingenuity in the West and may one day do so around the world.

De Soto is right about this much. Imagine a country, in other respects like yours, but in which there are no institutions of mortgage lending. Without lending institutions, the only people who can buy houses in such a country are those who can afford to pay cash up front. Would you be able to buy a house? Probably not. So what would you do? Rent an apartment? Probably not. After all, who could afford to build an apartment building in such a country if they would have to pay for the building with cash in advance? What would such a country be like, a country otherwise like yours with one little change: no mortgage lending industry and no way for anyone to get an affordable loan. With that one small change, the world you know would not be very much like what we call the West. It would be a developing country.

So it is in Peru, says De Soto. In rural Peru, how do you know when you cross from one owner's land to another's? Answer: a different dog starts barking. De Soto's point: you can't take your dog to the bank. If you want a loan, you need real, documented collateral. So, De Soto's answer to why capitalism works in the West and not elsewhere is that capitalism depends on the availability of credit. To obtain credit, one must establish a stable title to collateral so that lenders can afford the risk of low-rate lending.

De Soto concludes that globalization as such is not failing, but particular countries are failing to "globalize" their capital. Successful globalization won't be just about linking up elites. De Soto says that capital is the source of productivity, and consequently of the wealth of nations, but he adds that foreign capital investment, in the long run, is not good enough. The benefits of capitalism will not spread to remote parts of developing countries until the firm foundations of formal property are in place domestically. (And even that, we presume De Soto would admit, is only a start.)

There are cultures in which people are taught to hate the whole idea of buying on credit. The idea of a business that enables you to take out a mortgage so that you can buy a house in your twenties is often treated as the worst form of greed. But there is an element of the unseen here. What is the alternative? Where would you be if we had made it illegal for your parents to borrow enough money to buy a house?

The concept of being in the business of lending money, charging a fee—charging **interest**—for the service of giving customers a line of credit for buying a home, investing in a business, and so on, was a Mesopotamian invention around 3000 B.C. The lending industry has enabled movement and investment of capital ever since. To be sure, the Islamic nations were far ahead of the West in the sciences until the early modern period, and then something happened that prevented Islamic science from translating into technological and economic growth. There are many reasons why, of course, but one factor is that Islamic law treats lending money for interest as presumptively immoral. It has held them back.

WHEN FORMAL FREEDOM IS ENOUGH

Marx saw early capitalism in zero-sum terms. He was wrong, but still, he had a point. Marx was looking at capitalism's birth as a Western institution. From what he could see, early capitalism, with its sweaty sixteen-hour workdays, was justified only insofar as it was better than the bare subsistence of what had come before, and only insofar as early capitalism was leading to a world in which a work day would someday be only eight hours rather than sixteen, and only five days rather than six or seven. We cannot disagree. By today's standards, early capitalism between the times of Adam Smith and Karl Marx was horrible compared to what it eventually led to.

We all should be amazed by how much working conditions have improved since Karl Marx's time. Neither Adam Smith in 1776 nor Karl Marx in 1848 could foresee that life expectancy of the working class would someday exceed fifty years. Some contemporary political theorists talk about a static economy (a "stationary state") being desirable, as if we have reached the climax of technological innovation and the only thing left to discover is how to do better at distributing what we are now producing. People in Francis Bacon's time (the 1500s) talked as if everything worth knowing was already known by the time of Aristotle. As Bacon (one of the inventors of modern methods of observation-based science) would have predicted, there has not yet been a time when such ways of talking did not look foolish in retrospect.

This is not to say that progress does not come at a cost. There is always a cost. For example, progress in the sciences put us in a position to understand that we wanted to be able to paint our houses with something other than lead-based paint. We can be glad that we learned that lesson, even as we wish that we had learned that lesson earlier. Progress tends to be like that; it often consists of learning how to do better, and wishing that we had known earlier.

DISCUSSION AND EXERCISES

1. If farmland is so valuable, why do subsidies flow from those who do not own farms to those who do?
2. In market economies, people (engineers, entrepreneurs, money-lenders, inventors) who figure out how to make unskilled labor more productive get paid more than the unskilled laborers themselves. Why?
3. Where do people have the most access to the world's greatest art, music, and literature? Why?
4. How virtuous are people in market societies? Whatever your answer is, what evidence (if any) would make you change your mind?

5. Suppose we find, say, a certain banking system clearly working well—promoting peaceful commerce—in the United States and in Canada. Does it follow that the International Monetary Fund or the World Bank should be forcing African and Eastern European countries to adopt the North American system? What are some of the pitfalls of exporting institutions that seem to work well in a particular context?

6. How much economic freedom do we want? The question has many dimensions. Should we be free to buy and sell alcohol? Heroin? Abortions? Instruction manuals for building chemical or nuclear weapons? Should we be free to trade with people from other countries? Should employees be free to look for employers who pay more? Should employers be free to look for employees who cost less? Should manufacturers be free to market new and perhaps dangerous products? Under what conditions? What counts as fair warning?

7. Can a person be made less free by being given the option to take a low-paying job?

8. In your own words, explain the word "collateral." What does it take to convert a parcel of land into something that you can take to a bank and use as collateral to secure a loan?

Chapter 13

Production Possibilities Frontier

To understand trade, you first have to understand what is possible without trade. The Production Possibilities Frontier (PPF) is a graphical representation of what is possible, given certain underlying considerations. In other words, the PPF is a collection of points that shows the relationship between maximum possible production outcomes given a fixed set of resources over a period of time. These curves are sometimes called Production Possibilities Curves, or Production Possibilities Boundaries.

Imagine a man named Roberto on a deserted island. To keep it simple, suppose he can only produce two things: firewood and fish. His resources are the island itself and his time. If he spends all day collecting wood, he can collect three bundles. If he spends all day fishing, he can catch six fish.

Once you understand PPFs, you can use them as a tool to visualize and better understand the impact resources and productivity have on welfare. Later, they can also be very useful when examining the concept of Comparative Advantage.

PPFs are often used to present complex things, but we begin here with Roberto's Production Possibilities Curve on his deserted island, where we only have two things, wood and fish, to worry about. In table 13.1, Roberto's production is organized according to whether he spends his entire day collecting wood or catching fish. Notice that he can allocate some of the six days to collecting wood and some to fishing. The first row describes Roberto's production if he spends six days collecting wood and no days fishing. He manages to come up with eighteen bundles of wood, but no fish. The next row allocates five days collecting wood and one day to fishing. And so on.

Table 13.1. Determining Roberto's production possibilities over six days

	Days on WOOD	Production in WOOD 3 per day	Days on FISH	Production in FISH 6 per day
Spends all 6 days producing WOOD	6	18	0	0
Spends 5 days producing WOOD, 1 day on FISH	5		1	
Spends 4 days producing WOOD, 2 days on FISH	4		2	
Spends 3 days producing WOOD, 3 days on FISH	3		3	
Spends 2 days producing WOOD, 4 days on FISH	2		4	
Spends 1 day producing WOOD, 5 days on FISH	1		5	
Spends 6 days producing FISH	0	0	6	36

Table 13.2. Roberto's production possibilities over six days

Production in WOOD 3 per day	Production in FISH 6 per day
18	0
15	6
12	12
9	18
6	24
3	30
0	36

If you fill in the missing numbers in the table, you notice that as Roberto shifts from collecting wood to catching fish, the number of fish caught rises and the amount of wood collected falls. Those pairs of numbers (amount of wood, number of fish) represent the maximum production he can achieve given the way he allocates his time.

Roberto can always choose to produce less. He would produce less if he decided to take a day off, for example.

Let's suppose that if Roberto is at maximum production and decides to collect wood for three days and fish for three days, then he would collect nine bundles of wood and catch eighteen fish.

The only way Roberto can get more fish is by dedicating more days to fishing, which means giving up time collecting wood. If he increases his fishing time by one day, those six additional fish will cost him three bundles of wood. When he is at his most productive, he has to give up three bundles of wood to get six more fish. Even if he were willing to split his day between the two activities, every fish he caught would cost him one-half of a bundle of wood. In other words, choosing to produce one more fish has a cost, an opportunity cost, of a half bundle of wood.

The same goes if he wants to produce more wood. The opportunity cost of producing one more bundle of wood is two fish. Table 13.1 shows this relationship clearly, but graphing that information makes things clearer still. Figure 13.1 shows what this information looks like in graphical form if we put bundles of wood on the horizontal, or *x*-axis, and fish on the vertical, or *y*-axis. This graph is the PPF. Everything to the left of the line is a possible outcome. Everything to the right of the line is an impossible outcome. All of the points exactly on the line represent the maximum number of fish and bundles of wood Roberto can accumulate. How much of one or the other he accumulates is up to him.

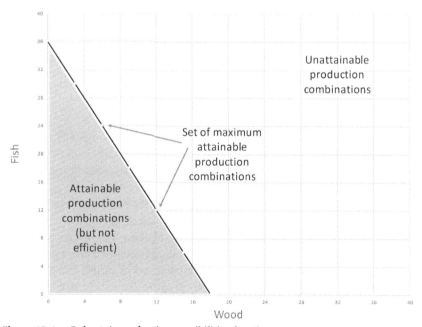

Figure 13.1. Roberto's production possibilities frontier

PPFS' NEGATIVE SLOPE

PPFs have a negative slope. This is because resources are finite. The slope is the ratio of the change in the *y*-axis variable, fish, over the change in the *x*-axis variable, wood. This is referred to as the "rise over run." The negative slope indicates that once Roberto is at maximum production, there is an opportunity cost, or tradeoff, to increasing production of one good. If the line is straight, that means the opportunity cost is constant at every level of production.

With fish on the vertical, or *y*-axis, and wood on the horizontal, or *x*-axis, the slope of Roberto's PPF is a constant −2. If the axes were switched, the slope would be −1/2. But this would simply be saying the same thing in two different ways. Interpreting the slope as the opportunity cost of one good in terms of the other will work no matter how the axes are designated. In simple terms, the opportunity cost of a bundle of wood is two fish, and the opportunity cost of one fish is half a bundle of wood.

Remember that Roberto can always choose to produce less than any of these pairs by deciding to work less than six full days. Under-employing his resources is represented as any point inside the PPF, which is the shaded region of figure 13.1.

While everything to the right of the line is unattainable as production possibilities, they are not unattainable as consumption possibilities. Roberto can consume more wood and fish than he can produce, by trading. For now, though, there are still some things left to consider with Roberto's PPF. As it turns out, anything that changes Roberto's productive capacity, for good or for ill, will change his PPF. And they can change in two ways.

PPF PIVOT

PPFs can pivot. Imagine that Roberto is strolling along on his island picking up wood when he happens upon a fishing net. This is a lucky day for Roberto, because now he can catch more fish. As a matter of fact, with his new net, he can catch nine fish a day rather than six.

This would increase Roberto's production of fish, but his ability to collect wood would not change. Still, he is better off after finding the net than he was before. If he spends six days fishing with his new net, he can now catch 54 fish! When change affects only one output, as was the case with the net, the PPF pivots outward if it is a positive impact, and inward if it is a negative impact. Figure 13.2 illustrates a positive pivot in Roberto's PPF when his ability to catch fish is improved.

PPF SHIFT

PPFs can also shift. This means that Roberto's ability to do everything can change for better or worse. Roberto can discover some new corner of the

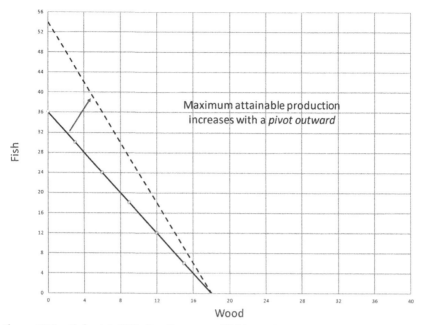

Figure 13.2. Roberto's PPF after discovery of fishing net

island which has all kinds of wood handy and a better fishing spot to boot. This would be a positive shift in his PPF. On the other hand, Roberto could sprain an ankle, which would shift his PPF negatively. Remember, a PPF is simply a graphical representation of Roberto's underlying situation. When the details of his situation change, so does his PPF.

If we control for the size of the population, the PPF can indicate the relative wealth of a society, just as it indicated Roberto's relative wealth in our simple example. Shifts or pivots out indicate an increase in wealth. Shifts or pivots in indicate decreasing wealth.

Production possibilities, at least in theory, are relatively straightforward, but real questions are always what a society will actually produce and what it will consume. Not surprisingly, actual PPFs get a little more complicated than Roberto's. This is largely because opportunity cost, which is at the heart of the PPF, is not usually constant. More often, opportunity cost increases. With a **constant opportunity cost**, Roberto's PPF is simply a straight line. But a more realistic story would show that Roberto can collect a number of bundles of wood when he first starts, but that wood becomes harder to find the more he collects. The same sort of thing is true of fish too. This is **increasing opportunity cost**. PPFs that take increasing opportunity cost into account have curved rather than straight lines. The slope is different everywhere, increasing absolute value as you move from left to right (for good x, the output on the horizontal

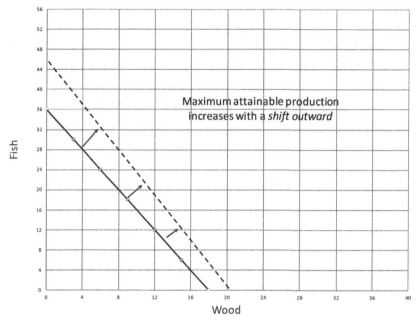

Figure 13.3.   Roberto's PPF with overall increase in productive capacity

axis), and increasing in absolute value of the inverse slope as you move from right to left (for good *y*, the output on the vertical axis).

DISCUSSION AND EXERCISES

1. What does a production possibilities curve show? How can you determine whether production is using resources efficiently?
2. Suppose that you can produce hamburgers or fries. Represent this situation with a PPC and describe what your figure shows.
3. Describe the difference between a PPF pivot and a PPF shift.

Chapter 14

What Seems Like Progress

People sometimes say wars and natural disasters are good for economies. They help society make progress. Why? Because they create jobs.

Can that be right? Is destruction good for an economy? You might think this is impossible. But let's think about it. When a disaster like a hurricane strikes, its path of destruction is widespread and obvious. In its wake, people do what they always do: they rebuild. When they do, they employ all kinds of people: bricklayers, construction workers, roofers, accountants and insurance adjusters.

French philosopher and politician Frédéric Bastiat wrote about this phenomenon in the 1840s. He was quick to give due credit to government for its role in securing France's borders, maintaining the nation's roads, and any number of other basic functions government typically carries out. But, Bastiat asked, should we also depend on government to create jobs?

Read Bastiat's essay on "What Is Seen and What Is Unseen." Check our online resources for a condensed version of Bastiat's essay.

Here is Bastiat's analysis. Bastiat asks us to imagine that a person, good fellow's son, breaks a window. What happens next? Someone gets hired to fix the window. Suppose the glazier (the person who repairs windows) charges six francs for the service. The easily seen cost is six francs. The easily seen benefit is that a window gets fixed.

What else is going on? Bastiat asks, what is unseen here? Is there an unseen benefit, namely that a repairman has a job fixing the window? Perhaps. Is there also an unseen cost?

Bastiat makes an interesting point. He notes that there is an unseen cost, namely that the six francs that got spent fixing the window would otherwise have been used to hire someone to do something else. Therefore, if we want to understand the big picture, we should ask, what is the net effect of using six francs to hire a glazier that otherwise would have been spent to hire someone else? What is the cost? It is this: whatever the six francs would have produced is not produced. *Opportunity cost* tends to be unseen. It is what would have been done with the money.

What increases the stock of wealth is getting work done. Breaking windows is the exact opposite of getting work done. Breaking windows is undoing work, making it necessary to do it over again.

So, Bastiat would hear people say there is a silver lining to natural disasters. What is the silver lining? Bastiat understood that government's make-work programs create jobs, but warned of something that should be obvious: the point of jobs is to create wealth. Rebuilding a city like New Orleans in the wake of a hurricane is not a way of creating wealth. Rebuilding is good, but *needing* to rebuild is bad. If New Orleans had not been damaged in the first place, that work would have gone into creating new wealth rather than into rebuilding what was lost.

Bastiat wanted his readers to think about what is seen and what is obvious. But he also worried about the unseen cost, the cost we fail to notice. This unseen cost, he said, would look small, not because it is actually small, but because it is spread out among many people in the form of taxes, and thus hidden from view. Bastiat never said we should not have government. He never said government is too expensive. Bastiat instead asked a very specific question: What is the opportunity cost of creating a job?

So why didn't Hurricane Katrina make New Orleans rich? Katrina was a Category 5 hurricane that hit New Orleans in 2005, bringing with it a path of destruction that made it one of the biggest natural disasters in American history, impacting over 93,000 square miles. It left around 300,000 homes uninhabitable, and deposited 118 million cubic yards of debris. There was plenty of work to be done the minute the floodwaters receded, and work creates wealth. Or does it?

When wealth is destroyed, by natural disaster or anything else, we have to rebuild, but we are not making progress. We are just coping with a setback as best we can. The rebuilding effort is simply a struggle to get back to where we were before disaster struck. New Orleans will get over Hurricane Katrina, without question. But neither New Orleans nor the United States will be as rich as they would have been if Katrina had not happened.

In Bastiat's terms, New Orleans was one gigantic broken window. And we are all prone to thinking of broken windows incorrectly, because of the seen and the unseen. What do we see? We see a broken window that needs to be fixed, and we see a glazier fixing it. The glazier is better off for having the work. He is richer. But what is unseen?

Bastiat wants you to think about the hidden worker, the person (or people) who would have been employed in place of the glazier if not for the broken window. The shopkeeper would not have replaced a perfectly good window, after all. He would have used that money on something else, be it a suit, or meat for dinner, or a new sign for his business. Who was the big loser when his window was broken? Well, he was obviously, but so were the tailor, the butcher, and the sign maker. And when we think government can simply create jobs, thereby creating wealth, we do not consider any of them.

Intuitively you know this is true. No one would think breaking every window in a neighborhood would be good for the economy, even if the neighborhood glazier would have work for the foreseeable future. Other people need work too, after all. What would we do next? Slash all the tires on all the cars to keep the tire shop in business? Burn down the grocery store? Dig up the streets? In the end, everyone we could think of would have more work, yet everyone would be worse off. And what is the biggest thing we would have lost along the way? All of the new, productive things everyone would have otherwise done with their time: actual wealth.

TWO STEPS BACK, ONE STEP FORWARD

Part of Bastiat's point is to make fun of the idea of "stimulating the economy" by first taking money out of the economy only to put it back in. What if we told the glaziers to take responsibility for creating their own jobs by breaking the windows themselves? What about the tire sellers? Should we encourage them to take the initiative in making work for themselves by turning them loose to go around slashing tires? We normally think of these things as crimes, but if destruction is ultimately good for the economy, then why not take the initiative?

Or, perhaps we needn't go through all the trouble. Instead of actually breaking all the windows and slashing all the tires, the neighborhood could just pretend it happened and pay the glaziers and tire shops as if their services had been needed. This is clearly better than causing damage to stimulate the economy, but it's still a terrible idea. In the end, people will spend their money fixing things that need fixing. They will also spend their money on things they want and enjoy. And when they do that, new things are created for them. Wealth is created.

BEWARE OF CREATING JOBS

It might take one worker one hour to dig a trench using a bulldozer. If you thought that the wealth of a nation is all about creating jobs, you might think that you could create a lot of wealth by getting rid of the bulldozer and instead using ten workers to dig the trench with shovels over the course of a whole day. Maybe even better would be to get rid of the shovels and use a hundred workers to spend a whole week digging the same trench with spoons. Replacing bulldozers with shovels would create jobs. Replacing the shovels with spoons would be even better if the point is to create jobs. So, what is wrong with this logic? What do we get wrong when we say creating jobs is the key to social progress?

THE CIRCLE GAME

Work makes a country richer because it adds to stock of wealth. Destroying wealth makes work, but misses the point. Adding services to the economy takes the economy a step forward. When any disaster strikes, whether natural or manmade, that is a step back. If taking a step forward is a good thing, then it isn't good to take a step back first.

Here's another illustration of the unseen (from David Friedman's *Machinery of Freedom*):

> Imagine a circle of 100 taxpayers. You are the tax collector. You go around the circle, taking a penny from each and then you pick one taxpayer out of the hundred and give that one a 50-cent windfall. That one person is now delighted, and thinks taxes are a good thing on balance.

Now do the same thing another hundred times, picking a different person each time for a 50 cent windfall. In end, we've taken one hundred from each taxpayer, we have given back fifty to each, and everyone is happy and thinks taxes are a good thing on balance.

Why are they happy? Because they see the 50 cent windfall, and may even come to depend on it.

They do not see the hundred cents they paid for that 50 cent windfall because the hundred cents were taken from them one cent at a time. The way the pennies add up is unseen.

Apply David Friedman's circle game to Bastiat's broken window question. Go around the circle, breaking one hundred windows. Make the glazier happy. Go around again, slashing one hundred tires. Now the tire store is happy. Eventually, everyone is working, and everyone is happy to have work, but everyone is poorer than they would've been. They feel lucky to have jobs because that is the only way they can afford to keep paying for all the damage to their own property. But there is no silver lining to working overtime just to stay afloat instead of working to add something new to the stock of a community's wealth.

DISCUSSION AND EXERCISES

1. Here are reasons for using tax money to pay high salaries to public officials. Which one does Bastiat single out as an especially bad reason?

   a. It creates jobs.
   b. It draws more talented people toward public service.
   c. It will increase tax revenues.
   d. It is needed to make progress on public works.

   Here is a tough question. It is tough because all of the answers have a grain of truth. Nevertheless, one answer is better than the others.

2. What is the unseen cost of using tax dollars to create jobs?

   a. Transaction cost
   b. External cost
   c. Opportunity cost
   d. Net total cost

3. According to Bastiat, why wouldn't hiring soldiers with tax dollars stimulate the economy and create jobs? Again, this is a tough question in a sense, because each answer has a grain of truth that you could defend. But still, if you understood Bastiat, you will see that one answer is better than others.

   a. Corrupt politicians steal the money; it never reaches the soldiers.
   b. Soldiers do not do productive work.
   c. Soldiers spend too much money abroad, which increases the trade deficit.
   d. The tax dollars had to be removed from the productive sector.

4. Think about two groups. Both groups build a house in Period 1. Then in Period 2, Group A erects another house, house #2. At the same time, Group B tears down house #1 and rebuilds it. Then in Period 3, Group A builds house # 3, while Group B tears down and rebuilds house #1. Then in Period 4, Group A builds house #4, and Group B tears down and rebuilds house #1. And at some point, if you are able to observe both groups, the opportunity cost becomes plainly visible. So, Bastiat asks you, is there really any silver lining to being in Group B, and never having more than house #1?

5. Imagine a country hit by a major hurricane every day. Obviously that
   would not make a country rich. But why not? Explain. (It sure would create jobs!) If being crushed once is a good thing, why isn't it ideal to be
   crushed every day? Or if there is no silver lining to being crushed, even
   once, why would creating jobs ever be a silver lining?
6. Explain the "broken window" fallacy. What is the fallacy involved in
   thinking that breaking stuff is a form of wealth creation? What is the fallacy involved in thinking that "two steps back, one step forward" is the
   same thing as one step forward? Think of this as a question of unseen cost.

Part III

UNDERSTANDING TRADE

Trade enables us all to make ourselves useful to each other. When people exchange goods and services, they make each other better off. In short, the more people trade, the more their communities flourish.

How, though, do we settle on the terms of exchange, which means, ultimately, how do we settle on the prices at which our services are exchanged? Are price changes predictable? Can they be made more predictable? What is a cooperative surplus? How is it generated? How is it distributed? How are these things affected by market structure, regulation, and current events?

Chapter 15

Conditions for Trade

Our prior discussion of trade and exchange has been simple. Isn't it all about mutual advantage? Now we need to step back, because the possibility of mutually advantageous trade depends on such factors as individual differences, the ability to communicate, the ability to transport, and an institutional framework that facilitates trust.

HETEROGENEOUS ASSORTMENTS

This strange phrase refers to the simple idea that people are not the same, and what they bring to the table is not the same. If everyone came to the table wanting to sell nails and buy butter, but no one brought any butter to sell, that would be a homogenous, rather than heterogenous, assortment, and that homogenous marketplace would have limited potential for gains from trade. When people show up wanting different things, and offering different things, there is more potential for gains from trade.

However, it is worth mentioning that even with homogenous assortments, trade can occur. Imagine that Paul and Leonard each own two rare collectible cars: one Porsche and one Lamborghini. Each of the Porsches is the same year, color, and model; has zero miles on it; and in perfect condition. The same is true of the two Lamborghinis. It would seem that if each party has a homogenous assortment (both have one of each), then trade could not occur. But wait: Paul and Leonard may both believe that it would be better to own two identical cars than one of each. Therefore, even if Paul and Leonard come to the table with identical bundles, gains from trade are still possible. In general, however, heterogeneity increases the potential for gains from trade.

COMMUNICATION

To trade, people need to communicate. They need to be able to present offers, discuss price or terms of trade, ask questions, and answer them. Think about how hard it would be simply to buy groceries if you could not speak the local language. Would you be able to get help reading a label to find out whether you were buying yogurt or sour cream? We often take for granted how much communication and how much shared background knowledge is involved when we trade.

DELIVERY

Communicating is one thing. Actually delivering is another. Trade presupposes parties who can deliver as promised. The product itself has to be available, and various tools for packaging and transporting may be needed. Getting the product to where it needs to be may require storage, refrigeration, or insurance.

INSTITUTIONS

We noted that people invent institutions as frameworks for mutual expectation. For trade to occur, institutions are necessary. We continued that thought by observing that human progress works though the development of institutions of trust. Contract law, judicial arbitration services, and insurance policies are among the institutions that set the stage for our being able to afford to trust each other, which, in turn, sets the stage for more trade.

MUTUAL GAIN

One further crucial condition for trade is that mutual gain must be both possible and predictable. People need to see that everyone can be better off after trading than before.

DISCUSSION AND EXERCISES

1. What are some of the preconditions that facilitate trade? Which are essential?
2. What conditions might prevent trades from taking place? Can these conditions be overcome?
3. What is the difference between heterogeneity and homogeneity?

Chapter 16

Comparative Advantage

Comparative advantage is an application of opportunity cost. Simply put, a lower opportunity cost is a comparative advantage in the production of that service.

How are you going to make a living, and contribute to your community? To answer this question, you need to understand your comparative advantage. The key idea, in any market economy, is that you do not need to be the absolute best in order to succeed. All you need is to have something to contribute, and everyone has something. Everyone has a comparative advantage so long as there are differences between people.

How can we be so sure? Let's start by asking why people trade at all. Why do people specialize in providing one service rather than another?

Comparative advantage is one answer. Imagine that LeBron James is the best basketball player in the world. But it is not hard to imagine that if LeBron wanted to be a shelf-stocker at the local grocery store, he would be the absolute best at that as well. He is taller than you. He is stronger. He has longer arms. Therefore, if absolute advantage is what matters, then LeBron will out-compete you every time. But in fact, absolute advantage is not what matters. In fact, LeBron James cannot compete with you for that job stocking shelves. Why not? Because LeBron James cannot afford to compete with you. The time LeBron spends entertaining people on basketball courts is too valuable for him to take time away from that to compete for your job at the grocery store. In fact, you have an overwhelming advantage, but your advantage is a comparative advantage, not an absolute one. You cannot compete with LeBron on the basketball court, but you can find your niche somewhere, and once you find it, you will find that LeBron James cannot compete with you in your niche. He cannot afford to compete with you.

Both individuals and entire countries have comparative advantages. Once we understand our comparative advantage, we both produce those things we can produce, and trade for those things we cannot. And trade can enable countries to consume at a level above their productive capacity—that is, outside their PPF.

This explains the concept of comparative advantage as a bit of simple common sense. What follows is a standard economic "proof of concept." Don't let the arithmetic confuse you. To prove the concept in mathematical terms, we return to Roberto's desert island, where Roberto is about to get some company.

ROBERTO

Roberto can still produce only two things: firewood and fish. If he spends the entire day collecting wood, he can collect three bundles. If he spends the entire day fishing, he can catch six fish. If we create a table that describes Roberto's production possibilities over six days, we can see the full range of his productive capacity.

The last two columns of table 16.1 show the maximum amount of wood and number of fish Roberto can produce in six days. We can graph these pairs of output with wood on the horizontal axis and fish on the vertical axis. The negative slope of the line indicates that once Roberto is at maximum production, there is an opportunity cost to increasing production of either of the things Roberto can produce.

The slope of his PPF is a constant -2, which means that increasing production of bundles of wood by one decreases production of fish by two. In

Table 16.1. Roberto's production possibilities over six days

	WOOD: 3 per day	FISH: 6 per day
Spends all 6 days producing WOOD	18	0
Spends 5 days producing WOOD, 1 day on FISH	15	6
Spends 4 days producing WOOD, 2 days on FISH	12	12
Spends 3 days producing WOOD, 3 days on FISH	9	18
Spends 2 days producing WOOD, 4 days on FISH	6	24
Spends 1 day producing WOOD, 5 days on FISH	3	30
Spends all 6 days producing FISH	0	36

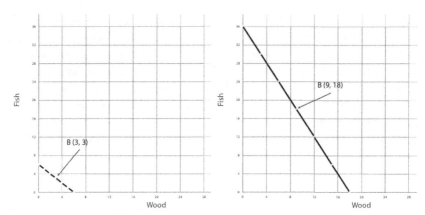

Figure 16.1. Cate's and Roberto's PPFs

other words: the opportunity cost of a bundle of wood is two fish. Without trade, Roberto can only consume within his PPF. Combinations beyond the frontier, to the right of the line, are not available to him if he relies solely on his productive capacity. If Roberto prefers more fish and wood to less of either or both, he will consume somewhere right along the PPF, not to the left of the line.

Like most people, Roberto prefers a mix of goods rather than just one thing. In our simple example, this means he likes having both wood and fish, so let's choose a point of consumption for Roberto somewhere between the two extremes. Let's have (9,18) be Roberto's optimum when he is constrained by his productive capacity. Let's call this point "B" for "before trade." See the right side of figure 16.1.

CATE

As it turns out, Roberto is not completely alone in his world. There is a nearby island inhabited by Cate, and she can produce the same two things as Roberto: firewood and fish. Just like Roberto, her productivity depends on how much time she spends collecting wood and fishing, but Cate's capacity to do both of those things differs from Roberto's. If she spends the entire day collecting wood, she can collect one bundle of wood. If she spends the entire day fishing, she can catch one fish.

Cate's PPF is so simple; a table is not necessary to summarize her productive efforts over six days. Her PPF appears below to the left of Roberto's. Since we are going to compare Roberto and Cate's output, their PPFs are drawn to the same scale with the same axes. We indicate the intercepts first. If she spends six days collecting wood, she collects six bundles of wood and catches no fish (6, 0). If she spends six days only catching fish, she collects no wood and catches six fish (0, 6). Since Cate has a constant opportunity cost of one fish for one bundle of wood, we know her PPF is a straight line connecting the two intercept points.

If Cate prefers more fish and wood to less of either or both, she will consume somewhere along her PPF, not in the interior. Let's choose a point of consumption for Cate somewhere between the intercepts. Let's assign (3, 3) as Cate's optimum when constrained by her productive capacity. Let's call this point "B" as well.

ABSOLUTE ADVANTAGE

Clearly, Roberto is more productive than Cate. Cate's PPF is so small that it fits entirely inside of Roberto's. Roberto has an absolute advantage in wood production over Cate because he can out-produce her (18 > 6). He also has an absolute advantage in catching fish (36 > 6). It seems he is better at everything than Cate. See figure 16.2.

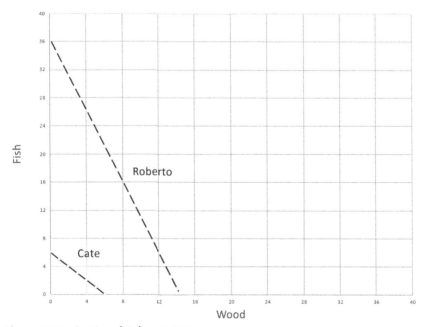

Figure 16.2.   Cate's and Roberto's PPFs

Is there is any reason, why Roberto would want to trade with Cate? Does she have anything to offer?

VOLUNTARY TRADE: FINDING A WIN-WIN SET OF OUTCOMES

Here is one of the keys to human trade and human prosperity. It doesn't matter if Roberto is richer than Cate or that she makes the same items Roberto makes or that Roberto makes so much more of each of them. What matters is whether a trade makes both of them better off.

We can figure out if there is a mutually beneficial trade Roberto and Cate can make. To do this, we return to their respective PPFs. First, determine what area on Roberto's PPF graph represents points guaranteed to make Roberto better off. The gray area in the graph indicates at least as much wood (9) and fish (18) as Roberto enjoys at "B" (9, 18). See figure 16.3. Simply put, if Roberto could be at a point to the northeast of "B," that would be better for him than being at "B." The same goes for Cate. If Cate could obtain a point in the area to the northeast of (3, 3), she would be better off.

A TRADE

Someone has to make a move. Suppose that Cate realizes she needs to make an offer that would make Roberto better off in order to make him want to

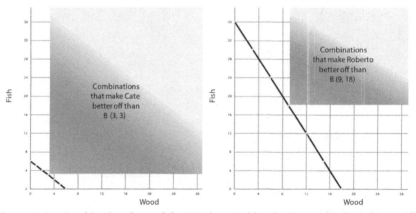

Figure 16.3.   Combinations beyond the PPF that would make Cate and Roberto better off

trade with her. She would also need to make an offer that would make her better off, too, or the whole thing would be pointless. What relevant information does she have? She knows this: her own cost for wood is one fish (remember this is her opportunity cost).

If Cate offers Roberto two bundles of wood for three fish from him, would she be proposing a deal they would both benefit from? As a matter of fact, the answer to that question is yes. To produce three fish, it would cost her three bundles of wood. If Roberto accepts her offer, then the cost of acquiring three fish is only two bundles of wood, not three.

Is this a good deal for Roberto? The answer to this question is also yes. Producing two bundles of wood costs Roberto four fish. If he accepts Cate's offer, then the cost of acquiring those two bundles of wood is only three fish, not four. Not only has each of these two people benefitted from the trade, they now have a path forward through which they can always benefit from this sort of trade, even though it seemed unlikely given Cate's lower production numbers when we first considered the trade.

If both Cate and Roberto adjust their production away from producing for their personal consumption, and instead produce for trade (i.e., for consumption by their trading partner rather than by themselves), gains from trade begin to emerge in pretty clear terms. If Cate increases her wood production by two and decreases her fish production by two, her production changes from "Before" (3, 3), to "Specialization" (5, 1). Now, if Roberto increases his fish production by three, and decreases his wood production by one-and-a-half, Roberto's production changes from "Before" (9, 18), to "Specialization" (7.5, 21). See figure 16.4.

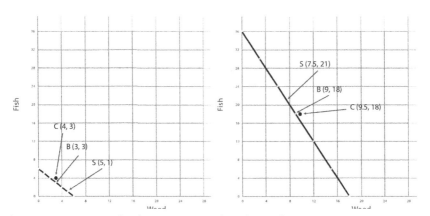

Figure 16.4. Cate's and Roberto's consumption after trade

Now let them go through with the deal. We label their final consumption "C" in figure 16.4.

Roberto's path to a trade

Roberto started at the most favorable point on his PPF, B, where he produced nine bundles of wood and eighteen fish. Hoping to trade with Cate, Roberto specialized in producing fish where he has the lower relative opportunity cost. His specialization yielded S, where he produced seven-and-a-half bundles of wood and twenty-one fish. He then traded three of his fish for two bundles of wood. This means that after trading, his consumption, C, rose to nine-and-a-half bundles of wood and eighteen fish, which means that Roberto is better off at C than B.

Cate's path to a trade

Cate started at the most favorable point on her PPF, B, where she produced three bundles of wood and three fish. Hoping to trade with Roberto, Cate specialized in producing wood where she has the lower relative opportunity cost. Her specialization yielded S, where she produced five bundles of wood and one fish. She then traded two bundles of wood for three fish. This means that after trading, her consumption, C, rose to three bundles of wood and four fish, which means that Cate is better off at C than B.

Here is the amazing thing about both trade and human cooperation: the only thing that changed for Roberto and Cate was that they adjusted what they were producing so they would have something to trade with each other. In this story, there are no resource discoveries or new technologies. The only thing Roberto and Cate needed in order to make progress together was to specialize in the production possibility in which they experienced a lower relative opportunity cost.

COMPARATIVE ADVANTAGE

If you know that Roberto and Cate have different opportunity costs, you also know that each of them must have a comparative advantage. You can also know this by looking at the slopes of their respective PPFs. Their PPFs have different slopes, so each must have a comparative advantage in something. Roberto has relatively inexpensive fish production (½ bundle of wood to Cate's one bundle of wood). Cate has relatively inexpensive wood production (one fish to Roberto's two fish). Even in this extreme example where Roberto is better at everything, he is still not the person to do everything. No one is.

The terms of trade that Cate proposed (two bundles of wood for three fish) are not unique. Any terms of trade where Roberto pays less than two fish for one bundle of wood and Cate pays less than one bundle of wood for a fish would push both Roberto's and Cate's consumption beyond their PPF.

It is important to note that Roberto and Cate would not benefit from specializing if they didn't have the opportunity to trade. The opportunity to trade is the primary reason for specialization.

One important concept we have set aside thus far in this analysis is transaction cost. Transaction costs are the costs of getting goods and services from sellers to buyers. An example of transaction costs between Roberto and Cate would be the cost of transporting the wood and fish between the two islands. As you might imagine, sometimes transaction costs are high enough to limit trade.

What we said here about Roberto and Cate applies not only to individual traders but to larger trading entities like countries or regions. Entire nations benefit from trade just as individuals do. As you can imagine, the potential benefits of trade are greater if there is a wider range of opportunity costs and differing resources between trading partners.

DISCUSSION AND EXERCISES

1. Roberto and Cate live in a simple world in which each of them has a clear comparative advantage. Can you think of other examples in your own life?
2. Explain why even though someone may be at an absolute disadvantage in everything, that person, and people with absolute advantages, can still gain from trading with each other.
3. Explain how looking at the PPFs of two (or more) people helps to clarify where gains from trade can be had.

Chapter 17

Division of Labor

The division of labor creates opportunities to serve and be served by vast multitudes. In an advanced commercial society, people produce things for customers they may never meet. Indeed, these producers may be only dimly aware of their customers' purposes, or even of their very existence. They know only that sales are good; someone judges the product to be worth its price. That is all that an ordinary producer needs to know. This is the ground on which modern society and modern prosperity are built.

DIVISION OF LABOR, ECONOMIES OF SCALE, AND SPECIALIZATION

Robinson Crusoe, published by Daniel Defoe in 1719, is the story of a sailor marooned on an island for twenty-eight years, who learns to survive on his own. We all have met people who seem more or less self-sufficient, but when we call them self-sufficient, we are not comparing them to Robinson Crusoe. They come nowhere near to producing enough to meet their own needs in the way a hermit would need to. When we call them self-sufficient, we have something else in mind. Namely, as we develop trading relationships, opportunities emerge for social animals to be self-sufficient in a new sense, not by producing to meet their own needs directly so much as by producing to meet other people's needs.

Plumbers (for instance) go to the market to offer their plumbing skills to other people, and after a series of trades, they go home with plenty of food for their families without ever growing a grain of food. They are self-sufficient, sustaining themselves not in isolation but in collaboration. They obtain goods by offering valuable services—something their trading partners consider more valuable under the circumstances than what they are giving up.

Our next topic extends the same point from individuals to whole countries. Whole countries can try to sustain themselves in isolation, but whole countries, like individuals, are better off sustaining themselves in collaboration with trading partners.

MERCANTILISM

When Adam Smith wrote his *Wealth of Nations* in 1776, European governments saw themselves as having a direct role in promoting commerce by protecting domestic industry from foreign competition. Smith is remembered as a defender of free trade, but his practical goal was to repudiate mercantilism's way of protecting domestic industry at the expense of consumers.

The guiding thesis of mercantilism is that a country prospers by exporting more than it imports, thus maintaining a positive cash flow. In practice, this involves imposing tariffs and other restrictions designed to limit imports and thereby protect politically influential domestic producers from foreign competition. Smith commented, "It is the industry which is carried on for the benefit of the rich and the powerful, that is principally encouraged by our mercantile system. That which is carried on for the benefit of the poor and the indigent, is too often, either neglected or oppressed."[1] Ordinary consumers pay more for protected goods than if there were foreign competition to discipline those who otherwise monopolize domestic markets.

Smith's main point was that, in the long run, nations get rich by being productive and by making goods cheaper, not by subsidizing unproductive enterprises and making goods more expensive. Stated so simply, the principle seems obvious; yet, as Smith says, most economic policy in his day attempted the opposite. Smith claims that the typical result of providing monopoly rights or tariff protection to any industry is to divert capital from more productive to less productive work (such as tending vineyards in Scotland).

What sort of foreign policy goes with mercantilism? A feverish one, Plato might have said; and 2000 years later Adam Smith (who studied Plato) would have agreed. If one believes that buying foreign products makes us losers in a zero-sum game, then one will want to acquire foreign products by some means other than paying for them. By the same token, if one believes in self-sufficiency as an economic ideal, then merely avoiding trade with neighboring countries will not be enough. One will want to acquire their land and working populations, thereby moving closer to the ideal of national

---

1. Adam Smith, *Wealth of Nations* (New York: Oxford University Press, originally published 1776). Book IV, chap. 8, p. 644.

self-sufficiency. If one is a mercantilist, one begins to think of military force as a first resort, and voluntary trade as a last resort. Mercantilists see neither game as mutually advantageous. On one hand, they see trade—paying to import wanted goods—as a way of losing. They see military force, on the other hand, as a way of making the other side lose. So, in the name of protecting domestic industry from international competition, and partly from desire for glory, mercantilist European states began building empires.

Smith wanted to dismantle the mercantilist system. According to him, nations become wealthy by expanding their markets, thereby expanding the opportunities for people to become more specialized producers of sophisticated products for millions of Europeans rather than for dozens of fellow villagers. The opening pages of *Wealth of Nations* explain how the division of labor in a market economy makes workers thousands of times more productive than they would be otherwise, and Smith was not exaggerating.

Returning to an earlier example, if you want pizza today, you can acquire a slice of it in exchange for a few minutes of work. But if you tried to make a pizza all by yourself, eschewing all reliance upon the division of labor, you would not live long enough to see that pizza. On your own, you would not even be able to get started. You would not be able to smelt the iron to make the oven and other basic tools.

Along similar lines, Smith notes that the occupation of *porter* could not exist in a village. There are no porters except where there is enough commerce to support hotels. There may be a carpenter in a village, specializing in anything involving wood. A carpenter in London, though, might specialize in cabinets. Or, a factory might specialize in making nails, thereby enabling thousands of people around the world to earn a living as carpenters by making the tools of their trade affordable; a factory might be able to make millions of nails per year and profit by selling them for a penny each. However, before there can be any economic point in being so specialized, there have to be economies of scale that drive down production costs. And before manufacturers can operate at large scale, they need access to a large customer base. Thus, Smith points out, specialization is limited by the extent of the market. A system of extended trade allows for goods to become progressively cheaper, and thus it allows people to become wealthier.

SPECIALIZATION

Smith thought that part of what made specialization work was the fact that people would specialize at what they, compared to others, were best at. Forty-one years after the publication of the *Wealth of Nations*, David Ricardo, in inventing our modern way of thinking about comparative advantage, argued that successful specialization and mutually beneficial trade do not require people to be the best at what they do. Company presidents hire teenagers to mow the lawn not because teenagers are better at lawn mowing, but because company presidents have better things to do with their time. Therefore, teenagers will always compete successfully for entry-level jobs, not because teenagers are the best, but because the best are too busy running the company to compete for a job mowing the lawn. Because teenagers have a lower opportunity cost, they have what economists call a comparative advantage: no matter how much more skilled the president may be at manual labor, teenagers still outcompete presidents for manual labor jobs because presidents would have to give up too much to compete for such jobs.

Similarly, even if France could produce better wool than Britain, France might buy English wool rather than produce its own because France has better things to do with its own farmland—for instance, France can grow grapes and produce wine. If France mistakenly considered it important to be self-sufficient in wool and devoted land to raising sheep—land that could instead be producing the world's best grapes—an opportunity would be lost both to France and for those who would otherwise have been eager to buy French champagne.

Smith had some success in rolling back the tide of mercantilism and in reducing trade barriers. The result? Angus Maddison noted that, since 1820, the "volume of exports per head of population rose 103-fold in the UK, 114-fold in the U.S. [Trade] eliminated the handicap of countries with limited natural resources. It was also important in diffusing new products and new technology."[2] John Nye gives the following figures: Between 1820 and 1910, exports as a percentage of the GDP in the UK and France went from just under 10 percent and 5 percent, respectively, to about 20 percent. Imports as a percentage of the GDP went from 5 percent to 20 percent in France and from 15 percent to about 35 percent in the UK. Thus, in a ninety-year period, the UK went from 25 to 55 percent of its economy being based on international trade, while France went from 10 to 30 percent of its economy being based on international trade.[3]

The works of Marx and Charles Dickens naturally lead us to be glad that we are not living through the early years of the industrial revolution. Life is better now. But is life better now because of the rise of industry, or despite it? Or, if we doubt that life is better now, and suspect that the early days of the industrial revolution were relatively good times, what would we count as evidence, one way or the other? We might have enough information to document changes in life expectancy, literacy, and per capita real income. Different scholars have different views. Our most recent information,

2. Angus Maddison, *The Resurrection of Western Europe and the Transformation of the Americas* (Washington: The AEI Press), p. 74.
3. John V. C. Nye, *War, Wine, and Taxes: The Political Economy of Anglo-French Trade, 1689–1900.* Princeton: Princeton University Press (2007).

however, favors the view that the industrial revolution was liberating from the very beginning. Peter Lindert and Jeffrey Williamson, for example, estimate that real wages in England for the working classes doubled between 1819 and 1851—the earliest and hardest days of the industrial revolution.[4]

Adam Smith, writing in the 1700s, was optimistic that if law, custom, and appropriate caution limit the opportunities to enrich oneself at other people's expense, and if commerce within the rule of law enhances the opportunities to enrich oneself in ways that contribute to the prosperity of the community in general, then the community will be a mutually advantageous and increasingly prosperous cooperative venture. Whether free trade within the rule of law approximates this greatest of blessings is a big question.

DISCUSSION AND EXERCISES

1. *Robinson Crusoe* was about a man forced to become completely self-sufficient. What would that take, and what kind of life might a self-sufficient person be able to achieve?
2. What were the central tenets of mercantilism?
3. Does it make sense for countries to specialize and trade with one another, or to be perfectly self-sufficient?

---

4. Peter Lindert and Jeffrey G. Williamson, "English Workers' Living Standard During the Industrial Revolution: A New Look." *Economic History Review* 36 (1983): 1–25.

Chapter 18

Buyers

When people make decisions about which goods and services to buy, they exhibit a predictable pattern of behavior concerning how much they are willing to buy over a given period of time. We call that pattern of behavior **demand**.

Buyers can be individuals, households, firms, or governments. Regardless of who the buyer is, we assume buyers do the best they can with what they have. This assumption is often referred to in economics as the "rational agent" or "rational actor" assumption. When people willingly choose to do something not in their best interest, we would classify that as a failure of rationality.

FACTORS THAT INFLUENCE WILLINGNESS TO PAY

People doing the best with what they have has predictable implications regarding what they are willing to pay for goods and services. Several factors influence people's willingness to pay for goods and services. Pizza provides a good example.

TASTE

Whether people are willing to pay for pizza depends first on whether they like and want pizza. Some people don't. Beyond this, there is a larger group of people who will not eat pizza for any number of other reasons, and this is a matter of taste, too. As with most things, information affects people's desire for pizza. Negative news, news like the health effects of a diet too rich with carbohydrates or gluten, for example, will influence people away from buying more pizza. Positive news, regarding the antioxidant properties of tomatoes, or the heart benefits of a diet rich in olive oil will move people in the opposite direction.

OWN PRICE

"Own price" is one of those terms economists use that seem more than a little awkward, but it means something specific that we have to understand. It refers to the price of a thing, its *own* price, rather than the price of related things. The price of the pizza is likely to influence buyers' willingness to pay for pizza. If you walked into a pizzeria with a group of friends on your way home from school, each thinking you wanted two slices at $2 each, only to find out the actual price of a slice was $10, your purchase would likely end up being different than you first expected. Your purchase might likely change if you learned slices were on special for 50 cents. Typically, people are willing to buy more of a good or service at lower prices.

RELATED GOODS AND SERVICES—COMPLEMENTS AND SUBSTITUTES

Of course, there are also things you like to enjoy with your pizza. Goods and services that are consumed together are referred to as **complementary** goods and services. These are things like hot dogs at a baseball game, hot chocolate at a skating rink, and cold drinks with hot pizza. The cost of these complementary goods matters too. Your purchase bundle will look quite different if sodas are $5 each, or $1 with free refills.

Not all goods are complements. Some goods are substitutes. For example, you may also like burgers, or fried tofu, or salad. What do any of these options cost? It matters, because these are **substitute goods**. You can walk away from an expensive pizza and have a less expensive burger as a substitute.

As we noted earlier, we call the price of something we are focusing on (like pizza in this case) *own* price. We call the price of a related good, *other* price. If we are talking about the prices of other goods and want to know how those prices affect demand, we need to know whether the second good is a complement (consumed *with* the first) or a substitute (consumed *instead* of the first). Because complements are consumed together, changing the price of one complement effectively changes the price of the whole consumption bundle. Consumption will shift away from bundles that become relatively more expensive. By contrast, the impact of changing the price of a substitute has the opposite effect. If the substitute becomes relatively less expensive, then we expect to see consumption shifting in the direction of the relatively less expensive substitute.

INCOME

When you decide how many slices of pizza to buy at $2 each, you normally take into account how much money you have to spend. So, if you find a $20 bill on the sidewalk outside of the restaurant, your calculations may change. An economist calls pizza a "normal good" if you buy more when you have more money. By contrast, if you instead buy less pizza when you have more money—maybe you buy lobster instead—then economists call pizza an "inferior good." This means that as your income goes up, and you can afford to buy more, you actually buy less. You shift your spending in the direction of what had been a relatively more expensive substitute.

EXPECTATIONS

Our expectations about the future also influence our willingness to buy a good or service. For instance, if we expect our income to go up in the near future, we may be more willing to make a purchase today.

PUTTING ALL THE FACTORS TOGETHER TO UNDERSTAND DEMAND

Individual demand, the desired quantity of a given good or service over a given period of time, is a function of many factors.

Quantity demand is a function of all the things we listed earlier: own price, price of complements, price of substitutes, income, tastes, expectations of all those things, and anything else that people care about.

Many factors influence an individual's demand: tastes, price, price of related goods, and income. Our expectations about these things will influence our demand. We can convert these two sentences into this expression:

$$q_d = f\,(P,\ Pc,\ Ps,\ I,\ T,\ E[P,\ Pc,\ Ps,\ I,\ T,\ \ldots\ ]\ \ldots)$$

where
q_d = *quantity demanded*
P = *own price*

P_c = *price of complements*
P_s = *price of substitutes*
I = *income*
T = *taste*
E = *expectations about any of these factors*
. . . = *anything else people care about*

Of all these factors, we consider own price (P), which is simply what a thing costs, to play the biggest role in explaining demand (q_d). To see how one factor influences an outcome that depends on many things, you must do a thought experiment in which you hold all the other factors constant. For example, if income changes halfway through your observations, you will get answers that depend on both income and prices changing. You won't know the impact of a price change; you will only know the impact of both income and prices changing.

A simple example will help in unpacking all of the variables that need to be considered to understand demand. Imagine being in a group with five of your classmates. You are in charge of taking the pizza order for everyone. You do not know the exact price of pizza, but you describe the one pizza option you have, and you give a range of prices so you can make the order without having to come back to the group once you find out the price.

Say you jot down a list like this on a scrap of paper:

PRICE	# PIZZAS (q_d)
$10	___
$5	___
$2	___
$0	___

If any of the factors discussed earlier change, people's willingness to pay for pizza might change, and the poll you took may no longer be valid. You can be fairly sure, though, that while you take a poll with your group, the other factors are going to remain constant. In the three minutes you need to take the poll, no one's income is going to change, the price of cold drinks is not going to change, news is not going to break about the price of burgers plummeting, and we hope that no one is going to start hating pizza.

By taking the poll of your classmates, you just made a **demand schedule**, which is a way to show the relationship between quantity demanded and own price.

The demand schedule is simply the relationship between quantity demanded and own price, holding all other factors constant. Here it is indicated by keeping the factors in the notation but indicating that they are held constant by putting them in **bold**.

$$q_d = f (P, \textbf{Pc, Ps, I, T, E[P, Pc, Ps, I, T \ldots] \ldots })$$

We will make one more simplification. We drop all those factors held constant in the notation and denote the short form of the function as the *demand curve*:

$$q_d = f (P)$$

We use the word *curve* here rather than function to remind us that it is just a relationship between two things—own price and quantity demanded—and holding constant other factors. If other factors change, the demand curve will need to be reexamined. Put in the simplest terms, demand curve is a function of the price of a thing, provided none of the other details change. The demand curve is a relationship between two variables: q (quantity) and P (own price, or price), and we can graph this relationship in two dimensions.[1]

You can graph your demand schedule for pizza, price on the vertical axis and quantity on the horizontal axis. If you didn't have the opportunity to come up with one, do a quick thought experiment and fill in numbers that make sense to you.

Make sure your axes match the labels in figure 18.1. You can have different numbers on the quantity of pizza axis, but price doesn't need to go much higher than $10. Pizza is just not that expensive.

You can now connect the four points you drew, and if your intuition about how much pizza people are willing to buy at various prices is correct, you will notice that your graph is downward sloping. And what should your intuition be? When pizza gets more expensive, people will buy less of it. Another way to talk about the relationship between q_d and P is to say it is a negative relationship. As one variable goes up, in this case price, the other goes down, in this case, the quantity of pizza demanded. This negative relationship, or downward sloping curve, is so robust that it is called the "law of demand."

---

1. In the relationship between price and quantity, price is often described as the independent variable. We asked, "How many pizzas are we willing to buy when *p*=$2? When *p*=$4?" We didn't start from the other way around. If price is the independent variable (quantity demanded depends on price), mathematical convention says it should go on the horizontal axis. In economics, we put *p* on the vertical axis. It may seem counterintuitive, but we continue that practice here.

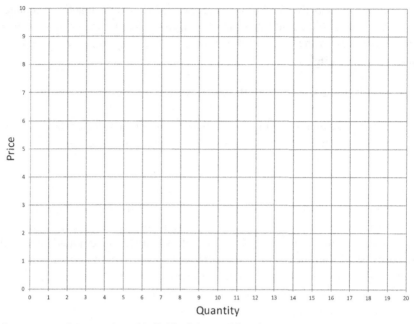

Figure 18.1.   Construction of individual demand for pizza

Table 18.1. Demand schedule for pizza, Group 1

Price	# Pizzas (q_d)
$10	0
$5	2
$2	5
$0	8

If your demand curve isn't downward sloping, then try again. Sketch your demand schedule and graph the one summarized in table 18.1 for Group 1's demand for pizza.

DEMAND IN A DYNAMIC WORLD

We just did the "willingness to pay for pizza" thought exercise. We assumed that those numbers would hold over a short period. We would not expect those values to represent the group's demand schedule next year or even next month. People live in a dynamic context and the factors that influence their willingness to pay for goods or services will change over time.

OWN PRICE CHANGES

You have full information about how many pizzas Group 1 will purchase when the price is $0, $2, $5, or $10. If the price is $5, Group 1 purchases two pizzas. If the price goes up to $10, they don't buy any. You can see this by looking at table 18.1. If the own price changes, you see the change in quantity demanded just by looking at the demand schedule. If something else besides own price changes, the demand schedule needs to be updated to incorporate those changes.

Now you know how many pizzas your group will purchase at those prices as long as nothing else changes for the members. But any number of things could change. Let's revisit the things that could happen to impact the demand for pizza.

PRICE OF A COMPLEMENT CHANGES

Remember that cold drinks and pizza are complements. Say the price of a cold drink doubles from $2 to $4. How might this impact the original demand schedule for pizza? Your intuition should be that demand would decrease because the total expense of what we might call "the pizza experience" would rise. And your intuition would be right.

Use the numbers suggested in table 18.2 to construct a fresh graph. Draw the original demand curve and the new demand curve when the price of a complement has gone up. Label the original curve (**Pc = $2**) and the new curve (**Pc = $4**). When the demand is lower in a new circumstance, we say "demand has decreased" or "demand has shifted to the left." We might even say "demand has gone down," but we don't mean to imply that at every quantity, less is paid, we mean that at every price, less is demanded. This is why we emphasize a decrease in demand is a shift to the left.

Table 18.2. Demand schedule for pizza, Group 1, change in the price of a complement

Price	# Pizzas (q_d when $P_c = \$2$)	# Pizzas (q_d when $P_c = \$4$)
$10	0	0
$5	2	0
$2	5	3
$0	8	6

Table 18.3. Demand schedule for pizza, Group 1, change in the price of a substitute

Price	# Pizzas (q_d when $P_s = \$4$)	# Pizzas (q_d when $P_s = \$8$)
$10	0	1
$5	2	3
$2	5	7
$0	8	10

PRICE OF A SUBSTITUTE CHANGES

Say burgers are a good substitute for pizza. Say further that the price of burgers doubles from $4 to $8 each.

No matter what the price of pizza is, the original demand schedule was made up based on the assumption that the price of the substitute was, let's say, $4. Now burgers are twice as expensive. Some people may shift from buying burgers to buying pizza. When the price of a substitute goes up, it increases demand for the good, in this case pizza.

Use the numbers in table 18.3 to construct a graph of the original demand curve and the new demand curve when the price of a substitute has gone up. When the demand is higher in a new circumstance, we say that "demand has increased" or "demand has shifted to the right." We might even say that "demand has gone up," but we don't mean to imply that at every quantity more is paid, we mean that at every price, more is demanded. This is why we emphasize an increase in demand is a shift to the right.

INCOME CHANGES

Now the hungry students find $20 bills on the sidewalk. They just got richer. How will this impact their decision to buy pizza? Let's assume pizza is a normal good, which means that it is a thing that people buy more of when they feel like they have more money. Again, construct a graph with two demand curves, representing the original demand curve and the new demand curve when income has gone up. Use the numbers in table 18.4.

We have used pizza for all these examples, but you can do the same thing with any good or service that is traded. You just need to keep in mind what the good is, what its complements are, what its substitutes are, if it is normal or inferior, and what could impact taste for that good or service. In this respect, Lattes, blue jeans, flip-flops, iPhones, apartment rentals, haircuts, manicures, house cleaning services, and taxi rides are no different than pizza.

Table 18.4. Demand schedule for pizza, Group 1, increase in income

Price	# Pizzas (q_d original income)	# Pizzas (q_d higher income)
$10	0	2
$5	2	4
$2	5	8
$0	8	8

Table 18.5. Demand schedules for pizza, Groups 1–4

Price	Group 1 (q_d^1)	Group 2 (q_d^2)	Group 3 (q_d^3)	Group 4 (q_d^4)
$10	0	0	1	1
$5	2	1	2	1
$2	5	2	5	4
$0	8	6	8	5

TOTAL MARKET DEMAND

We are interested in individual demand, but we are more interested in how an entire population will react to changes in the economy. If we know all individual demand curves, we can find the total market demand curve. For instance, say there were four groups of students, and they all did the same pizza poll. Say they are the entire population that will be purchasing pizza.

If you graphed the demand curve for each group in table 18.5, you would find that each one is downward sloping: less is demanded at high prices than low prices.

Just as individual demand curves represent the amount individuals (or small groups of individuals) are willing to buy at given prices, **total market demand curve** represents the amount everyone in the market is willing to buy over a given period of time at given prices. We can sum individual demand schedules ($qd^1 + qd^2 + qd^3 + qd^4$) at each price before we graph, or we can sketch the demand curve and add each group's demand for each price point successively. This is called summing horizontally at each price point. Either method yields the same total market demand curve.

The total market demand is a sum of all the individual demand functions, so anything that can make an individual demand function shift can also make total market demand shift. In addition to all the factors that impact individual demand, changes in population size will affect market demand. If we let **N** be the population size, the market demand function can be represented with the following notation:

$$Qd = f (P, Pc, Ps, I, T, E[P, Pc, Ps, I, T], N \ldots).$$

Table 18.6. Sum of individual demand = Total market demand

Price	Group 1 (qd^1)	Group 2 (q$_d^2$)	Group 3 (q$_d^3$)	Group 4 (q$_d^4$)	Total market demand (Q$_D$)
$10	0	0	1	1	2
$5	2	1	2	1	6
$2	5	2	5	4	16
$0	8	6	8	5	27

DISCUSSION AND EXERCISES

1. Graph the total market demand curve schedule in table 18.6. Does the total market demand curve slope downward?
2. Does it seem flatter or steeper than an individual demand curve? Why do you think this is?
3. Assume there is a newly added Group 5 that behaves just like Group 4. How does this affect total market demand?
4. Sketch the new total market demand, including Group 5, on the same graph as the first four groups.
5. The new total market demand curve is to the right of the old one. Is it steeper or flatter than the old one?

Chapter 19

Sellers

Just like buyers, sellers can be individuals, households, firms, or even governments. No matter who the seller is, we assume sellers do the best they can with what they have. We should be able to observe a predictable pattern of behavior over time regarding their willingness to sell goods and services at various prices. We call that pattern of behavior supply.

For this exercise we also assume that the seller cannot dictate the amount sold. Sellers can only offer to sell an amount at any given price. This is similar to the power that we assumed buyers have. Buyers can choose to buy or not at any given price. In other words, we are assuming no haggling. Sometimes this is referred to as being a "price taker," meaning the agent takes the price as given and doesn't try to manipulate it. When buyers and sellers take prices as given, that is referred to as a competitive market. That may sound strange since they don't seem to be acting competitively, but this is how a competitive market is defined in economics—each actor, whether on the buyer or seller side, behaves as if he or she cannot influence price. We use this assumption on behavior here and explore other behaviors later.

THE PROFIT MOTIVE

The story on the seller's side is a bit simpler than the story on the buyer's side. Sellers are motivated to earn a profit. Profits are simply revenue minus cost of production. Revenue is sales (price of item multiplied by the number sold, or $p \times q$). We consider the cost of production to include the cost of inputs involved in making the good or service.

Accounting profits are profits an accountant would report. This is the common use of the word "profit." For our purposes here, profits mean economic profits. Economic profits are profits that take all costs, including opportunity costs, into account. The accounting costs are typically lower than the true cost of operating a business. For instance, one of the biggest costs not accounted for is what the business owner could have otherwise done over the same period.

Saying that sellers are motivated by profits may sound controversial. One implication of that assumption is that sellers who want to continue to operate over time are motivated to keep an eye on costs. This is true for operations that have a "not-for-profit" status. Charities want to do the most good (their measure of sales) with the staff and donations they have (their inputs).

Profits break down into two major components: revenue and cost.

REVENUE

We know that revenue is price multiplied by quantity sold. We know that the seller can't determine price, so the question is how does the price influence a seller's willingness to sell?

As a thought exercise, imagine someone in your class was thinking about getting into the pizza business. Imagine how many pizzas that person would want to sell if pizzas were $20 each? $10 each? $5 each? Or $2 each? What if the price for pizza was $0?

COST

When deciding how much to sell at a given price, sellers consider their cost of production. The cost of production includes cost of inputs (rent, wages, interest rates, regulation, and all other expenditures). Improvements in technology are adopted by a firm to make overall costs go down. Expectations about any of these factors impact the opportunity cost of production.

FACTORS THAT AFFECT WILLINGNESS TO SELL

We have just told a story that two factors, price and opportunity cost of production, influence how much an individual motivated by profit is willing to supply. We say that individual supply is a function of price and cost of production.

Individual Supply = f (Price, cost of production)

Or

$$q_s = f(P, c)$$

where
q_s = *quantity supplied by one firm*
P = *own price*
c = *(opportunity) cost of production.*

Of all of these factors, we consider own price (P) to play a key role in understanding firm supply (q_s). When we examine how own price impacts willingness to supply, we must hold all the factors contributing to the cost of production constant.

It helps to think of a specific good and time frame. Say your friend Marie is thinking about making pizzas and selling them. Say this is a seven-inch pizza with sauce, cheese, and some great spices. If she didn't know what the going price for such a pizza was, she might put together a schedule like the one given here. This schedule represents how many pizzas she is willing to sell in a day at various prices. See table 19.1.

As price goes up, Marie is willing to offer more pizzas. Does this make sense? Sure it does. At very low prices, it doesn't pay for Marie to use up a lot of resources to make pizzas. At $2, she could be willing to supply a few pizzas. If pizza can get a higher price, she would be willing to use more resources and make more revenue. So far, this looks like supply is a positive relationship, as price goes up so does the amount offered for sale.

We will make one more simplification. For the supply schedule, everything except own price is held constant, we drop all those factors held constant in the notation and denote the abbreviated form of the function as the **supply curve**:

$$q_s = f(P)$$

Table 19.1. Marie's supply schedule for pizza

Price	# Pizzas Marie (q_s)
$0	0
$2	6
$5	30
$10	100

We use the word "curve" here rather than function to remind us that it is just a relationship between two things—own price and quantity supplied—and doesn't represent all the other factors we are holding constant to create the supply schedule.

This simplification is worthwhile, because now we can graph this relationship in two dimensions: q and P. Here we will continue the practice of putting P on the vertical axis.

Remember if the cost of production changes, it may impact the willingness to offer for sale. And the supply schedule may no longer be valid.

As an exercise, graph the supply schedule for pizza, with P (price) on the vertical axis, and q (quantity) on the horizontal axis.

Go ahead and connect the five points you drew. Your graph should be upward sloping.

SUPPLY IN A DYNAMIC WORLD

OWN PRICE CHANGES

You can see the impact of a price change on supply by looking at the graph you drew, or at the supply schedule. If the price of pizza changes, you can see the change in quantity supplied just by looking at your graph or the supply schedule. You have full information about how many pizzas Marie is willing to sell when the price is $0, $2, $5, $10, or $20.

How many pizzas Marie will be willing to supply is described by her supply curve as long as nothing has changed regarding wages, interest rates, rent, regulation, technology of the pizza business, or even her outside opportunities. Let's go through a couple of things that would disrupt Marie's supply schedule.

COST OF PRODUCTION: WAGES FOR WORKERS CHANGE

It turns out that Marie is having a hard time hiring and keeping good pizza makers. A big restaurant has set up nearby and has started offering higher wages. To keep the pizzas coming, Marie has to pay her workers more. How might this impact the original supply schedule for pizza?

Draw the original supply curve and the new supply curve when the price of an input has gone up. Use the values in table 19.2 and label each curve.

Table 19.2. Marie's supply schedule for pizza with higher wages

Price	# Pizzas original wages (q_s)	# Pizzas new, higher wages (new q_s)
$0	0	0
$2	6	4
$5	30	20
$10	100	60
$20	1000	700

When the supply curve is lower in a new circumstance, we say that "Supply has decreased" or "Supply has shifted to the left." We might even say that "Supply has gone down," but we don't mean to imply that at every quantity offered, less is paid. We mean that *at every price, less is supplied*. This is why we emphasize a decrease in supply is a shift of the entire supply curve to the left.

A shift left is a decrease in supply, but to an untrained observer, it might look like the newly drawn, decreased supply curve lies "above" the original supply curve, giving the illusion of an increase in supply. This can be a real pitfall. We read the graph horizontally. When we ask how much is supplied at a given price, the answer is less to the left, or more to the right.

COST OF PRODUCTION: INTRODUCING NEW TECHNOLOGY

Say there is a new piece of software that can help Marie predict when her buyers will want pizza. She can schedule her workers more effectively, thereby reducing her costs. This will increase Marie's willingness to offer pizzas at every price. See table 19.3. Draw the original supply curve, and then the new supply curve when new technology is introduced. When the supply is higher in a new circumstance, we say that supply has increased, or that supply has shifted to the right. We emphasize that an increase in supply is a shift to the right.

We have used pizza for all these examples, but you can do the same thing with any good or service that is traded. You just need to keep in mind exactly what the good is, what inputs are used to create and distribute the good, and how technology and expectations might impact the production process. Try these: lattes, blue jeans, flip-flops, iPhones, apartment rentals, haircuts, manicures, house cleaning services, and taxi rides.

Table 19.3. Marie's supply schedule for pizza with new technology

Price	# Pizzas original wages (q_s)	# Pizzas new, technology (new q_s)
$0	0	0
$2	6	10
$5	30	50
$10	100	150
$20	1000	1600

Table 19.4. Supply schedules for three pizza producers

Price	# Pizzas seller 1 (qs^1)	# Pizzas seller 2 (qs^2)	# Pizzas seller 3 (qs^3)
$0	0	0	0
$2	6	10	14
$5	30	40	20
$10	100	90	120
$20	1000	750	1250

TOTAL MARKET SUPPLY

We know that individual supply is the relationship between own price and quantity demanded for one seller, holding all the elements of production costs constant. If we assume that an entire industry is made up of firms that are motivated much like Marie's, we can find the total market supply curve. The total market supply curve shows the relationship between price and amount all sellers are willing to sell.

As an example, say there were only three possible sellers of pizza in your town. Those three sellers are the entire population that will be producing pizza. We can call them the pizza industry for this region. Table 19.4 summarizes their individual supply schedules.

If you graphed the supply curve for each group, you would find that each one is upward sloping: more is supplied at high prices than at low prices.

Just as individual supply curves represent the amount, individual sellers are willing to offer at given prices, total market supply curve represents the amount all sellers in the market are willing to offer at given prices. We can sum individual supply schedules ($q_s^1 + q_s^2 + q_s^3$) at each price before we graph or we can sketch the supply curve and add each seller's supply for each price point successively. This is called summing horizontally at each price point. Either method yields the same total market supply curve. See table 19.5.

Table 19.5. Supply schedules for three pizza producers and market supply curve

Price	# Pizzas seller 1 (qs¹)	# Pizzas seller 2 (qs²)	# Pizzas seller 3 (qs³)	Total market supply (Q_s)
$0	0	0	0	0
$2	6	10	14	30
$5	30	40	20	90
$10	100	90	120	310
$20	1000	750	1250	3000

The total market supply is a sum of all the individual supply functions. Any factor that changes and causes an individual supply curve to shift can also make total market supply curve shift. In addition to all the factors that impact individual supply, changes in the number of sellers will affect market supply.

$$Qs = f(P, c, \mathbf{N} \ldots)$$

where $\mathbf{N}$ is the population size.

More sellers will make the market supply increase. A decrease in the number of sellers will make the market supply decrease.

DISCUSSION AND EXERCISES

1. As an exercise, graph the total market supply schedule from table 19.5. Does the total market supply curve slope downward or upward?
2. Does it seem flatter or steeper than an individual supply curve? Why do you think this is?
3. Assume a new seller comes to town and has the same costs as Seller 3. That is, the new seller has the same individual supply schedule. How does this affect total market supply? Sketch the new total market supply on the same graph as the market supply with only the first three sellers.
4. You will find that the new total market supply curve is to the right of the old one. Is it steeper or flatter than the old one?

Chapter 20

A Market: Supply and Demand

Supply and demand curves help us to predict how much will be traded and at what price under particular circumstances.

The easy part is putting both curves, supply and demand, on the same graph. Each curve is constructed in the same way, with price of the good or service on the vertical axis and quantity of the good or service on the horizontal axis. The supply curve has a positive slope. As the price goes up, sellers are willing to sell more pizzas. The demand curve has a negative slope. As the price falls, people are willing to buy more pizzas. The intersection of these two curves is called the market equilibrium.

Equilibrium is a state in which opposing forces or influences are balanced. In this case, the opposing forces are buyers who tend to want to buy at a lower price, and sellers who tend to want to sell at a higher price. See figure 20.1.

JUSTIFYING THE INTERSECTION AS THE EQUILIBRIUM

Take for example the equilibrium in the pizza market. The supply and demand intersect where P = $5 and Q = 1000. See figure 20.1.

Choose a price below the intersection. At any price below the equilibrium, the quantity demanded is larger than the quantity supplied (1200 > 800). See figure 20.2. We call this excess demand. That condition, which can be thought of as more buyers than sellers, puts upward pressure on the price. That upward pressure persists until the quantity demanded equals the quantity supplied.

Choose any price above the intersection. At any price above the equilibrium, the quantity demanded is less than the quantity supplied (~1170 > 800).

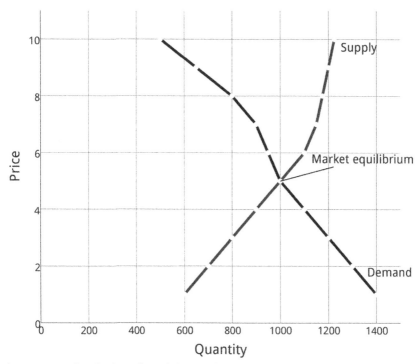

Figure 20.1.   Sketch of supply and demand for pizza

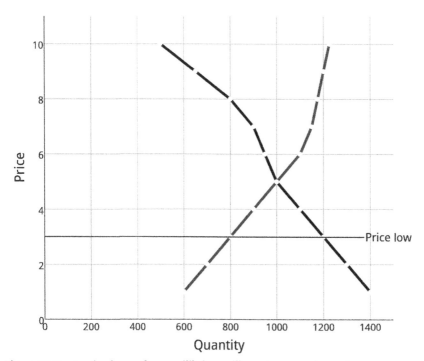

Figure 20.2.   A price lower than equilibrium will create excess demand

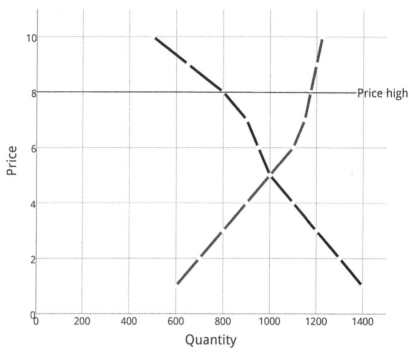

Figure 20.3.   A price higher than equilibrium will create excess supply

See figure 20.3. We call this the excess supply, and that condition puts downward pressure on the price. That downward pressure persists until the quantity demanded equals the quantity supplied.

Any price other than the equilibrium price creates either excess supply or excess demand, driving the price down or up toward the equilibrium.

EQUILIBRIUM AND EFFICIENCY

An equilibrium price uses society's resources in the most efficient way possible given what people want.

Suppose someone wanted pizza makers to make 100 pizzas beyond what the market produced on its own. We can tell by looking at the supply curve that it would take a $6 price per pizza to induce pizza makers to make those extra pizzas. A supplier would be using up $6 to produce pizzas that are only worth $4 to buyers. How do we know those extra pizzas are only worth $4 to buyers?

We use an interpretation of the demand curve called the inverse demand curve. The demand curve is a function of P, for example, Q(P). The inverse demand curve Qd(P)⁻¹, or P(Qd), is merely the inverse of demand function, where we solve the demand function in terms of Q rather than P. The inverse interpretation shows us what 1100 pizzas are worth to buyers and what those pizzas cost sellers. P(Qd) shows the "willingness to pay" for given quantities. P(Qs) shows us at what price sellers would willingly accept given quantities. At an output greater than the equilibrium output (any point to the right of the equilibrium), making pizzas ends up costing sellers more than buyers are willing to pay. Therefore, any quantity traded greater than the equilibrium quantity is inefficient.

On the other side, say there was a desire to limit the amount produced to 900 pizzas, 100 fewer than the equilibrium quantity. When so few pizzas are traded, each is valued at or above $7. (See the demand curve to the left of q=900 in figure 20.5.) At most, those 900 pizzas will cost $4 each to produce. (See the supply curve to the left of 900 pizzas in figure 20.4.) If trades stopped at q = 900, a quantity lower than the equilibrium quantity, there is a lost opportunity to society to create value for those willing to pay a price

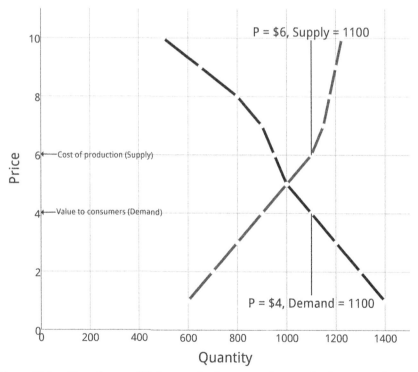

Figure 20.4. More than equilibrium production causes lower valued output to be produced at higher cost

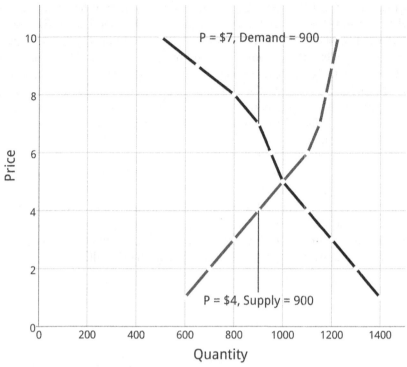

Figure 20.5. **Less than market equilibrium production causes higher valued needs not to be met by lower cost output**

higher than the cost of production. In other words, any quantity lower than the equilibrium quantity is inefficient.

DISCUSSION AND EXERCISES

1. What is an equilibrium price?
2. Why does the price in a market tend to move toward an equilibrium price? Describe the process involved.
3. What is meant by efficiency? How is efficiency related to equilibrium?

Chapter 21

A Market Responds: Price and Quantity

Now that we understand and have constructed demand and supply curves, we can use them together to interpret the impact of economic changes on market outcomes. Supply and demand curves help us to predict how much will be traded and at what price under particular circumstances. When those circumstances change, we update the curves and compare the resulting predicted price and quantity to the original market outcomes. With this simple tool, we can interpret the qualitative impact of economic changes on market outcomes.

We constructed supply and demand curves with many variables fixed. Both curves are constructed with the price of the good or service being the independent variable. This construction allows us to see how price movements influence the quantity demanded and the quantity supplied.

The supply and demand curves for one market (an identical good or service over the same period of time) can be put on the same graph. We can then see where the tension between buyers (wanting more at a lower price) and sellers (wanting to sell more at higher prices) resolves in equilibrium. At the equilibrium price, all buyers who want to buy and all sellers who want to sell can do so. You can think of an equilibrium as the only condition where there are no unsatisfied buyers bidding up the price, and no unsatisfied sellers offering discounts.

DEMAND SHIFTS

If the price of a related good (substitute or complement) on the consumer side changes, it will shift the demand curve. If income, tastes, expectations, or the number of buyers change, it will shift the demand curve. If the number of buyers change, the market demand curve will respond with a shift in the same direction.

A demand increase (shift right) is indicated in the image on the left in figure 21.1. What could have caused the increase in demand? An increase in the price of a substitute, a decrease in the price of a complement, an increase in income, a positive change in taste for the good or service, or an increase in the number of buyers would all cause an increase in demand. Notice that the supply curve did not change in the image on the left. However, more quantity is supplied in the updated market. Demand increased, and the quantity supplied increased. Notice what happened to the equilibrium price with an increase in demand.

SUPPLY SHIFTS

Anything that can cause an increase or decrease in the cost of production will shift the supply curve. If the number of sellers changes, the supply curve will respond with a shift in the same direction.

A supply decrease (shift left) is indicated in the image on the right in figure 21.2. What could have caused the decrease in supply? An increase in the price of an input, an increase in government regulation, an increase in taxes, or a decrease in the number of sellers would all cause a decrease in supply. Notice that the demand curve did not change in the image on the right where the supply curve shifted. However, less quantity is demanded in the updated market. Supply decreased and the

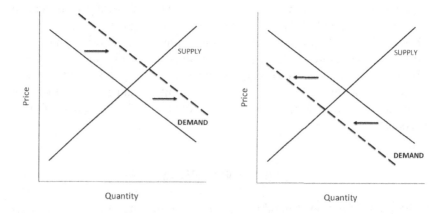

Figure 21.1.   Demand shifts

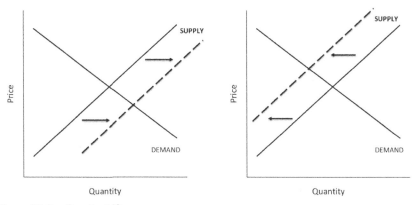

Figure 21.2. Supply shifts

quantity demanded also decreased. Notice what happens to the equilibrium price with a decrease in supply. Does falling supply have the same effect on equilibrium price as rising demand?

Typically, if something shifts one curve, it will not shift the other curve. There are exceptions, but typically, the major impact of a change in market conditions will be on one curve.

OTHER INFLUENCES ON EQUILIBRIUM

Price regulations (price controls) and quantity regulations (quotas) will also influence a market. Both topics are covered later.

DISCUSSION AND EXERCISES

Apply what you have learned about supply and demand to predict the impact of the following events:

1. People moved away from New Orleans after Hurricane Katrina and settled in Baton Rouge. Let Q be the number of homes and P be home price in Baton Rouge. What do you think happened to home prices and the quantity of homes sold in Baton Rouge? Support your answer with a graph.
2. After a long absence from the oil market, Iran has reentered the international oil market. Let Q be the number of barrels of oil and P be the price

of a barrel of oil. What do you think will happen to the price of oil? Support your answer with a graph.

3. The price of milk has gone down. Milk is used to make lattes. What impact will this have on the market for lattes?

4. The price of milk has gone down. Many people use milk with boxed, ready-to-eat cereal (e.g., Honey Nut Cheerios). What impact will this have on the market for Cheerios?

5. Milk is used to make cheese. The price of cheese has fallen because milk is so inexpensive. What influence will this have on the market for cheese pizzas?

Chapter 22

Economic Surplus

Surplus is a direct result of a beneficial trade. Surplus is the value generated by trading. Without trade, there is no surplus generated for buyers or sellers. The amount of surplus generated in a market depends on the quantity traded, and who is trading.

Economic surplus is another word for total welfare resulting from trade. Welfare, or surplus, is attributed to both sides of the market: buyers and sellers. **Consumer surplus** is the gain obtained by buyers when they can purchase a product for a price that is lower than the price that they would be willing to pay. **Producer surplus** is the gain obtained by sellers because they can sell at a market price that is higher than their willingness to sell. See figure 22.1. When buyers and sellers can trade, and prices are flexible, surplus is maximized when the highest value buyers and lowest cost sellers trade.

Surplus is a direct result of a beneficial trade. Without trade, there is no consumer surplus or producer surplus. The amount of surplus generated in a market depends on the quantity traded and who is trading. The higher the buyers value the goods and services and the lower the goods cost to produce, the higher the surplus generated for a society.

DISCUSSION AND EXERCISES

1. What is surplus and why is it important?
2. What do economists mean by consumer and producer surplus? How are they measured? Why are they important?
3. What are the sources of consumer and producer surplus? How might we increase them?

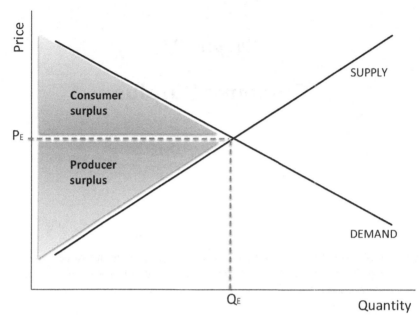

Figure 22.1.   Total surplus generated in a market

Chapter 23

Price Signals and Spontaneous Order

Prices enable people to form mutual expectations. Prices help people to coordinate in complex ways as they individually decide what to produce or consume.

Think about language for a moment. What is a language? There are artificial languages, computer languages, for example, but most languages are what we call natural languages, which means no one invented them. They just happened. A language is an unending process of people adjusting to each other. No one had to design the process by which languages evolve. Interestingly, all languages are products of human action but not products of human design. To suppose a rational society would design its language from the ground up is contradicted by our actual history. Language helps us communicate because language is a never-ending process of agents on the ground adjusting to each other. Languages are highly refined, effective adaptations to the evolving communication needs of particular populations.

As with language, prices are a form of communication. How do we know what it will take to get our product to whoever wants or needs it most? We might take bids. As we (and our rivals) take bids for a service, that service comes to have a price. As with language, prices enable people to form mutual expectations. Prices help people to coordinate in complex ways as they individually decide what to produce or consume. To think that an authority needs to decide what the price of rice ought to be is like thinking that an authority needs to decide what sound people ought to make when they want to refer to rice. In fact, no one needs to decide. Coordination emerges spontaneously.

One of the most interesting facts here is that price signals enable and encourage people to respond to information they do not have. Perhaps the cost of drilling has changed, or a cheap substitute has been discovered, or political unrest has made a key ingredient harder to acquire. Having no inkling of such variables, buyers nevertheless respond appropriately because they know the one thing they need to know: the price. As F. A. Hayek wrote in his 1945 essay "The Use of Knowledge in Society":

> Assume that somewhere in the world a new opportunity for the use of some raw material, say, tin, has arisen, or that one of the sources of supply of tin has been eliminated. It does not matter for our purpose—and it is very significant that it does not matter—which of these two causes has made tin more scarce. All that the users of tin need to know is that some of the tin they used to consume is now more profitably employed elsewhere and that, in consequence, they must economize tin.[1]

What emerges from the haggling is not only a deal, but something larger: a community. There was no central decision about who should produce tin, or whether anyone should; no central decision about who should consume tin, or whether anyone should; no central decision about what to give in return for tin. All that happened is that some people guessed that if they had a way to bring tin to market, there would be enough consumer demand to make the venture worthwhile. When some of these guesses prove correct, and people begin to trade, a market in tin emerges and becomes part of what brings people together as partners in mutually beneficial ventures.

Price signals economize on information, eventually leading to patterns of cooperation involving large networks of people all over the world. Cooperation evolves among people who need not share a language, need not be aware of each other's existence, and need not be aware of their mutual dependence. They may be involved in a business that depends on "tongue crimp terminals" without ever having heard of a tongue crimp terminal. You may not know what tongue crimp terminals are, but if you use a keyboard like the one on which we are typing these words, you depend on them. People are only vaguely aware of thousands of jobs that need doing so as to supply them with inputs that enable them to have a finished product to sell. Particular agents seldom if ever have more than a glimpse of a big picture, yet their efforts make up society as a cooperative venture for mutual benefit.

We may understand the system's logic well enough to make important predictions at a general level, for example, that a rising money supply leads to rising prices. We may be able to predict that a population of insects will evolve resistance to a pesticide, or that a fluid sufficiently chilled will crystallize and become a solid, even though we could hardly begin to predict the behavior of any particular element of that system. Likewise, we may be able to predict that

---

1. F. A. Hayek. "The Use of Knowledge in Society," *American Economic Review* 35 (1945), pp. 519–530.

a society that declares war on drugs will ultimately lose that war. However, although there is a certain logic to the system, the fact remains that economies are technically chaotic, chaotic to such a degree that even something as straightforward as next week's oil prices are at best a matter of educated guesswork even for experts. Crucially, beyond the question of what we can predict, the further point is that there is a drastic limit to what we can simply decide. No one can decide against people responding to incentives, in the same way that no one can decide against bacteria becoming resistant to antibiotics.

PRICE MECHANISM

Free-floating prices have ethical importance. If you charge whatever it takes to cover your production cost, then the competition will not be able to undersell you unless they can produce at lower cost. If they can produce at lower cost, and therefore can undersell you, that is a signal that you should be producing something else, something that you can provide to a level of excellence that enables you to compete successfully for customers. If you do not have any competition, then you are in a position to charge a premium. In the short run, the extra profit will enable you to cover your cost of research and development. In the long run, the profitability of your business will attract competitors and drive prices down, eventually driving further research into ways of lowering production cost. That logic explains why the price of services that use new technology tends to fall over time, even in otherwise inflationary conditions.

We can expect a rule of law to evolve into a framework that brings people together and begins to generate information in the form of prices. Reliable information about prices, when people have it, tells them how to be of greatest service to others and how to prosper in the process. Yet prices must be flexible, not just knowable. Why? Because when prices are flexible, that is when prices become a **signal**. Changing prices are a signal of changing facts about what buyers and sellers want from each other. So, as Hayek taught us, prices can't be fixed, or even planned. For prices to be able to teach us what people want right now, and how much they are willing to do in exchange for getting what they want, prices must rise and fall with supply and demand.

DISCUSSION AND EXERCISES

1. What does it take for people to have a reason to economize? What does it take for people to want to conserve a resource, and use it wisely? What does it take to signal a consumer to treat something as scarce?

2. Is there a difference between the incentive effect of charging a single up-front fee for an all-you-can-eat buffet versus having to pay the marginal cost of each additional item you order?

3. Take a look at the price for any service. Has that price changed recently? Has the price changed historically, over the long run? See if you can find out why. Prices change for a reason.

Chapter 24

Price Controls

Price controls are restrictions in the movement of prices, and they come in two forms: price ceilings and price floors. Price ceilings are maximum allowable prices. To be effective, price ceilings must be set below where prices would have been in the absence of celings. Price floors, on the other hand, are minimum allowable prices. To be effective, price floors must be set above where prices would have been in the absence of floors. Effective price controls will tend to result in a reduction of the quantity traded plus a loss in surplus when compared to a market uncontrolled in this way.

Prices are the result of buyers and sellers each looking for the best price they can get in a marketplace. Prices rise and fall in response to changes in market conditions that affect supply or demand. However, price floors and price ceilings each prevent prices from responding in predictable ways to changes in supply or demand.

A **price floor** makes it illegal to buy or sell for anything less than a mandated price. Along the same lines, governments sometimes guarantee producers a certain price for their product, even if no other customer is willing to pay that high a price for it. This is called a price support. A price floor or support is effective only if it is above what the price would have been without the floor.

You can see from figure 24.1 that a relatively high-price floor intersects the demand curve at a lower quantity, and the supply curve at a higher quantity. How much will actually be traded in this market? The lower quantity will be traded. The extra offered for sale at the relatively high price floor will go unsold in this market, causing an excess supply.

Two examples of price floors are price supports (e.g., guaranteed minimum prices for some agricultural products) and minimum wage laws. If a

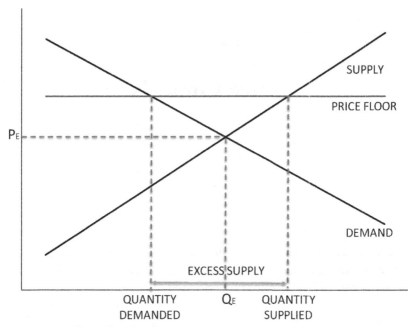

Figure 24.1.   Effects of a price floor

minimum wage law were changed, for example, to mandate a thousand dollars an hour wage for teenaged employees, then no one would hire teenaged workers.

What happens to the surplus value generated in these markets when a price floor is imposed? Who wins and who loses?

Price ceilings are maximum allowable prices. To be effective, price ceilings must be below where the price would have been without the ceiling. You can see from figure 24.2 that the relatively low price of the ceiling intersects the supply curve at a low quantity and intersects the demand curve at a high quantity. Producers won't produce as much at the lower price, while consumers will demand more because the goods are cheaper. How much will be traded in this market? The lower quantity will be traded.

A price ceiling makes it illegal to buy or sell for higher than a mandated price. Sometimes a price control is *effective*, and sometimes not. If a government makes it illegal to sell a textbook for more than a million dollars, no one's decision to buy or sell will ever be affected. A price ceiling for textbooks of one dollar, on the other hand, would be all too effective, because it is below the predicted unrestricted price. Publishers would stop producing textbooks, and the market for these books would disappear.

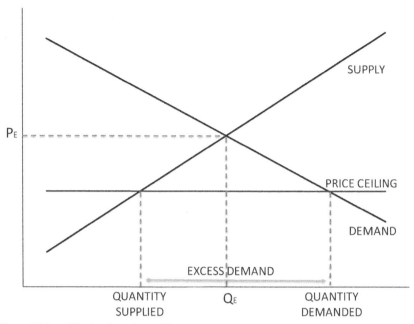

Figure 24.2. Effects of a price ceiling

An effective price ceiling lowers quantity supplied from what it would be at a higher price. Therefore, at this lower price, demand exceeds supply. Put differently, price ceilings create shortages.

The naming of ceilings and floors may seem backward. Effective ceilings are below the equilibrium price. Effective floors are above the equilibrium price. But it isn't confusing if you think of how they function in a market. Their point is to block activity. Ceilings set maximum allowable prices. The only way ceilings impact a market is by preventing prices from rising to the equilibrium. They must be below the market price to be effective. Analogously, floors set minimum allowable prices. They impact a market if they are set above the market price, not allowing the price to come down to reach its equilibrium level. If you ever forget, just choose a price and ask yourself if that price will prevent the market from reaching an equilibrium. If your answer is yes, you are placing the control where it will make a difference.

TESTING THE THEORY: EMPIRICAL EVIDENCE

Empirical evidence is never uncontroversial. If the minimum wage rises, we would predict teenage unemployment to rise in response, but the prediction will not turn out to be true in every case. Sometimes, something else happens at the same time that outweighs the impact of a rising minimum wage. If effective rent controls are imposed, that might make it easier to find housing that you can afford, or it might mean that when people look for housing, they learn to start paying side payments, on top of the rent, to landlords.

There is a fair bit of uncertainty here, even when we know a lot about the relationship between variables. This is a basic fact about the nature of science in general. To test a hypothesis, we need a well-controlled experiment, but observing how an economy reacts to a policy change will never be a well-controlled experiment. There always seem to be countless variables in play, and thus countless alternative explanations. We still want to be as scientific as possible, but the fact remains that, especially in the social sciences, good science is humble science. Our most reliable predictions are not always confirmed by the empirical evidence. Sometimes there is something wrong with the prediction. Other times it will mean that we don't have enough evidence yet. It may also mean that some hidden variable is overwhelmingly important under the circumstances or that our evidence is in some other way unreliable.

DISCUSSION AND EXERCISES

1. How is rent control likely to affect the market for housing in a city? When would you recommend such a policy?
2. What will happen to the number of people employed if the minimum wage were doubled? What if it were cut in half?
3. Price ceilings are often implemented in the form of "anti-gouging" laws in the wake of natural disasters. What happens with scarce goods (like power generators, gasoline, and water) when their prices cannot move given increased demand?
4. A ceiling is effective only if it is below what the price would have been absent interference. Can you explain why? When would a price ceiling be effective in a good way?
5. If rent controls are established, what effect would you predict on the supply of rental housing? How will rent controls affect the supply of affordable housing? Under what conditions?
6. When rent controls are imposed, who wins? Who loses? Overall, is more or less surplus generated in a rent-controlled housing market?

Chapter 25

Economic Science: Putting Theory to the Test

Price controls—floors and ceilings—prevent buyers and sellers from sending each other a signal. If the price cannot rise, then buyers can't signal to sellers that demand has increased. If sellers don't get the signal, and supply fails to respond to rising demand, then rising demand translates into shortages rather than into economic growth.

Some situations seem to call for price controls. Imagine an isolated mining town, where the mine is owned by a single company, and everyone in town works for the mining company. Even the saloon is owned by the mining company. The labor market in this town is what we refer to as a **monopsony**, which means that there is only one buyer of labor. Because of the town's isolation, there are no other buyers, and therefore there is no competition on that side of the market. There is no competition for labor. In that case, we could see a point in there being a minimum wage. Thus, we have an argument for a **price floor**.

Similarly, if some exogenous shock to the market, something like a hurricane or other natural disaster that threatens to cut off supply or otherwise causes demand to soar, then we might cap prices to prevent "price gouging." Thus, we have an argument for a **price ceiling**.

Arguments against free-floating prices tend to presuppose that markets are not competitive. This presupposition is sometimes correct, and under those conditions, economists have reason to accept that the general economic argument for free-floating prices does not apply.

So why do Western nations tend to shy away from sweeping systems of wage and price controls? One answer: Suppose we impose a price ceiling and thereby make it illegal for the price to rise. That might sound good, but if the price can't rise, then buyers can't send a signal to producers that demand exceeds supply and that increasing supply would increase gains from

trade. But unless producers increase supply, rising demand results in shortages rather than in economic growth. We know this from standard economic
theory and from sad experience as well.[1]

JUST PRICE AND EXPERIMENTAL PHILOSOPHY

A society where people are free to trade will be a cooperative venture for
mutual benefit. As long as there is a window of opportunity for mutual advantage created by downward sloping demand and upward sloping supply (so
long as transaction costs are not prohibitive), there will be gains from trade.

IT'S NOT THE PRICE; IT'S THE SURPLUS

Crucially, whether we realize gains from trade require only that we trade.
They do not require that we trade at any particular price within that window
of opportunity. Perhaps gains won't be fairly distributed, but gains there will
be nonetheless. Being obsessed with just price makes trading less likely,
which tends to squander some of the cooperative surplus.

Accordingly, we want to beware of focusing on price prematurely. We do
not want to lose sight of the fact that there is a time and place for thinking about
economic growth and about the wealth of nations. Obviously, as individuals,
when we buy or sell services, we all want the best price we can get. But from
a larger perspective, what should we want? Should we want people to have
as much as possible to offer each other? Should we want people to be able to
get accurate information about how much others are willing to pay for their
services? One implication of standard economic analysis is that the wealth of
a nation has everything to do with gains from trade and nothing to do with the
particular prices at which goods are traded. In figure 25.1, there are gains from
trade to be had. How much is gained depends on how much is traded. The maximum number of trades occurs at the equilibrium price. At that price, the number
of widgets supplied rises to meet the number that consumers wish to purchase.
Above that price, fewer trades are made because fewer buyers wish to buy.

Figure 25.2 depicts the creation of a price ceiling that prevents suppliers
from selling at a price higher than what someone has decided is "fair."

When the market clears at an equilibrium price, every customer who
wants a widget at its equilibrium price can get one. By contrast, the problem

---

1. For example, see Virgil Henry Storr, Stefanie Haeffele-Balch, and Laura Grube, *Community
Revival in the Wake of Disaster* (New York: Palgrave MacMillan (2015). Most recently, see Ste-
fanie Haeffele and Ann Hobson, *The Need for Humility in Policymaking* (London: Rowman &
Littlefield, 2019).

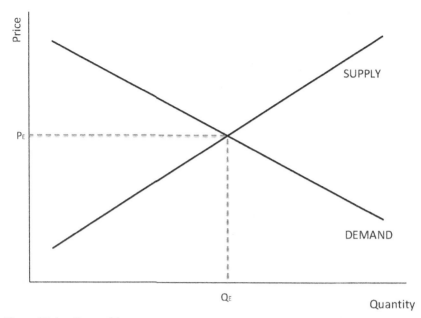

Figure 25.1. Competition

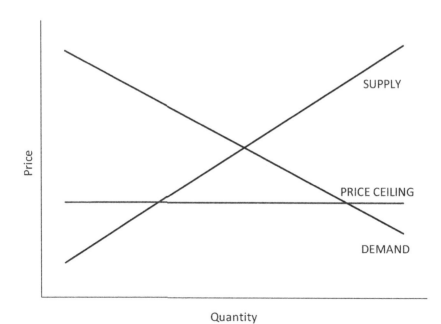

Figure 25.2. Price ceiling

revealed in figure 25.2 is that when supply is cut off by a ceiling, there is unmet demand. Buyers who would have been well served by an opportunity to buy at a higher price are instead shut out. Figure 25.3 shows the standard representation of what is known as the "deadweight loss" of price ceilings.

Here is the twist. The standard picture of deadweight loss (depicted as an *unshaded* triangle in figure 25.3, representing mutually beneficial trades prevented by a price ceiling) implicitly assumes that the agents systematically shut out are the lowest-value buyers (the buyers who are willing to pay the least) and highest-cost producers (the sellers whose production cost is higher). In fact, in a real marketplace (and this is not merely a theoretical possibility but a typical outcome in experimental auctions), buyers who go away empty-handed are not necessarily the ones who are least willing to pay and who thus are systematically outbid.

Auction experiments reveal that buyers who succeed in making a purchase are a random selection of buyers who happen to be in the right place when an artificially scarce item comes up for sale. For the sake of example, imagine there has been a terrible storm, followed by a power failure. Refrigerators are not working, and people want ice. However, without refrigerators, ice is hard to get. Therefore, without price controls, price-gougers can charge much higher than normal prices for precious ice. If price-gouging sellers charge much higher than normal prices, then buyers who want ice only to chill their warm beer will not be able to compete with buyers who need ice to chill

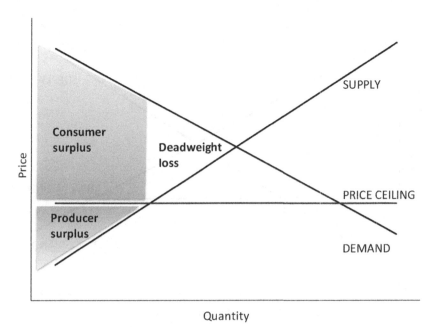

Figure 25.3. Standard image of surpluses and deadweight loss

insulin or baby formula. Those high-value buyers will bid the price up to a level that shuts out beer drinkers. Beer-chilling $2 ice disappears from the market. Life-saving $12 ice remains plentiful.

By contrast, if the price is legally prevented from rising above $2, two things happen, not one.

First, as per the standard model, supply will be low because suppliers will not supply as much ice at a lower price.

Second is a tragic distributive implication overlooked by standard analysis. Namely, if prices are capped at $2, then those who want ice only to chill their beer *remain in the market.*

Beer drinkers will consume some fraction of scarce supply that a free-floating price would have reserved for insulin users who needed it more. If we just look at a deadweight loss triangle on the standard model, as in figure 25.3, we don't see this. The true scope of the tragedy of price controls, though, is larger than the standard unshaded triangle of figure 25.3.

The tragedy is a consequence of a particular mirage, a mirage that we need to make sure prices are fair, and should not settle for everyone being better off.

By capping price of ice at $2, we ensured that rising prices would not signal low-value consumers that they should defer to high-value consumers.

Figure 25.4 illustrates a typical result of running a classroom auction with a dozen or so buyers and sellers. (You can try this in your own class! Check

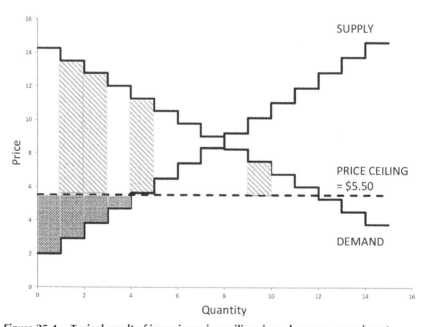

Figure 25.4. Typical result of imposing price ceilings in a classroom experiment

the QR code for more information.) Without price controls, buyers and sellers, knowing nothing beyond their own resale value or cost of production, can wander around, and in three minutes make trades later revealed to have converged on a market-clearing competitive equilibrium, typically with all potential gains from trade being realized.

With price ceilings, successful sellers still tend, systematically, to be a cluster of low-cost producers; sellers with higher production costs are shut out. On the other side of the equation, though, successful buyers are a random selection of positive-value buyers who happen to be in the right place at right time when a seller announces an offer.

CONCLUSION

If we are in the grip of a mirage that prices must be low to be fair, we will think we have reason to impose a price ceiling to keep prices from rising to a level that exceeds some people's ability to pay. If we take this concern to its logical conclusion, we would cap prices at $0, because, for any price above zero, we can imagine a desperate would-be consumer unable to afford that price. Capping prices at zero, however, ensures that no consumer has more than a fair share by ensuring that no one has any share at all.

Price controls cannot possibly solve the problem that moral philosophers see with free-floating prices, namely the problem of guaranteeing that access to needed goods will never be limited by the ability to pay. Wherever price exceeds zero, there is no guarantee. If what bothers us is a theoretical prospect of people's being unable to afford the cost of producing an item they need, then we are concerned about a problem that price controls cannot solve.

Ability to pay is inevitably a serious issue. It will appear to be *the* issue when we view a snapshot of life in the marketplace and abstract from the logic of how producers and consumers respond to rising prices. In a regime with no price ceiling, we can imagine beer drinkers so rich that they would pay any sum at all for ice and thereby outbid those who need ice to chill their insulin. However, if such beer drinkers exist and make it outlandishly profitable to be a seller of ice, then the market will be flooded with ice, flown in by helicopter if necessary. Where the price of ice is free to rise, high-demand consumers create conditions under which ice becomes plentiful, thereby solving the problem for everyone. By contrast, if we impose price controls where some beer drinkers are willing to pay any price at all, *including out-waiting or out-begging insulin users lined up for ice*, then the outlandish demand of these imaginary beer drinkers is still part of the problem. The difference is that under price controls, their outlandish demand is not simultaneously part of the solution because price controls stop outlandish beer drinkers from giving suppliers an overwhelming reason to get ice to that market.

Setting aside cases of life and death emergency, widespread access to new products depends on early adopters who pay premium prices, thereby financing the ramping up of production. Free-floating prices drive a dynamic equilibration of supply and demand that eventually brings prices into the neighborhood of the cost of production. Moreover, the same process of equilibration drives investments in research and development that lower production cost, thereby allowing prices to fall even more. When some consumers are willing to pay any price for a portable telephone, they create conditions that eventually result in cell phones of improved quality becoming affordable for teenagers and even rural peasants in developing countries. In the long run, widespread access to laptop computers, smartphones, and cheap sandwiches (with ingredients from all over the world) happens because of the economic coordination that free-floating prices make possible. Whether late adopters can afford to bide their time and wait their turn cannot be guaranteed—either in theory or practice. It depends on the circumstances of particular agents in particular cases. As a rule, though, it is a tragic mistake to prevent price signals from informing entrepreneurs about where society most values their efforts to lower production cost.

In conclusion, standard economic analysis overlooks the reality that deadweight loss does not necessarily fall on low-value buyers. The reality is that deadweight loss to buyers tends to be randomly distributed. To the extent that the impact is randomly distributed, price controls squander more wealth—more potential gains from trade—than standard economic analysis suggests. The impact also will be more arbitrary, thus arguably more unfair, than what is indicated by the standard picture. If we see fairness as requiring that goods and services flow systematically to consumers who need them most, then we had better not see fairness as an issue to address with price controls.

DISCUSSION AND EXERCISES

1. How are prices related to fairness? Is a low price always better than a high price?
2. What can we learn about economics from experiments?
3. Why might experimental results differ from real-world results? How should we account for these factors?

Chapter 26

Progress and Wealth Creation

Adam Smith believed that nations become wealthy when they are free to produce whatever is in the greatest demand and sell it wherever demand is greatest.

Why do nations become wealthy? This is the question that Adam Smith tried to answer roughly 250 years ago. Smith wrote during the early stages of the industrial revolution. He concluded that nations become wealthy when they efficiently produce surplus tangible goods that they then can exchange with other nations for economic currency or other tangible goods. Keep in mind that this was at a time when global telecommunication was still 200 years in the future. Transport was mostly by water or horseback, and proceeded at roughly three miles per hour. Airplanes had scarcely been imagined. What we call the Information Age was a long way off. People measured the wealth of a nation in terms of its stock of tangible goods.

Today when we evaluate the wealth of a nation, we might look first at its stock of knowledge and skills. Even more radically, we might think of tangible goods as valuable mainly in terms of whether we can make use of them or whether they serve our purposes. In other words, are they of service? That is the idea underlying what is now called **Service-Dominant Logic**.

GOODS-DOMINANT LOGIC

People and nations have become wealthy, but how did this happen? One way of analyzing commercial activity uses what we call "goods-dominant logic." Humans took the land and other natural resources (things like soil, oceans,

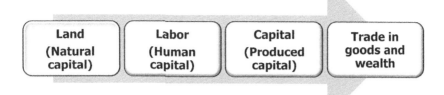

Figure 26.1. Goods-dominant logic process

and forests) and applied labor or human capital to transform natural resources into manufactured products. Figure 26.1 illustrates this process.

Adam Smith in *Wealth of Nations* explained that as we become increasingly specialized, and as the marketplace becomes a place increasingly defined by the division of labor, labor becomes more efficient. Over time, we move from a condition in which nearly everyone does everything for himself or herself to one in which we can observe workers performing a specialized activity such as putting the right front wheel on a car as it moves down the assembly line.

Industrialized nations with a high division of labor produced more goods than they needed, and thus were able to export goods to other countries in return for other natural resources, manufactured products, or money. This is the goods-dominant view of wealth creation.

SERVICE-DOMINANT LOGIC

If you view service as the application of knowledge and skills (something inherently intangible) then perhaps the path to wealth is the exchange of services. Or stated alternatively the exchange of knowledge and skills.

A different way of analyzing commerce might look like the one shown in figure 26.2. This analysis begins not with natural resources, but with intangible capital: knowledge and skills of people, organizations, and nations. In the marketplace, which has increasingly become a marketplace of ideas, people and organizations interact with each other to integrate resources (natural, produced, and intangible) to provide services to one another.

One thing not shown in this model is institutions. Institutions are essential to wealth creation because of their role in coordinating market actors.

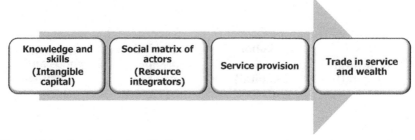

Figure 26.2.   Service-dominant logic process

DISCUSSION AND EXERCISES

1. Compare goods-dominant and service-dominant logics. Describe modern examples that fit each model.
2. Do you expect the future to be more oriented to the production of goods or services? Why?

Part IV

TRUST, AGENCY, AND BYSTANDERS

Communities are networks of cooperation. Successful communities grow, and the networks that compose them become more complex. Particular companies within a growing community sometimes expand along with their community. As a company begins to expand, it too comes more complex. It becomes a community unto itself. As a company expands, owners can no longer do everything themselves. Owners have to delegate. Companies begin to hire large teams of employees, and employees are the ones that owners have to trust to manage relationships with clients, partners, shareholders, trustees, contractors, and any number of people directly or indirectly involved with the business. Eventually, an owner needs to trust an employee not only to be an extra pair of hands, but also an extra pair of eyes and ears. Employees are the owner's agents. As a company grows, owners increasingly have to trust employees to understand and care about what the company is trying to do.

Chapter 27

Principal-Agent Framework

When a company's operation becomes complex enough that owners need to delegate responsibility, they can run into a problem. They have to think about how to align the interests of the various parties to whom they have delegated responsibility. How does a company give its employees a reason to care whether its products actually work, whether its products are safe, or whether its advertising is honest and accurate?

How does a company give its employees a reason to care whether the company is a good neighbor, and does not pollute its environment?

There is a potential for a **principal-agent problem**. A principal-agent relationship is an arrangement where one person, the principal, relies on another person, the agent, to act on the principal's behalf.

What could go wrong? If you are the principal, you are counting on someone else to act as your agent. You need to see, from the beginning, how your interests and the interests of your agent might fail to align. The potential for conflict stems from the simple fact that agents are supposed to represent the interest of a principal, but agents have interests of their own. For example, if your financial advisor advises you to buy a particular product, but you know that the advisor works part-time as a salesman and gets paid a commission for selling that same product, there is a conflict of interest. You need to take his advice with a grain of salt. Your agent's advice may serve his interest rather than yours.

Another aspect of the risk is that principals do not know everything. Agents have information that principals lack. So, principals have to trust agents to do what needs to be done.

Information about the details of time and place is always going to be unique to each person. Suppose the principal has no way to know how hard the agent is working. When key information is directly available only to the agent, the principal has a problem. So, in order to be able to trust an employee (the agent), an owner (the principal) has to ask, "Does my employee *know* enough about what I want?" and also "Does my employee *care* enough about what I want?" Think about how complex any realistic example would be. If you own a football team, then you can expect that your quarterback shares your desire to win games. But your quarterback may want to call plays in a certain way in order to be the hero and get extra credit for the win, which to you is a pointless way of diminishing your chance of winning. You can expect that your quarterback shares your desire to protect him from injury, but your quarterback may enjoy racing motorcycles in the off-season, which to you is a pointless way of putting your investment at risk. Or, perhaps your quarterback has already injured himself, but conceals the injury from you. You need to trust the quarterback to share information with the team doctors, and for the team doctors to understand how much information should be shared with you. If they tell you too much, the quarterback stops trusting them, and that would be bad for you. So, in all kinds of ways, your employees will have information that you lack, and you have to be okay with that.

Various mechanisms can help to align the interests of agent and principal. In employment, employers (principals) may seek to reward agents only for their measurable production rather than pay them by the hour. This is why some employees work on commission. If the principal wants the agent to produce widgets, then paying the agent per unit produced tends to align incentives better than paying the agent for putting in time. There are many other mechanisms by which employers or other principals try to link rewards to measurable forms of success.

DISCUSSION AND EXERCISES

1. Think about relationships between owner and manager, manager and employee, lawyer and client, patient and doctor, or home buyer and real estate agent. For each of these pairs, which of the two is the principal? Which is the agent?
2. In the classroom, between the instructor and the student, who is the principal and who is the agent? Is the teacher an agent for the student, parents, school principal, school district, society, or all of these people? Why do teachers test the students?
3. Suppose you are a quarterback with a multimillion-dollar contract. You need your linemen to protect you. But their contract isn't precisely tied to how well they protect you. What could you do?

Chapter 28

Cost to Bystanders

A negative externality, or external cost, is a cost of a transaction paid by bystanders who were not consulted, and whose interests were not taken into account. A transaction may also create positive externalities, that is, have external benefits.

Any given transaction has costs and benefits. If a seller sells a widget to a buyer for $1.50, the benefit of the transaction to the seller is $1.50, minus whatever it cost to bring that widget to market. Presumably, both parties are better off. They both agreed to the deal, after all. If the seller produced the widget for 79 cents, he makes a profit by selling it for $1.50. If that widget enables the buyer to complete some job more quickly and thereby earn money more quickly, then it looks like everyone is better off. What can go wrong?

An **external cost** is a cost imposed on bystanders, including neighbors. Even if the buyer and seller are both happy with the deal, they may not be the only people who are affected. Suppose using the widget makes a horrible noise, and when the buyer uses it at 4 am, neighbors are unable to sleep. In that case, the widget turns out to have costs to neighbors. The deal affects a whole neighborhood, not just the buyer and seller. An external cost has been imposed. Because of that unknown negative impact on neighbors, it is no longer clear whether society as a whole is better off as a result of the buying and selling of widgets.

A transaction may also create positive externalities, that is, an **external benefit**. Examples are easy to see once you know what to look for: farmers plant trees, beekeepers raise bees that pollinate neighbors' trees, and corporate security systems sometimes make entire neighborhoods safer despite the fact that the neighbors do not help to pay for the private security guards and improved lighting. These are all positive externalities. By contrast, when companies pollute the air and water, make a lot of noise, or cause traffic patterns to be disrupted, we experience negative externalities.

EXTERNALITIES, COMMON SENSE, AND BEING A GOOD NEIGHBOR

Sometimes externalities are not worth eliminating. When people live miles apart, we don't bother to develop laws regulating the shooting of guns into the air. At some point, though, as population density rises, an external cost becomes more serious. Likewise, there is an external cost to driving. If you are on the road, then sharing the road comes at some cost to you. But of course, we don't want people to stop driving. We simply want to monitor the risk and the cost to make sure they do not exceed reasonable levels.

Completely eliminating external costs is not the aim. When we think about what it means to be a good neighbor, it always involves managing a tradeoff between two things. First, we have to be slow to take offense and we have to tolerate minor irritations. We might prefer not to hear neighbors talking too loudly next door, but good neighbors tolerate minor irritations. On the other side of the equation, it is also true that good neighbors want to avoid causing those minor irritations. So, if we are having a party, we tell our guests to keep their voices down because we don't want to irritate our neighbors. Alternatively, we might invite the whole neighborhood to the party. Or we might ask neighbors for their permission to host a noisy celebration. If they are good neighbors, they probably will tell us to go ahead, and instead of being irritated, they will think we showed respect because we asked their permission. In short, we want to be sensitive enough to avoid disturbing them, but we also want to dial down our own sensitivity a bit in order to avoid being disturbed by them.

One crucial lesson here is that there is no perfect substitute for being considerate. We can't just pass a law against being irritating. No system of law will enable us to be good neighbors simply by obeying the law.

Being a good neighbor, or a good trading partner, almost always involves being considerate in a way that goes beyond simply obeying the law. Laws can help us all to understand the minimum standards, but good neighbors go beyond the minimum standards. Good neighbors are thoughtful.

SOCIAL COST IN A MARKET FRAMEWORK

We can use the supply and demand framework to show how externalities impact market outcomes.

Recall that the market demand curve represents the amount everyone in the market would buy at any given price. Another way to think about the demand curve is that it represents the *private* marginal benefit of consumption. The values represented along the curve are benefits to potential purchasers of the good or service, no one else.

We learned that the market supply curve represents the amount all sellers in the market are willing to offer at any given price. In the same way that the demand curve represents private values, the supply curve represents the *private* marginal cost to sellers of each unit of potential production.

Demand and supply curves are categorized as private benefits and costs, because these benefits and costs go to the actors involved, not third parties. To model the benefits and costs to third parties, we need to construct a curve that incorporates their costs or benefits. When we introduce externalities in the supply and demand framework, we need to reconstruct demand or supply curves so that they accurately reflect the cost to whole communities.

Externalities can occur in the good's *production* or in its *consumption.* If an externality arises in the course of producing the good, for example, a factory is polluting a nearby river used for drinking water, then the true cost to society of producing that good is higher than what producers consider in making production decisions. In other words, *Social Marginal Cost (Social MC) > Private Marginal Cost (Private MC, or supply).* Figure 28.1 illustrates

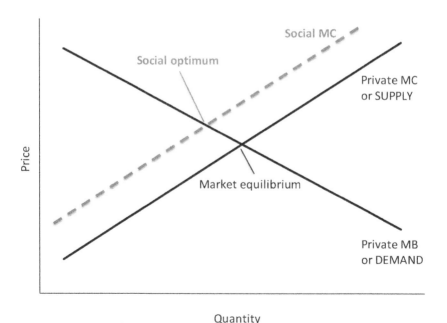

Figure 28.1. Negative externality in production

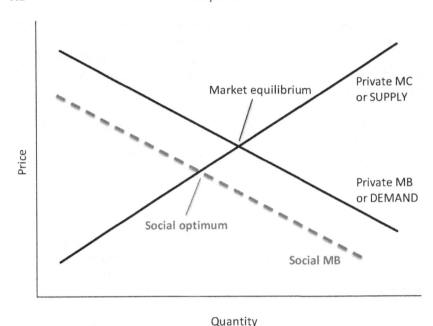

Quantity

Figure 28.2. Negative externality in consumption

society's higher cost of production with the introduction of the social marginal cost curve. Theoretically, the Social MC illustrates the supply curve if all costs, including those imposed on third-parties, were considered in the production decision.

If an externality occurs through the consumption of the good, second-hand smoke, for example, then the true benefit to society of consuming that good is less than what consumers consider in making consumption decisions. In other words, *Social Marginal Benefit (Social MB) < Private Marginal Benefit (Private MB or demand)*. Figure 28.2 illustrates society's lesser benefit with the introduction of the social marginal benefit curve. Theoretically, Social MB illustrates the demand curve if all benefits, including those imposed on third-parties, were considered in the consumption decision.

IMPLICATIONS OF NEGATIVE EXTERNALITIES

The intersection of the original demand and supply curves will indicate the market equilibrium price and quantity. When there are no externalities, this price and quantity will tend to converge on levels that maximize the value to society. When there are externalities, the original demand and supply curves no longer fully represent the costs and benefits to society. Market outcomes may not maximize surplus. Social efficiency occurs where Social MC = Social MB. (If there are no externalities, then Social = Private.)

If we have a negative externality on the production side (figure 28.1), then drawing a vertical line through the market equilibrium shows that the Social MC is higher than the Private MB (demand). What does that tell us? That tells us that at the margin, it is costing society more to produce that good than the good is valued by consumers. Social MC = Private MB to the left of the market equilibrium. This means there is overproduction.

When there is a negative externality on the consumption side (figure 28.2), we can see that the Social MB is lower than the Private MC (supply). At the margin, members of society are benefiting less from the consumption of that good than it costs to produce it. Private MC = Social MB to the left of the market equilibrium. This means there is overconsumption.

TAX ON NEGATIVE EXTERNALITIES

Taxes on negative externalities are intended to increase the cost of producing or consuming the good, therefore aligning the private and social benefits and costs. A **tax** is a charge imposed by a governing body. A tax can be in proportion to the price paid for a good or service or a fixed amount. A tax on the producer shifts the supply curve in the same direction as the Marginal SC curve. A tax on the consumer shifts the demand curve in the same direction as the Marginal SB curve. Either tax would lower the amount traded, and increase the price paid by consumers.

This is one case where shrinking a market increases value for society.

Creating a tax that performs this function is complicated. First, the cost of the tax needs to approximate the social cost of the externality. Measuring social cost is difficult. What is the cost of pollution from a car, for example? Sometimes demand is not responsive to changes in price, and a tax will not reduce demand much. Adult cigarette consumption, for example, seems less responsive to price increases than adolescent cigarette consumption. Beyond this, managing a taxation scheme is not free. It is itself an activity that consumes scarce resources. There are costs associated with monitoring, collecting, and enforcing taxes. If we put a tax on cigarettes, people may consume fewer of them, and the profitability of manufacturing cigarettes may fall. In the case of cigarettes, reducing consumption might be a good thing.

Of course, the relationship between what we intend and what actually happens can be complicated indeed. When we tax an activity, there is less incentive to engage in the activity, and we would expect that the activity level to fall. But sometimes the activity goes underground instead. People continue to engage in the activity, but instead of conducting the activity in plain sight, they start to hide it in order to avoid the tax.

Note that this is one of the places where it helps to study ethics and economics together. We all make moral choices, but the economic fact remains: human behavior is robustly and predictably responsive to incentives. Suppose that when we increase the fees for dumping at the landfill, it leads to an increase in illegal dumping. We all can agree that it is immoral for people to dump waste in dangerous and obnoxious ways. But what does that imply? One seemingly clear implication is that morality is asking the rest of us to avoid giving people an incentive—making it pay—to dump waste in dangerous and obnoxious ways.

We may pass a law because we want people to do a certain thing, but what actually happens when we pass that law will not be a story about what we intended. *The real story is always about what the law gave people an incentive to do.* Even when we all agree on exactly how we want our story to end, it can be amazingly hard to know how to pass laws that actually move our story toward that conclusion.

DISCUSSION AND EXERCISES

1. List some important examples of externalities. What makes them important?
2. Does a market typically account for positive externalities? Will the market produce an efficient quantity?
3. When we think about what we *would like* to happen, how much attention should we pay to how people will react?

Chapter 29

Competitors Are Not Bystanders

We imagined a case where someone buys a widget that makes a horrible noise that keeps neighbors awake. That noise is an external cost. What the buyer pays for the widget is a cost that fails to reflect the price that neighbors pay. Therefore, demand for the widget will be higher than it should be, that is, higher than what the demand would be if its true full cost were taken into account. The widget will be over-used. And in a way, that kind of over-use is a moral problem. The price mechanism does not teach buyers to take into account the price that neighbors pay.

Now consider a second case. Suppose you invent a less expensive process for manufacturing gizmos. You now can profitably sell gizmos for $1.99 rather than for their previous going rate of $3.14. As a result, competitors who had been selling gizmos for $3.14 are worse off. How does this differ from the first case?

In both cases, someone is worse off, but somehow the second case is perfectly fine in a way the first case is not. The first case—waking people up in the middle of the night by making an ear-splitting noise—is a form of trespass. By contrast, the second case—selling gizmos for $1.99—leads angry competitors to accuse you of "stealing" their customers, but the truth is that those customers are not their property, and never were. You are not stealing anything. Your rivals are competing to provide customers with a better service, and they are losing that competition, nothing more, nothing less. No trespass has occurred, even though your competitors may understandably hate to lose their customers to a better provider.

PECUNIARY EXTERNALITIES

Here is the underlying economic point. Externalities that affect people's welfare only by affecting the price of what they are trying to sell are called **pecuniary externalities**. From a social perspective, pecuniary externalities are not a problem. Superficially, pecuniary externalities look and feel like external costs to competitors, but they are not externalities at all They are not external costs. In this case, there is no social cost that prices are failing to take into account. Instead, the price of gizmos is falling in response to genuine changes in the cost of providing customers with gizmos.

The price mechanism in this case is succeeding, not failing. It is the success rather than the failure of the price mechanism that your rivals are complaining about. There are no bystanders being made worse off in a way that prices fail to reflect. There are only competitors. Your rivals are receiving an efficient price signal that customers no longer value their product, and they need to offer customers a better service if they want to stay in business. The economy is sending them a clear signal. If your competitors are listening, they will hear morality sending them the same signal: their community needs them to figure out a better use for their resources. Their community no longer wants gizmos that cost $3.14.

No one wants their customers to be stolen, but if you want to earn your customers' loyalty, the solution is not to try to make it illegal to provide your customers with a better service, but to become the provider of the better service. And people and businesses often try to use the law to their advantage in this way, and they have for a long time.

EXTERNALITIES AND THE COMMON LAW

In 1707, the case of *Keeble* vs. *Hickeringill* came before the Queen's Bench of England. Keeble was a farmer who used decoys to lure waterfowl into traps, and then sold the birds in town. His neighbor, Hickeringill, began to fire guns into the air in order to frighten the birds away and interfere with Keeble's business. Keeble filed suit. Judge Holt ruled in favor of Keeble. Holt reasoned that Keeble was minding his own legitimate business and Hickeringill had no right to interfere.

Chief Justice Holt's verdict included a reference to another case in which a defendant interfered with a neighbor's school by starting a better school. The defendant won in that case because the students were not the plaintiff's property. The plaintiff had no right to be protected against the defendant "stealing" students by offering students a better alternative. Holt next considered a hypothetical situation where a defendant interferes with a neighbor's school by firing guns into the air and frightening students away. That would be an intentional trespass, because the defendant would be aiming to sabotage the plaintiff's product. What is wrong in the last case is that the defendant is not aiming to offer customers a better product, but is instead aiming to lower the value of a rival's product.

What makes this case intriguing is that Justice Holt saw the difference between the concepts of genuine and merely pecuniary externalities centuries before those technical terms were coined. Justice Holt saw that a commercial society needed to be able to make that distinction. He refined the property system in order to limit genuine externalities, while leaving intact the liberty to compete in the marketplace, thereby making it easier for us to live, and make a living, together.

DISCUSSION AND EXERCISES

1. Imagine yourself in the position of competitors who find themselves losing business to new and more efficient providers. You fought your way to the top, and now you are losing the battle to stay on top. Recall a lesson from the earlier discussion of **comparative advantage**. Namely, you do not have to be the absolute best at anything in order to find work. Especially when you are just starting out, you have a low opportunity cost. That is an advantage, and if you are willing to work with that advantage, it will turn out to be enough to get you started. Having to start over, especially if that means you have to start at the bottom and work your way up all over again, can seem painful. But it happens. Life can surprise you. That is one reason why the material on personal finance is important. It can help you plan for the challenge of suddenly needing to adjust to a smaller income.
2. What is the difference between a pecuniary externality, a positive externality, and a negative externality? Give examples of each.
3. Did Justice Holt decide *Hickeringill* correctly? Why or why not?

Chapter 30

The Logic of the Commons

Suppose there is a plot of land. The land has a **carrying capacity**, which is a level of use that the land can sustain more or less indefinitely. One word of caution: the concept of carrying capacity points to something real, because there are real limits to what the land can support. However, these limits are not rigid. Instead, carrying capacity is somewhat fluid, and a function of many variables. For example, can Kruger Park in South Africa carry 15,000 elephants? The answer depends on whether we want to leave room for rhinos. But whether we want to leave room for rhinos is something we have to decide, partly by deciding what kind of world we want to live in. It is not simply an ecological issue.

With that understood, here is a simple example of what can go wrong.

Suppose a parcel's carrying capacity is one hundred animals. The land is owned jointly by ten shepherds, each of whom owns ten animals for a total flock of one hundred animals. The land is thus at its carrying capacity. As things stand, each animal is worth (to keep the arithmetic as simple as possible) $1 to its owner, so that, at carrying capacity, one hundred animals are worth $100. Crucially, although the ten shepherds treat their individual flocks as private property, they jointly treat the land as one large communal pasture, with no internal fences, so each of their flocks grazes freely.

10 shepherds × 10 animals each = 100 animals. Individual flock's value = 10 animals × $1 = $10 Total flock's value = 100 animals × $1 = $100

Now suppose one shepherd adds an 11th animal. We now have 101 animals altogether, thus exceeding the land's carrying capacity. There is not quite enough food per animal now; therefore, they are a bit leaner, and the

168

value per animal drops to, let's say, 95 cents per head. The total stock of 101 animals is now worth $95.95, which is $4.95 less than the total stock was worth before when it was within the land's carrying capacity.

Total flock's value = 101 animals × $0.95 = $95.95

Obviously, this looks like a losing proposition. So, why would a shepherd add the extra animal?

At the original carrying capacity, the individual flocks of ten were worth $10. Having added one more sheep, the shepherd now has eleven, and each of the eleven is worth 95 cents. That works out to $10.45, which means that the individual shepherd made a profit of 45 cents by adding the extra animal, even though the value of the total stock went from $100 to $95.95.

Individual shepherd's flock with the extra sheep = 11 animals × $0.95 = $10.45

Although the total cost to the group of adding the extra animal exceeded the total benefit, the cost to the individual shepherd was less than the benefit to that shepherd.

The reason there is a difference is due to the logic of the commons. Specifically, the individual shepherd receives 100 percent of the benefit of adding the eleventh sheep, while paying only 10 percent of the cost. The other 90 percent is paid by the other nine shepherds; they own 90 percent of the animals, so they suffer 90 percent of the loss involved in the falling price per head. Individual shepherds, however, see only individual costs and benefits and act accordingly. The same decision that was a net cost to the group is a net benefit to the individual shepherd. The logic of the commons has begun its seemingly inevitable grind toward its tragic fate.

COMMONS PROBLEMS ARE EXTERNALITY PROBLEMS

A commons becomes a **commons tragedy** when the collective use of a commune or open access commons exceeds its carrying capacity. The tragedy of the commons is one version of the more general problem of **externalities**. An externality, also called a "spillover" cost, is the price that innocent bystanders pay for other people's decisions. We say cost is "**internalized**" when the arrangement is changed so that decision makers now bear the entire cost of their decisions. One general purpose of property institutions is to internalize externalities, preventing people from shifting the cost of their activities onto others. New externality problems emerge frequently. Someone had to invent mobile phones, for example, before texting while driving could become the problem that it has become.

A system is likely to be economically and ecologically sustainable only to the extent that agents pay the true cost of their decisions. Traces of commons tragedies can be seen in everything from overfishing of coral reefs to socialized health care systems, where access to health care service is limited only by a patient's willingness to wait in line. Worries about commons tragedies are implicitly common in debates about famine relief (should we bring food to the people?), immigration (should we bring people to the food?), and population control (how many more shepherds do we have a right to add?).

PRIVATE PROPERTY SOMETIMES SOLVES COMMONS PROBLEMS

In an unmanaged commons, individual shepherds decide for themselves whether to step up their level of use. They do not pay the full cost of their overuse, though, because the cost falls mainly on other members of the communal user group. The payoff of overuse is negative for the group, but positive for the individual who elects to overuse.

Is there nothing those shepherds can do? One option would be to cut their jointly owned territory into ten smaller parcels, so each shepherd owns a small parcel with its individual carrying capacity. Under this new arrangement, instead of dispersing the environmental degradation over the entire commons, the damage is concentrated on the offender's private land. Thus, in the hypothetical example, instead of dispersing damages worth $4.95 over one hundred animals and ten owners, the damage is concentrated within the individual shepherd's own parcel. To keep the example simple, suppose the parcel covers an area one-tenth the size of the original communal plot. Suppose also that when the damage is concentrated in one-tenth of the area, the resulting damage is ten times as great per square foot. In that case, the flock of ten, which had been worth $10, is now a starving flock of eleven, worth about $5.05. The value of each animal has been cut roughly in half, a painfully obvious mistake. Consequently, under a system of individual parcels, shepherds learn fast not to add the eleventh sheep.

Private ownership gives an owner a right to exclude. By conferring a right to exclude, a system gives an owner an opportunity to conserve a resource. In giving the opportunity, the system also provides an incentive, because whatever owners save, they save for themselves.

AN ALTERNATIVE SOLUTION: COMMUNAL MANAGEMENT

Separating the land into private parcels often is a good alternative to managing land as an unregulated commons, but it is not always the only alternative. Another option is for the shepherds to leave the territory in a common pool. Then, instead of each tending a small flock of ten sheep, ignoring the costs they impose on each other as they add more sheep, they could pool their flocks and become joint owners of a single large flock of one hundred. Each shepherd now has an interest in all of the sheep. Under a communal arrangement, a shepherd considers not whether to add the eleventh sheep, but whether to add the 101st. Adding the 101st sheep means that for each shepherd, the result is not that the value of his flock goes from $10 to $10.45. Instead, the value goes from a 10 percent ownership stake in $100 to a 10 percent stake in $95.95.

Therefore, under the communal arrangement, no one would want to add the extra sheep. Here, too, as in the case of switching to private parcels, an external cost has been internalized, and each of the ten shepherds now has a self-interested reason to respect the land's carrying capacity. The communal shepherds will need to process more information than a small private owner would, and communal shepherds will have less incentive to be diligent in gathering and processing information because their stake in the decision is only 10 percent. Further, since each voice would only be one vote out of ten, no one shepherd would possess the deciding vote. Still, all things being equal, they would want to make decisions that accord with sustainable use.

Regardless of whether shepherds cut their land into parcels or pool their flocks of sheep, the fact remains that in the real world, a community of ten people has an opportunity to create and enforce rules governing the land's use that will enable them to avoid collective suicide. There is still an additional issue to consider.

THE OPEN ACCESS COMMONS: A DIFFERENT SORT OF PROBLEM

Suppose the group has gone communal, pooling both their land and their livestock. So far, so good. Next, the ten shepherds devise rules to regulate the addition of extra animals. But suppose they have a different kind of problem. Namely, they can't stop an *eleventh shepherd* from entering the picture with yet another flock. With a fixed and known set of players, viable conventions tend to emerge, but if a community is not able to restrict the inflow of new users, then we have an **open access** commons, which makes the tragedy far more likely.

Sometimes, everything depends on whether it is possible to add the extra player rather than for existing players to add the extra animal. For a community to manage itself successfully, it must be able to control negative externalities among members of the community, but historically it is even more critical that the community be able to restrict access, controlling the size and membership of the community of users. A **commune** is a restricted access commons, in other words, it is not open access. In a commune, property is owned by the group rather than by individual members. People exercise a right to exclude as a group. Normally, communes draw a sharp distinction between members and non-members, and restrict access accordingly. By analogy, think of your household as like a commune. Your children are members of the household, which means they are free to help themselves to whatever is in the refrigerator. However, you draw the line between your children and complete strangers. You would not want strangers to feel free to come and go the way your children do. Free access is restricted to members of the household.

Some medieval commons lasted, non-tragically, for hundreds of years. Nobel laureate Elinor Ostrom describes a Swiss commons whose written records date back to the thirteenth century. Cattle were privately owned but grazed in communal highlands in the summer. People grew private crops on individual plots in the valleys, intending to use part of their crops to sustain their cattle over the winter. The basic limitation on communal summer grazing was that owners could send only as many cattle to the highland meadows as their private land parcel could sustain over the winter with fodder grown during summer.

Letting individual owners freely decide whether to add to their individual stock is above all what governors of a commons cannot do. To avoid tragedy, governors of a common pasture must manage the overall livestock population, based on their estimate of the pasture's overall carrying capacity. There are several ways to do this. Managers can allow a given owner to graze cattle on common land only in proportion to (a) how much hay that owner produces, (b) what proportion of the land belongs to that owner, or (c) the number of shares that owner owns in the cooperative. In the Swiss commons, Ostrom says, no citizen could send more cows to the communal pasture than he could feed during the winter. In this way, the Swiss commons was able to avoid tragedy for hundreds of years.

In a commune, partners recognize an imperative to take the option of overgrazing out of the hands of individual partners. History indicates, though, that members of successful communes internalize the rewards that come with that collective responsibility. In particular, they exclude nonmembers. A successful commune does not run itself as an open-access commons.

DISCUSSION AND EXERCISES

1. Explain the "eleventh sheep" problem. Then explain why the "eleventh shepherd" problem can be even harder to solve.
2. Today the word "tragedy" is used to refer generically to any terrible outcome. The word has an older meaning, though, referring to literary works stretching back to the ancient Greeks, works that depict a protagonist caught up in events that are fated to end badly regardless of what the protagonist chooses. So, what is it about commons tragedies that makes them tragic? When people do the opposite of managing scarce resources in a responsible way, and the result is like a Greek tragedy, what makes the tragedy seem inevitable, or at least predictable?
3. Why do problems emerge with commons in the first place?

Chapter 31

Environmental Tragedies

Here are two stories about tragedies of the commons. They illustrate why it matters whether we have a good system of property law.

CORAL REEFS

The first story comes from the coral reefs of the Philippine and Tongan Islands. People once fished those reefs with lures and traps, but then began bleach-fishing, which involves dumping bleach into the reefs. Fish cannot breathe bleach (sodium hypochlorite). Suffocated, they float to the surface where they are easy to collect. Fishermen have recently pumped hundreds of thousands of pounds of cyanide per year into Philippine reefs for this very reason.

The problem is that the coral itself is composed of living animals. The coral suffocates along with the fish, and the dead reef is no longer a viable habitat. Still another technique, blast-fishing, involves dynamiting the reefs. The concussion produces an easy harvest of stunned fish and dead coral. Perhaps your first reaction is simply to be horrified, and to say people ought to be more responsible. They ought to preserve the reefs for their children.

But that would miss the point, which is that individual fishermen lack the option of saving the coral for their children. Individual fishermen obviously have the option of not destroying it themselves, but what happens if they elect not to destroy it? What they want is for the reef to be left for their children; what happens is that the reef is left for the next blast-fisher down the line. If a fisherman wants to have anything at all to give his children, he must act quickly, destroying the reef and grabbing the fish himself. It does no good to tell fishermen to take responsibility; they *are* taking responsibility—for their children.

174

Existing institutions do not empower them to take responsibility in a way that would save the reef.

Under the circumstances, they are at liberty not to destroy the reef themselves, but they are not at liberty to do what is necessary to save the reef for their children. To save the reef for their children, fishermen would need the power to restrict access to the reef. They would need the right to exclude blast-fishers. Whether they stake that claim as individuals or as a group is secondary, as long as they succeed in restricting access. One way or another, they must have, and effectively exercise, a right to restrict access.

ATLANTIC GREEN TURTLE

The second story comes from the Cayman Islands. The Atlantic Green Turtle has long been prized as a source of meat and eggs. The turtles were a commonly held resource, and were being harvested in an unsustainable way. In 1968, when by some estimates there were as few as 3000 to 5000 left in the wild, a group of entrepreneurs and concerned scientists created Mariculture Ltd. (sold in 1976 and renamed Cayman Turtle Farm) and began raising and selling captive-bred sea turtles. In the wild, as few as one-tenth of 1 percent of wild hatchlings survive to adulthood. Most are seized by predators before they can crawl from nest to sea. Cayman Farm, though, boosted the survival rate of captive-bred animals to 50 percent or more. At the peak of operations, the farm was rearing over a hundred thousand turtles. The farm released 1 percent of its hatchlings into the wild at the age of ten months, an age at which hatchlings have a decent chance of surviving to maturity.

In 1973, commerce in Atlantic Green Turtles was restricted by CITES (the Convention on International Trade in Endangered Species) and, in the United States, by the Fish and Wildlife Service, the Department of Commerce, and the Department of the Interior. Under the newly created Endangered Species Act, the United States classified the Atlantic Green Turtle as an endangered species, but Cayman Farm's business was unaffected, at first, because regulations about commerce in Atlantic Green Turtles covered only wild turtles, implicitly exempting Cayman Farm's captive-bred animals. In 1978, however, the regulations were published in their final form, and although exemptions were granted for trade in captive-bred animals of other species, no exemption was made for turtles. The company could no longer do business in the United States. Even worse, the company could no longer ship its products through American ports, so it no longer had access via Miami to world markets. The Farm exists today only to serve the people of the Cayman Islands themselves.

Cayman Turtle Farm tries to operate as a private business. Its owners had a plan for saving a particular endangered species, and under the original circumstances, their plan was financially sustainable. But the owners were not simply aiming to maximize revenue. They had an ecological agenda as well, and when it comes to real-world plans, the details always seem to matter. In this particular case, there was concern that farming turtles would spur demand, and that rising demand would lead to rising prices, which would mean an increased poaching pressure on wild populations. As a rule, though, it seemed more likely that the opposite would happen. When your rivals figure out a way to bring the same product to market at a much lower cost, price tend to fall rather than rise. (Recall our conversation about pecuniary externalities. Cayman Farm was "stealing" the customers of the wild poachers, but the poachers could not do much about it. They had no market for their wild and illegal product, so for the most part, they went to Turtle Farm and asked for jobs.) Poaching decreased rather than increased.

A different danger, though, is that large-scale farms, like salmon and cattle farms for example, breed disease that put wild as well as domestic populations at risk. As with any other new industry, there are always unanticipated problems and newly emerging externalities that need to be contained.

What do these stories tell us? One lesson is that leaving our environment in the commons is not like putting our environment in a time capsule as a legacy for future generations. There are ways to take what we find in the commons and preserve it—to put it in a time capsule—but before we can put something in a time capsule, we have to **appropriate** it, meaning that whale-oil consumption in we have to claim it as our property, which means we have to claim a right to decide what to do with it.

A private nonprofit organization, The Nature Conservancy, is pursuing such a strategy. It has acquired (by purchase or by gift) over a billion dollars worth of land in an effort to preserve natural ecosystems. Interestingly, this includes habitat for endangered species that have no market value. This is another case of market economies making people wealthy enough that they can afford to save something for the future: whatever is most precious to them.

HOW TO SAVE THE WHALES

We know why consumers are often so thoughtless. Water is a scarce good. When we subsidize it, as if we wanted people to consume more of it, people do consume more of it, and we run out.

Electricity is a scarce good. When we subsidize it, as if we wanted people to consume more of it, people do consume more of it, and we run out.

If we had heavily subsidized whale-oil consumption in the late nineteenth century, whales would likely be extinct. Would-be producers of alternative energy sources, like petroleum, would not have been able to compete.

Imagine selling food by charging each household a flat monthly fee, then simply turning people loose on the supermarkets, treating supermarkets as if they were an "all you can carry" buffet. If we imagine a fully stocked supermarket opening for business on those terms, how long would it be before its shelves were empty?

It seems safe to say that if we ran a supermarket like an "all you can carry" buffet, the supermarket would run out of food almost instantly. If we ran a whole country that way, the whole country would run out of food. A vast amount of food would be wasted. We would scold people for behaving that way, but it would be our fault, because we created the circumstances that made their behavior predictable.

From an environmental perspective, we want consumers to economize. We want them to exercise self-restraint. That will not happen unless consumers pay the true cost of consumption, and pay for whatever they use on a per unit basis. To make consumers stop to think before consuming an extra unit, the extra unit needs to have a price.

More generally, if you want to save whales, do not subsidize the consumption of whale oil. Do not give cash prizes to people for doing things you do not want them to do. When you subsidize consumption, you pay people to consume more than they otherwise would. If that is not your objective, eliminate the subsidy. Let prices rise. Let the market do its job of steering consumers and producers toward (for example) alternative energy sources.

From an environmentalist perspective, one of our primary policy responsibilities in setting public policy is to avoid unmetered consumption. Unmetered consumption is a prescription for irresponsible consumption, thus a prescription for future dilemmas.

Being moral is not simply a matter of following the right rules. Nevertheless, there are such things as moral principles (many more than can be enumerated in a useful written code) that carry considerable weight and that fairly reliably lead us in the right direction. One clear example of a moral principle is that we should always consider the consequences of our actions. This moral principle has to be coupled with another one: do not treat people as if they were merely numbers, so that it looks acceptable simply to sacrifice low numbers for the sake of high ones. Treat all people as having lives of their own to live. When people say, "It's my life" they are saying something that matters. People often do heroic things when they sacrifice their own hopes and dreams for the greater good. So, be prepared to sacrifice for what you believe in. That's what heroes do. But beware of the urge to sacrifice *other people* for the greater good. That's not what heroes do.

DISCUSSION AND EXERCISES

1. Coral reefs and turtles provide stark examples of how incentives alter human behavior. Can you apply that same lesson to other environmental concerns? How so?
2. What would happen if we placed a consumption tax on driving, either by charging tolls on various roads or by charging for metered usage?
3. We charge for metered usage for any number of things, like electricity to name just one. Can you think of others?

Chapter 32

Property

The term **property right** is used to refer to a bundle of rights that could include rights to sell, lend, bequeath, and so on. In what follows, the phrase refers mainly to the right of owners to exclude nonowners. Note that the right to exclude is a feature of property rights in general, including public property and communal property. It is not the defining feature of private ownership in particular. Private owners have the right to exclude nonowners, but so do communes. So does the National Park Service, and any number of other entities.

PROPERTY LAW

Property law is an ongoing search for ways to internalize what economists call externalities: positive externalities associated with productive effort and negative externalities associated with misuse of commonly held resources.

If all goes well, property law enables would-be producers to enjoy the benefits of productive effort. It also enables people to insulate themselves from external costs associated with activities around the neighborhood. Property law is not perfect. There is no such thing as getting things exactly right. Why? Because change is always just around the corner. The problem itself is about to change, and therefore what counts as a solution will change as well. Property laws are evolving adaptations to a constantly changing problem. For example, in 1936, air traffic was beginning to emerge, but it was not yet settled whether flying over someone's land at 10,000 feet counted as trespassing. How high up does your property line go? How would a judge decide?

How would you decide? Recall the case of Hinman v. Pacific Air Transport, mentioned in the section on Transaction Cost and Progress.

THE UNREGULATED COMMONS

Private property enables and incentivizes people to take responsibility for conserving scarce resources. It preserves resources under a wide variety of circumstances. It is the preeminent vehicle for turning negative sum commons into positive sum property regimes. However, it is not the only way. Evidently, it is not always the best way, either. We see public property everywhere we look, and it is not only governments who create it. It has a history of evolving spontaneously in response to real problems, enabling people to remove a resource from an unregulated commons and collectively take responsibility for its management.

An unregulated commons need not be a disaster. An unregulated commons will work well enough as long as the level of use remains within the land's carrying capacity. However, as use nears carrying capacity, there will be pressure to shift to a more exclusive regime. For a real-world example of an unregulated commons evolving into a regime of private parcels as increasing traffic began to exceed carrying capacity, consider economist Harold Demsetz's classic account of how property institutions evolved among indigenous tribes of the Labrador Peninsula. As Demsetz tells the story, the region's people had, for generations, treated the land as an open-access commons. The human population was small. There was plenty to eat. Thus, the pattern of use was within the land's carrying capacity.

With the onset of the fur trade, though, the scale of hunting and trapping activity went way up. The population of game animals began to dwindle. The unregulated commons had worked for a while, but the tribes came to face a classic "tragedy of the commons." The tragedy of the commons is one version of a more general problem of externalities. In this case, the benefits of exploiting the resource were internalized, but the costs were not, and the arrangement was no longer sustainable.

In response, tribal members began to mark out family plots. The game animals in question were small animals like beaver and otter that tend not to migrate from one plot to another. Thus, marking out plots of land effectively privatized small game as well as the land itself.

In sum, the tribes converted the commons in fur-bearing game to family parcels when the fur trade began to spur a rising demand that exceeded the land's carrying capacity.

One other wrinkle regarding the privatization of fur-bearing game: although the fur was privatized, the meat was not. There was still plenty of meat, so tribal law allowed people to hunt for meat on each other's land. Unannounced visitors could kill a beaver and take the meat, but they had to leave the pelt displayed in a prominent place, because that is how they sent a signal of respect to the owner. In effect, that pelt said, "Thank you for feeding me. Here is your pelt, which I cut and cleaned with care to show my respect."

The new customs went to the heart of the matter, privatizing what had to be privatized, leaving intact liberties that people had always enjoyed with respect to other resources where unrestricted access had not yet become a problem.

PROPERTY RIGHTS AND EXTERNAL COSTS

We can contrast the unregulated or open-access commons with communes. A commune is a restricted-access commons. In a commune, property is owned by the group rather than by individual members. People as a group claim and exercise a right to exclude. Typically, communes draw a sharp distinction between members and non-members, and regulate access accordingly. Public property tends to restrict access by time of day or year. Some activities are permitted; others are prohibited.

Many experts on the history of property rights believe that private, public, and communal property are each, in their own way, potentially effective responses to externality problems. Each kind of property serves social welfare in its own way. Likewise, each ownership regime has its own externality problems. Communal management leads to overconsumption and to slacking off on maintenance and improvements, because people receive only a fraction of the value of their labor, and pay only a fraction of the costs of their consumption. To minimize disincentives, a commune must monitor production and consumption activities.

In practice, communal regimes can lead to careless dumping of wastes, ranging from piles of unwashed dishes to ecological disasters that threaten whole continents. People get lazy and just don't care enough about the sorts of basic courtesy—simply cleaning up after themselves—that good neighbors care about. You have been around long enough to know what we are talking about. One advantage of private property is that owners can move to different parcels and in effect rearrange their neighborhoods so as to better serve common aims. For example, nuisance laws and zoning laws can help to create separate spaces so that neighbors who want peace and quiet can choose a location that puts some distance between themselves and neighbors who want to have loud parties. That is one way in which neighbors spontaneously take steps to reduce external cost. In other cases, the external costs may occur on a larger scale, and be so widespread that it is not easy to move away from them. Those cases might call for intervention by regulatory agencies.

DISCUSSION AND EXERCISES

1. What does it mean to own something? What rights does private property include?
2. What do you or your family treat as common property? Why?
3. What do you or your family *never* treat as common property? Why not?
4. Explain the sense in which the house you live in counts as property. Explain the sense in which national parks count as property.

Chapter 33

Parcels

Is it generally best to convert an unregulated commons to smaller private parcels, or manage it as a commune with power to exclude non-members? It depends on what kind of problem the property regime is intended to solve. In particular, not all problems are of equal scale; some are more local than others. As a problem's scale changes, there will be corresponding changes in which responses are feasible and effective. An individual sheep eating grass in the pasture is what some people would call a small event, affecting only a small area relative to the prevailing parcel size. If the commons is being ruined by small events, there is an easy solution: cut the land into parcels. We see this solution everywhere. If we can divide the land into parcels of a certain size, such that the cost of grazing an extra sheep is borne entirely by the individual owner who decides whether to graze the extra sheep, then we have internalized externalities and solved the problem. If we divide the pasture into private parcels, then what a particular sheep eats on a particular owner's pasture is no one else's concern. The grass is no longer a common pool.

For better or worse, events come in more than one size. For the sake of example, suppose six parcels are situated over a pool of oil in such a way that, via oil wells, each of the six owners has access to the common pool. The more wells individual owners drill, the more oil they can extract, up to a point. As the number of wellheads increases, oil pressure per wellhead declines. Not only is the reserve of oil ultimately limited, but the practically extractable reserve eventually begins to decline with the number of wells sunk.

This kind of problem occurs when an event is too large to be contained on a single parcel, or does not have a precise and confined location, or migrates from one location to another. For one reason or another, the event is large enough that its effects spill over onto neighboring parcels. Neighbors cannot solve the problem simply by putting up fences.

In an unfenced commons, there is, in effect, only a single parcel, so the words "small," "medium," and "large" would refer simply to the radius over which the effects of an event are felt, that is, small, medium, or large parts of the whole parcel. In a regime that has been cut into smaller parcels, the more interesting distinction is between a small event that affects a single owner, a medium event that affects immediate neighbors, and a large event that affects remote parts of the community. When land is divided into parcels, whether an event is small, medium, or large will depend on the size of the parcels. Whether a regime succeeds in internalizing externalities will depend on whether it succeeds in carving out parcel sizes big enough to contain events whose effects it is most crucial to internalize. In effect, if an individual owner's parcel size could be increased without limit, any event could be made "small."

Robert Ellickson says private regimes are clearly superior as methods for minimizing the costs of small and medium events. Regarding small events, the first point is that the external costs of small events are near zero. Neighbors do not care when we pick tomatoes on our own land; they do care when we pick tomatoes on *their* communal plot. In the former case, we are minding our own business; in the latter, we are minding theirs. In the end, there are no small events on communal land. Everything we do affects our neighbors. Even doing nothing at all affects our neighbors, given that we could instead have been helping to tend the communal gardens. The second point regarding private property regimes concerns the cost of monitoring. To internalize externalities, whatever the property regime, owners must be able to monitor other would-be users. In a private regime, though, it is only boundary crossings that need monitoring, and guard dogs and motion sensors can handle that. By contrast, the monitoring needed within a communal regime involves evaluating whether workers are just going through the motions, whether they are taking more than their share, and so on. As Ellickson said, "Detecting the presence of a trespasser is much less demanding than evaluating the conduct of a person who is privileged to be where he is." Thus, private parcels basically eliminate the external cost of small events, and monitoring, while still required, is relatively cheap and relatively unobtrusive in a regime of private parcels.

The effects of medium events tend to spill over onto one's neighbors, and thus can be a source of friction. So, a quiet dinner party might be a small event of no consequence to the neighbors, but when guests spill outside and crank up the music loud enough to rattle the windows of the house next door, it becomes a medium event. Nevertheless, privatization has the advantage of limiting the number of people having to be consulted about how to deal with the externality, which reduces transaction costs. Instead of consulting the entire community of communal owners, each at liberty with respect to the affected area, one consults a handful of people who own parcels in the immediate area of the medium event. A further virtue of privatization is that disputes arising from medium events tend to be left in the hands of people in the immediate vicinity, people who tend to better understand local conditions and thus are in a better position to devise resolutions without harmful unintended consequences. They are in a better position to foresee the costs and benefits of a medium event.

When it comes to large events, though, there is no easy way to say which mix of private and public property is best. Large events involve far-flung externalities among people who do not have face-to-face relationships. The difficulties in detecting such externalities, tracing them to their source, and holding people accountable for them are difficulties for any kind of property regime. It is no easy task to devise institutions that encourage pulp mills to take responsibility for the cost of dumping in the river while simultaneously encouraging people downstream to take responsibility for their welfare, and thus to avoid harm. For example, if downstream users take responsibility for regularly testing water quality, then they are doing the best they can to avoid harm, and obviously we would want them to do exactly that even as we try to address the problem at its source. Ellickson says there is no general answer to the question of which regime best deals with far-flung external costs of large events.

Large events will fall into one of two categories, depending on whether pertinent laws and community norms are settled. On the one hand, if everyone understands that the pulp mill has no right to dump toxic wastes into the river, then the pulp mill will not dump with impunity. If they release wastes by accident, the legal response should be relatively swift. On the other hand, if pertinent legal rights and community norms are not yet in place, and it is unsettled whether people have a right to use the river for fishing, swimming, irrigation, or dumping, then disputes can be ugly, difficult, frequent, and unending. Most problems arise when existing customs or laws fail to settle who (in effect) has the right of way. That is not a problem with parceling land *per se*, but rather with the ambiguity and uncertainty regarding which rights to common use remain in place and which have been overturned. So, privatization exists in different degrees and takes different forms.

Different forms have different incentive properties. Simply parceling out land or sea is not always enough to stabilize possession of resources that make land or sea valuable in the first place. Suppose that fish are known to migrate from one parcel to another. In that case, owners have an incentive to grab as many fish as they can whenever the school passes through their own territory. Thus, simply dividing fishing grounds into parcels may not be enough to put fishermen in a position to avoid collectively exceeding sustainable yields. It depends on the extent to which the sought-after fish migrate from one parcel to another, and on continuously evolving conventions that help neighbors deal with the inadequacy of their fences (or other ways of marking off territory). Clearly, then, not all forms of privatization are equally good at internalizing externalities. Privatization per se is not a panacea, and not all forms of privatization are equal.

The fundamental lesson here is that the real-world question about property rights, both from a moral and an economic perspective, has very little to do with the familiar but trite ideologies of private versus public property, or capitalism versus socialism. The real question is, how large do the parcels need to be in order to internalize the costs of the main activities being undertaken on those parcels? Parcels are too small when the *external* cost is higher than it needs to be. Parcels are too large when the *transaction* cost is higher than it needs to be. When parcels are large enough that people can mind their own business and enjoy their parcel without disturbing the peace, but also small enough that people do not need to spend hours commuting in order to get to the market or to their place of work, the parcel size is about what it needs to be in order for people to maximize the benefit and minimize the cost of having neighbors.

DISCUSSION AND EXERCISES

1. What is a parcel, and how is the concept used when thinking about property rights?
2. What are the relative advantages and disadvantages of small, medium, and large parcels?
3. Can you think of some things that are better cared for in common, and others in private hands? What differentiates the two lists?

Chapter 34

Communal Property

As we have seen, there are obvious difficulties with how private property regimes handle large events. The nature and extent of the difficulties depend on details. So, for purposes of comparison, Robert Ellickson looked at how communal regimes handle large events. Our first example is Jamestown.

The Jamestown Colony was North America's first permanent English settlement. Our story begins in 1607. Jamestown was a commune, sponsored by London-based Virginia Company. Land was held and managed collectively. The colony's charter guaranteed to each settler an equal share of the collective product regardless of the amount of work personally contributed. Of the original group of 104 settlers, two-thirds died of starvation and disease before their first winter. New shiploads replenished the colony; the winter of 1609 cut the population again, this time from 500 to 60. Colonist William Simmons wrote, "It were too vile to say (and scarce to be believed) what we endured, but the occasion was only our own for want of providence, industry, and government, and not the barrenness and defect of the country, as is generally supposed." In 1611, Eyewitness Ralph Hamor described soldier Thomas Dale (appointed by Governor Thomas Gates to administer the colony) arriving to find living skeletons bowling in the streets, waiting for someone else to plant the crops. ("Skeletons" is not the actual word chosen by eyewitness George Percy. The word he used was, if anything, even more horrifying. He called them "anatomies.") Their main food sources were wild animals such as turtles and raccoons, which settlers hunted and ate by dark of night before neighbors arrived to demand equal shares.

Colonist George Percy wrote that bad water accounted for many deaths, but most of the deaths were from starvation. Contemporary archeologist Ivor

Hume reacted with wonder. "The James Fort colonists' unwillingness or inability to work toward their own salvation," he has written, "remains one of American history's great mysteries." Newly arriving ship's crew members, fishing the Chesapeake Bay, caught seven-foot sturgeon and oysters the size of dinner plates, and left their fishing gear with the colonists. How could colonists starve under such circumstances? Moreover, Hume wonders, "Percy's recognition that bad water was the cause of many deaths leaves one asking why, then, nothing was done to combat its dangers. That foul water was bad for you had been known for centuries." Hume adds, "Although considering the geology of Jamestown Island, it would have been fruitless to try to reach sustained freshwater by digging wells, they were not to know that—but nobody even tried!"

New information on Jamestown continues to surface. By 2007, it had become apparent that the colonists had indeed tried to dig a well, but Hume's point still holds. When the well project failed, the colonists seem to have given up. Just as inexplicably, they seem to have torn down sections of the fort to use as firewood, even though eyewitnesses described the edge of the forest as "within a stone's throw." Apart from the need for firewood, the forest should have been cut back for the sake of securing the fort's perimeter.

In 1614, Thomas Dale, by this time Governor, had seen enough. He assigned three-acre plots to individual settlers, which reportedly increased productivity to a point where, as colonist Captain John Smith observed, a person working under the communal system would be glad to "slip from his labour, or slumber over his taske" and "the most honest among them would hardly take so much true paines in a weeke, as now for themselves they will doe in a day."

We (Johnson and Schmidtz) visited Jamestown in 2007. We talked to four historians who work there, and we read an extraordinary collection of eyewitness accounts. We now suspect that several factors exacerbated the communal charter's corrosive incentive effects. First, the Virginia company intended to make a profit, so someday skimming the produce of the colony was precisely the point. The colonists resented being misled about how difficult life would be, and the idea of working harder than required for their own subsistence, largely to profit the lying fat cats who had put them in their plight to begin with, was intolerable. Further, the colonists wanted to go home and had the idea that they could win a deadly game of "Chicken." The idea, as reported by a horrified Thomas Dale, was, "We will weary out the Company at home in sending us provisions, and then, when they grow weary and see that we do not prosper here, they will send for us home. Therefore let us weary them out."

The colony converted all of its land holdings to private parcels in 1619. They eventually established a "Headright" system under which settlers were given 50-acre plots, plus an additional 50 acres for each servant in their employ. The way it developed, a settler would plant tobacco, harvest a crop, then use the money to return to England to recruit new settlers. The recruiter would then collect the new settler's 50-acre grant. The new settler would get free transport to Virginia, plus some portion of the fifty acres in return for working the recruiter's land for a few seasons while learning the essential skills. Recruiters thus began to cobble together large plantations. New recruits, in turn, became recruiters themselves, and Virginia's tobacco economy began to gallop.

WHAT WAS THE POINT?

Why go communal in the first place? Are there advantages to communal regimes? One advantage is obvious: communal regimes can help people spread risks under conditions where risks are substantial and where alternative risk-spreading mechanisms, like insurance, are unavailable. The company was sending settlers to a frontier where, without help, something as simple as a sprained ankle could be fatal. The only form of insurance available was, in effect, mutual insurance among the settlers backed up by their ability to work overtime for less fortunate neighbors. But as communities build up capital reserves to the point where they can offer insurance, they tend to privatize. Insurance enables people to work with companies, managing individual risks with precision financial tools that do not cause avalanches of external cost that ruin communal regimes.

A communal regime might also be an effective response to economies of scale in large public works that are crucial in getting a community started. To build a fort, man its walls, dig wells, and so on, a communal economy is an obvious choice as a way of mobilizing the teams of workers needed to execute these urgent tasks. But again, as these tasks are completed and community welfare increasingly comes to depend on small events, the communal regime gives way to private parcels. At Jamestown, Plymouth, the Amana colonies, and Salt Lake, as Ellickson observes, formerly communal settlers, "understandably would switch to private land tenure, the system that most cheaply induces individuals to undertake small and medium events that are socially useful." The Legend of Salt Lake says the sudden improvement in the fortunes of once-starving Mormons occurred in 1848 when God sent seagulls to save them from plagues of locusts, at the same time as they coincidentally were switching to private plots. Similarly, the Jamestown tragedy sometimes is attributed to harsh natural conditions, as if natural conditions radically changed in 1614, multiplying productivity sevenfold while Governor Dale coincidentally was cutting the land into parcels.

Historically, the benefits of communal management have not been enough to keep communes together indefinitely. Perhaps the most enduring and successful communes in human memory are the agricultural settlements of the Hutterites, dating back to sixteenth-century Austria. They migrated to the Dakotas in the 1870s, then to Canada to avoid compulsory military service during World War I. North American Hutterite communities now contain around 40,000 people, mostly on the Canadian prairies. Hutterites believe in a fairly strict sharing of assets. They forbid radio and television, to give one example of how strictly they control contact with the outside world.

Ellickson says Hutterite communities have three special things going for them: (1) A population cap: when a settlement reaches a population of 120, a portion of the community must leave to start a new community. The cap helps them retain a close-knit society; (2) communal dining and worship: people congregate several times a day, which facilitates a rapid and intense monitoring of individual behavior and a ready avenue for supplying feedback to those whose behavior deviates from expectations; and (3) a ban on birth control: the average woman bears ten children (the highest documented fertility rate of any human population), which more than offsets the trickle of emigration. We might add that Hutterite culture and education leave people ill-prepared to live in anything other than Hutterite society, which accounts for the low emigration rate.

Ellickson discusses other examples of communal property regimes. But the most pervasive example of communal ownership in America, Ellickson says, is the family household. American suburbia consists of family communes nested within a network of open-access roadways. Family homes tacitly recognize limits to how far we can go in converting common holdings to individual parcels. Consider your living room. You could fully privatize, having one household member own it while others pay user fees. The fees could be used to pay family members or outside help to keep it clean. In some respects, it would be better that way. The average communal living room today, for example, is notably subject to overgrazing and shirking on maintenance. Yet we put up with it. No one charges user fees to household members. Seeing the living room degraded by communal use may be irritating, but it is better than treating it as one person's private domain.

Some institutions succeed while embodying a form of ownership that is essentially collective. History indicates, though, that members of successful communes internalize the rewards that come with that collective responsibility. In particular, they reserve the right to exclude non-members. A successful commune does not run itself as an open-access commons.

BIOSPHERE II, TUCSON ARIZONA:
OUR MODERN JAMESTOWN

In September 1991, eight people were sealed for two years inside Biosphere 2, just north of Tucson, Arizona. Biosphere 2 was a model plan for a self-contained community on Mars or the Moon: a three-acre artificial world.

Everyone saw the complexity of the engineering challenge and wanted to prove that it is possible to design a small, yet self-contained, ecosystem. John Allen, the self-described inventor of Biosphere 2, also saw the social and economic dimensions of the challenge. Allen knew that producing enough food would not be easy, but was counting on the motivating power of hunger. He noted that "biospherians could not obtain food by flashing dollar bills or credit cards at Safeway. They would only eat well if they learned Clever-Way. If they goofed off, they would eat less. Quick feedback makes learning curves more rapidly upward. I was confident initial production would increase" (*Me and the Biospherians*, p. 173). That is roughly what the planners of Jamestown thought. People will cooperate because they had no choice. Circumstances would force them to be free.

The eight people who made up the crew of Biosphere 2 lost an average of twenty pounds during their two-year stay. The loss was not life-threatening, but they were not trying to lose weight. They lost weight because their economy wasn't sustainable. Their economy was not big enough to sustain the kind of life-form that we now think of as a normal healthy human being. The crew of Biosphere 2 were intellectuals: unusually capable individuals, who were philosophically committed to harmonious communal living. They made mistakes, of course. They rejected opportunities to develop specializations within their community because they did not want to become a class society. They did not want one of them to become the janitor while someone else became the chef. But even if the Biospherians had understood the tragedy of the commons, and had understood the history of Jamestown, the most fundamental lesson taught by Biosphere 2 was not about a mistake but rather about the inherently limited potential of an economy with a population of eight. In a community of eight people, even with every advantage under the sun except for division of labor, a person inevitably must work all day just to survive. The Biospherians had fantasized that they would have eight or ten hours a day to read and write, because they would be liberated from the distractions of the outside world. They envisioned gardening as an aristocratic hobby that would take less time than driving across town to shop at a supermarket. The reality of a small, closed economy was nothing like that.

One of the crew members, Jane Poynter, gave a Ted Talk in which, she said,

I get to compare biospheres. And hopefully from that I get to learn something. So what did I learn? Well, here I am inside Biosphere 2, making a pizza. So

I am harvesting the wheat, in order to make the dough. And then of course I have to milk the goats and feed the goats in order to make the cheese. It took me four months in Biosphere 2 to make a pizza. Here in Biosphere 1, it takes me about two minutes, because I pick up the phone and I call and say, Hey, can you deliver the pizza?[1]

We should stress that what Poynter did in four months was genuinely impressive. She worked with imported tools, of course. She was in no position to build her own iron smelter. But she did plant the seed, grow the grain, harvest the grain, mill the flour, and then after all that, bake the crust. No one should doubt that what she did was pretty amazing. The point is that we also should be amazed by what the economy of Biosphere 1 enables people like Poynter to accomplish in two minutes.

One obvious lesson from all this is that the key to a successful community is the same as the key to a thriving ecosystem: resilience. *There is a challenge just around the corner. It will surprise you, and it will matter. The survival of your system will depend how it handles changes that no one sees coming.*

Biosphere 2 near Tucson imported oxygen, food, medical attention, tools, and other things too. Did they cheat? Yes, if being "self-contained" were meant to imply that they had zero contact with the outside world. On the other hand, if we were to imagine a colony on the Moon, we would not imagine a colony on the Moon never being visited by supply ships from Earth either. So, if we operate with a more realistic idea of how far a human community would want to go in the direction of being self-contained, then what Biosphere 2 did was not really cheating. The Biospherians aimed to learn the limits of their self-contained society and learn they did.

Human beings trade. That's what we do. We specialize. We aim to be the best we can be at what we do.

The poet John Donne once wrote one of the most striking lines in the English language: *No man is an island.* The line is quoted every day, mainly because it is such a haunting way of expressing the profound truth that human beings are social animals. Remember what we said in part II about Robinson Crusoe. Some social animals are more self-sufficient than others, precisely because they support themselves by being of service to partners of their choosing. But being self-sufficient does not mean being an island. It does not mean being a hermit.

If you want to live a decent human life, you live in a community, a marketplace. You seek out opportunities to cooperate in mutually beneficial ways. If you want to live well, you live in a very large marketplace. When people dream only about their own wants and needs, it takes four months to make

---

1. https://www.ted.com/talks/jane_poynter_life_in_biosphere_2?language=en&t-

a pizza. But people who dream about helping other people are the ones who figure out how to do it in two minutes.

DISCUSSION AND EXERCISES

1. Why would anyone launch a business such as Cayman Turtle Farm? In particular, they were releasing tens of thousands of yearlings into the wild every year, but why? There is no profit in doing that, so they must have had some further agenda, but what could it have been?
2. What went wrong with Biosphere 2? Compare and contrast what happened there with what happened at Jamestown.
3. Human beings trade because it is in their nature, and because it makes life better for them. Is there anything that you encounter on a daily basis that is not the result of trade, at least in part?

Chapter 35

Trust

Trust is the willingness to make oneself vulnerable to another person. In particular, if Roberto agrees to do something for you on Tuesday, and you make plans based on the assumption that Roberto will do what he agreed to do, then you trust Roberto. Economic interactions, especially market interactions, tend to be based on various forms of mutual trust.

THE INTERPERSONAL SIDE OF TRUST

The first big idea in economics, again, is that there are gains from trade. We are better off for trading with our neighbors. In economics, by assuming that people act in their own best interest, we can reliably predict who will trade, the amount of trade, and the prices at which commodities and services will trade, given market conditions.

The second big idea is that all economic interactions, especially market interactions, presuppose a level of trust. This relationship stems from the risk inherent in any trade, especially trades that come together over time and require an extended pattern of future interactions. We use contracts to specify the terms of trade over time, but, as any lawyer or economist will tell you, contracts are never complete. A complete contract specifies a proper response for every possible future development. However, not every possibility will be anticipated, and there is a limit to how much you want to write into a contract. It is important to keep it simple. (You don't want your contract to be so long that reading it is not humanly possible.) Realistically, not everything will be written into any real-world contract.

Recall our earlier discussion of transaction cost. One kind of transaction cost is the cost of obtaining information, including information about what kind of service we get for our money. Part of the point of a business having a policy like "satisfaction guaranteed or your money back" is to make trading less risky for customers.

That kind of transaction cost, the cost of finding out whether your partner is trustworthy, is right to the point here. Trust is an ever-present issue, a factor in just about every deal. The more two people trust each other, the lower the cost of making a deal. But to trust someone is to take a risk, so anyone who wants to have a reputation for being trustworthy has to earn it.

Institutions can help. Institutions can, for example, help people to insure themselves against the risks inherent in exchange. Institutions can provide a framework of contract law that enables traders to create a written record of some main elements of what they expect from each other going forward; in the process, the parties to the contract are giving themselves some right of recourse for the most blatant failures to deliver what one promised to deliver. But contract law is supposed to be the background, not the foreground. In a country where there is a rule of law, individuals are not supposed to need to spend their days in court protecting their rights. The bottom line is that people have to feel comfortable with the assumption that can afford the risk of trusting people. When people have reason to feel comfortable trusting each other, economies grow, and communities make progress. Further, whether people have reason to feel comfortable trusting each other begins with people feeling confident in the background institutions of contract law and property law, institutions that make it safe for people to show up at the bargaining table in the first place.

That is the theoretical explanation for a historical tendency. Highly productive patterns of cooperation get off the ground to the extent that basic rights regarding contract and property are secure.

THE INSTITUTIONAL SIDE OF TRUST

In moral philosophy, there has been much discussion of the following two cases. The first one is an imaginary case often discussed in ethics courses.

TROLLEY: A trolley is rolling down a track on its way to killing five people. If you switch to another track on which there is only one, you save five, but you kill one.

In the TROLLEY case, the obvious issue is that there are six lives at stake, and it is built into the case that we can't save everyone. The more subtle theoretical challenge is to say what else is going on, morally speaking. Perhaps it is simply five lives versus one, or perhaps the issue is about *killing* one versus *letting* five *die*, and killing versus letting die may not be the same thing as simply one versus five.

Here is the second case. Or is it the same case?

> *HOSPITAL:* Five patients are on operating tables dying for lack of suitable donors. A delivery person walks in, and you happen to know enough about everyone involved to know that the delivery person would be a suitable organ donor for all five patients. If you kidnap the delivery person and harvest her organs, you will be saving five and killing one. Should you do it? Why or why not?

Why isn't this simply a question of five versus one—the needs of the many versus needs of the few? The answer is that hospitals are institutions, and one characteristic of good institutions is that they provide people with a setting in which they can afford to trust each other. Hospitals cannot serve their purpose unless people can trust doctors and staff to treat patients and everyone else as rights bearers.

Institutions have utility by creating conditions under which people can trust each other not to operate in a utilitarian way, as if other people were simply pawns to be moved around in such a way as to maximize the overall good. Institutions get the best result not so much by aiming at the best result as by imposing constraints on individual pursuits so as to bring individual pursuits into better harmony with each other. Institutions like hospitals serve the common good by creating opportunities for mutual benefit then trusting individuals to take advantage of them.

Ultimately, there are two sides to the sense in which institutional utility is based on trust. First, people have to be able to trust their society to treat them as rights bearers, not as mere pawns. And second, society has to trust people to make use of opportunities that people have as rights bearers within society. Even from a utilitarian perspective, then, numbers don't always count. Simply treating values with respect sometimes is the best we can do to promote them.

The principle here is clear: Consider the consequences. However, when applying this principle, we must realize that even when considering consequences, there are times when the numbers do not count. The numbers can be like a snapshot of process of motion: a misleading picture of what is really at stake.

One of us (Schmidtz) tells the following story.

Wherever I present the Trolley case and ask people whether they would switch tracks, many will answer, "There has to be another way!" On a trip to

Kazakhstan, I presented the case to 21 professors from nine post-Soviet republics, and they said the same. I responded as I always did, saying, "Please, stay on topic. I'm trying to illustrate a point here! To see the point, you need to decide what to do when there is no other way." When I said this to my class of post-Soviet professors, though, they spoke briefly among themselves in Russian, then said, "Yes, we understand. We have heard this before. All our lives we were told the few must be sacrificed for the sake of many. We were told there is no other way. What we were told was a lie. There was always another way."[1]

GOING BEYOND CODES OF ETHICS

Being moral is not merely a matter of following a set, any set, of rules. It is an art as much as a science. It would be grossly unscientific—grossly unresponsive to reality—to pretend otherwise. Being moral takes some wisdom. It takes some experience.

Consider this fact: every code of ethics is a human invention, which means it is someone's attempt to predict what the problems are going to be and what will count as meeting a minimum standard.

Repeat: the code is a *minimum* standard. You can't afford to set your personal sights that low. You have to consistently expect more from yourself than that. You want to have a reputation, and to deserve a reputation for going the extra mile, and for doing your job to a level of uncommon excellence.

Reality does not promise to play fair. It will throw curves at you that will be beyond what any code-writer or any government regulator ever dreamt of. You will have to be ready for that as well. There are days when complying with the law will be easy compared to the challenge of making decisions you can be proud of.

The interpersonal side of ethics has always had, and always will have, something to do with internalizing externalities. Ethics will never be the same thing as economics, but good ethics and good economics will always keep an eye on each other. Good ethics and good economics both keep an eye on the idea of cooperation. Both respect a culture and a legal system that encourages agents in the marketplace to be on the lookout for opportunities to make mutually advantageous moves. Moreover, both good ethics and good economics will acknowledge that what it takes to realize opportunities for mutual advantage will always be an evolving problem.

---

1. David Schmidtz, *Elements of Justice* (Cambridge: Cambridge University Press, 2005), p. 171.

DISCUSSION AND EXERCISES

1. List ways in which you need to trust other people, and they need to trust you, in order for you to be able to live good lives together.
2. Is there a fundamental difference between the hospital and trolley examples? If so, what is it?

Chapter 36

Benefits for Bystanders

A positive externality occurs when consuming or producing something results in a benefit to a third party.

Market society is sometimes described as a tide that lifts all boats. In many ways, the metaphor is apt. It reminds us that the key to making a living and getting ahead in market society is to produce what other people value.

Profits are not normally made at other people's expense. People get rich when they market the light bulb, telephone, or computer, not because such inventions make people worse off, but rather because they make people better off.

Politician Elizabeth Warren once said,

"There is nobody in this country who got rich on their own. You built a factory out there—good for you. But I want to be clear. You moved your goods to market on roads the rest of us paid for. You hired workers the rest of us paid to educate. You were safe in your factory because of police forces and fire forces that the rest of us paid for. You built a factory and it turned into something terrific or a great idea. God bless! Keep a hunk of it. But part of the underlying social contract is you take a hunk of that and pay forward for the next kid who comes along."

There is a lot of truth in what Warren says. If a community is in proper working order, then life on the inside is far better than life on the outside. And it is better because of the hard work and great ideas of untold numbers of people who came before you and who are working beside you right now. If you are doing good work right now, then you ought to be paid for it. Everyone ought to be paid for the good work they are doing that makes life easier for all of us. It is not necessarily true that the police ought to be paying *you* or that *you* ought to be paying them. But whoever agreed to pay any given person ought to pay that person. When employers or customers do pay people for doing good work, the result tends to be good for everyone. If your customers agreed to pay you, then they ought to pay you. If you agreed to pay your employees, then you ought to pay them. And if there are public servants who are helping to keep public services in order—services on which we all depend—then they need to be paid as well. That is where Warren's point is important. Insofar as a society requires paid public servants, it also requires a way to pay them. That is the basic argument about why some taxes are morally justified.

Thomas Edison is credited with inventing the light bulb. In any case, he was one of the people who got rich by helping to make it possible for people to be able to see what they are doing, especially at night. Our life expectancy is now several decades longer than it was in Edison's time, and the light bulb (the fact that surgeons can now see what they are doing, for example) is one reason why. So, we can say (1) Edison got rich, (2) a lot of people helped him to get rich, (3) many of them also got rich in the process, (4) somebody made sure they got paid for their help, (5) some of them were public servants, and they were paid for their efforts along with everyone else, and finally (6) if Edison did not pay those public servants directly, then it seems fair that his share of the taxes paid would be proportionate to his share of the benefits received.

One more thought, then, about paying it forward: suppose we said that Edison had obligations beyond making sure that everyone around him got paid. Suppose we said Edison had obligations to future generations. As Elizabeth Warren puts it, he has obligations "to the next kid who comes along."

It is not obvious why that would be true, but suppose it is. In that case, the question becomes: What if Edison did, in fact, help the next kid who came along? What if Edison, in fact, passed on something incredible to the next kid? After all, he gave that kid the light bulb.

Suppose Edison had given every penny he ever made to a tax collector, for the sake of paying it forward. Seriously, even if Edison had given us every penny he ever made from the light bulb, it would have been nothing compared to benefit of giving us the light bulb itself. And of course, this is not only Edison who we are talking about. Any competent garage mechanic does far more to make the world a better place simply by getting motorists back on the road than he or she could ever do by paying taxes on the services he or she provides.

In the developed world—that is, the world built by people like you with a little help from people like Thomas Edison—ordinary people today can turn on a light and (at almost no cost!) see what they are doing after the sun goes down. Ordinary people can literally fly across the Atlantic Ocean. Ordinary people can literally talk to someone on the other side of the world. Someone can ask you where Thomas Edison grew up, and with the help of the Internet, you can provide a detailed report in two minutes. If you had been able to do these things in Thomas Edison's time, you would have been a comic book superhero. You may not be Thomas Edison, yet you can do things that Edison could hardly have imagined. What will kids be capable of doing a hundred years from now? That may depend on you.

You are something new under the sun. You have powers to make the world a better place that are unlike anything the world has ever seen.

POSITIVE EXTERNALITIES IN A MARKET FRAMEWORK

Just as we did for negative externalities, we can use a market framework of supply and demand graphs to show how positive externalities impact market outcomes. This section may seem like an echo of the negative externality section, and it should. We use the same tools, the Social MC and Social MB curves, but we find the opposite effect. The presence of positive externalities implies that free market outcomes produce too little of a good or service.

Remember that the demand curve represents the *private* marginal benefit in dollars of each unit of potential consumption, and the supply curve represents the *private* marginal cost in dollars of each unit of potential production. Remember too that a positive externality or external benefit is the benefit of a decision or transaction enjoyed by bystanders.

When we model positive externalities in the supply and demand framework, we need to construct a wholly new curve, one that includes the benefit bestowed on nonparticipating members of society. We have introduced the idea of social cost. This section shows how the idea can be represented in graphical form.

If an externality occurs through the production of the good or service, a new call center opens downtown, for example, and the employee traffic makes it safer for the other residents. It means that the true cost to society of producing that service is lower than what firms consider to be the cost of production. In other words, *Social Marginal Cost (Social MC) < Private Marginal Cost (Private MC, or supply)*. Figure 36.1 illustrates society's lower cost of production with the introduction of the social marginal cost curve. Theoretically, the Social MC illustrates the supply curve if all costs, not just firms' costs, were considered in the production decision.

If an externality occurs through the consumption of a good, by neighbors beautifying their homes, for example, increasing the value of all the homes in the neighborhood, it means that the true benefit to society of consuming that good is less than what consumers consider. In other words, *Social Marginal Benefit (Social MB) > Private Marginal Benefit (Private MB or demand)*. We show this great social benefit by introduction the social marginal benefit

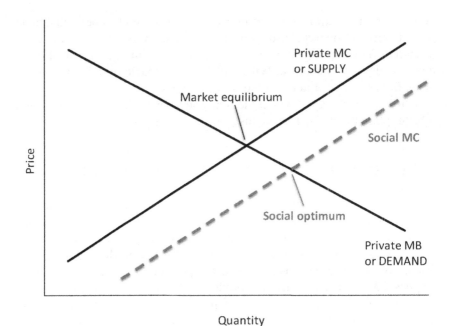

Figure 36.1.   Positive externalities in production

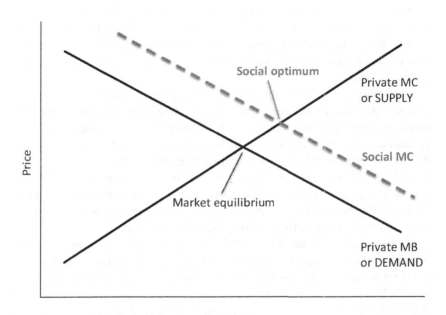

Figure 36.2.   Positive externalities in consumption

curve in figure 36.2. Theoretically, Social MB illustrates the demand curve if all benefits, including those enjoyed by third parties, were considered in the consumption decision.

IMPLICATIONS OF POSITIVE EXTERNALITIES

The intuition is exactly the same whether we consider positive or negative externalities. The intersection of the original demand and supply curves will indicate the market equilibrium price and quantity. When there are no externalities, the equilibrium quantity will maximize the value possible to society. When there are externalities, the original demand and supply curves will no longer fully represent the costs and benefits to society. Market outcomes will either overshoot or undershoot the optimal outcome. Social efficiency occurs where Social MC=Social MB. (If there are no externalities, then Social = Private.)

If we have a positive externality on the production side (figure 36.1), and we draw a vertical line through the market equilibrium, we can see that the Social MC is lower than the Private MB (demand). At the margin, it costs society less to produce that good than it is valued by consumers. The socially optimal outcome, Social MC = Private MB, is to the right of the market equilibrium. This means there is underproduction in the market.

When there is a positive externality on the consumption side (figure 36.2), we can see that the Social MB is higher than the Private MC (supply). At the margin, members of society are benefiting more from the consumption of that good than it costs to produce it. The socially optimal outcome, Private MC = Social MB, is to the right of the market equilibrium. This means there is underconsumption in the market.

SUBSIDIES ON POSITIVE EXTERNALITIES

Recall that taxes on negative externalities are intended to increase the cost of producing or consuming the good, therefore aligning the private and social benefits and costs, and reducing the amount traded.

For positive externalities, we have too little production, so we would want to boost the size of the market. We want the opposite of what a tax does. A negative tax is a subsidy. Instead of collecting a fee for an activity, a bonus is given for participating in the activity. The more consumed, the more the benefit. A subsidy for the production or the consumption of the good would increase the amount traded and increase the price paid by consumers. In the same way that a tax on sellers shifts the supply curve to the left, a subsidy on sellers shifts the supply curve to the right.

Subsidies on positive externalities are intended to decrease the cost of producing or consuming the good, therefore aligning the private and social benefits and costs, and increasing the amount traded.

The idea is that if we use subsidies to help make it more affordable to buy (or to supply) the good, then that should increase the volume of trade in the subsidized good. In theory, that should be a good thing. Of course, Bastiat would warn us not to ignore the hidden cost of diverting subsidy money from whatever purpose it would otherwise have served. Nevertheless, corn, wheat, soybeans, and other foods are subsidized, as are oil, ethanol, and housing. How would we decide whether subsidizing those products is worth the cost?

DISCUSSION AND EXERCISES

1. Find an existing subsidy and determine if there is a positive externality associated with the consumption or production of the good subsidized?
2. Give three examples of positive externalities that you experience regularly in your life.
3. When Elizabeth Warren made the claim that no one gets rich on his or her own, she echoed a theme that we have been developing throughout this book: no one lives a life completely free of other people, nor should anyone want to. If that is true, how much of our individual success do we owe one another? In what form should this debt be addressed?

Chapter 37

Market Power

If an entity can influence the price either by setting the quantity traded or by setting the price, that entity is said to have "**market power**." Market power, when used, affects the market outcome resulting in a less than efficient outcome.

In the model known as **perfect competition**, companies are assumed to have zero market power—no power to manipulate prices.

At one extreme, we have perfect competition: no market power for buyers or sellers. At the other extreme, we have total market power: monopoly power (one seller, setting the price higher than the perfectly competitive price) or monopsony power (one buyer, setting the price lower than the perfectly competitive price). In reality, markets can approximate either extreme or anything in between.

There are many models of market structure and predicted conduct between the extremes of perfect competition and monopoly/monopsony. We even have terms like "oligopoly" (few sellers) and "duopoly" (two sellers) to refer to some of the points between the extremes. Theories have been developed that link market structure to conduct and performance. Under certain conditions, a duopoly (in the form of a cartel) can perform like a monopoly, and under other conditions, just two firms can perform like a perfectly competitive market. Theoretically, the perfectly competitive outcome is the gold standard. It is the best that a market can do. Evaluating behavior in a market always comes down to comparing the amount of trade being generated to the amount of trade that would occur under perfectly competitive conditions. This isn't always easy, but it is the goal.

In a dynamic world, sellers often possess some degree of market power. Firms that are successful in putting resources to their best use, by lowering costs and serving customers, for example, will tend to enjoy periods of market power and higher profits.

DISCUSSION AND EXERCISES

1. Can you think of a single perfectly competitive market? What are its characteristics? What makes it perfectly competitive?
2. Can you think of a few companies operating today that have a tremendous degree of market power? How did they achieve it? Is there necessarily a problem when firms achieve overwhelming market power?
3. If the "perfectly competitive outcome is the gold standard," what would make this outcome possible? Would this outcome ever be likely?

Chapter 38

Monopoly Power

A monopoly is a market in which there is only one seller. If there is only one seller, then the seller has pricing power. In a market served by one seller, a monopolist, the price may rise above competitive level.

Monopolists, like other firms, are firms that are interested in earning profits. Unlike other firms, monopolists have pricing power on the selling side of the market.

Suppose we assume that a monopolist chooses a price and quantity to produce in order to maximize profits. As a reminder, the owners of a competitive firm choose the quantity they desire to supply at the market price. (See Sellers in part III.) The owners of competitive firms do not have the opportunity to choose the price, they merely choose how much they would like to supply to the market at the going price. Competitive firms are called **price-takers**.

One criticism of monopolists is that they charge higher prices and supply lower quantities in a market than we would expect to see in a competitive market. See figure 38.1. The market served by a monopolist is summarized by the market demand curve (with no relevant market supply curve). The monopolist is free to experiment with price and quantity combinations to maximize profit. A monopolist, sometimes referred to as a **price-maker**, understands the demand curve is downward sloping and charges a price as maximize profit.

If sellers in a market make positive economic profits, they can anticipate that other firms will enter the market. New firms will enter because positive economic profits imply that resources are highly productive in a given industry, and there is further opportunity to gain from their employment.

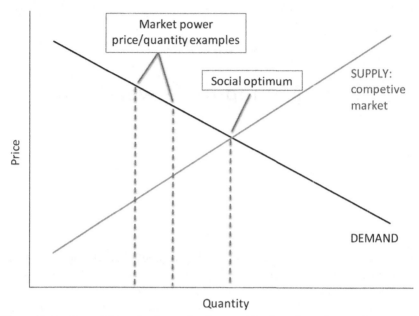

Figure 38.1.   Potential production and price combinations for a firm with monopoly power

Herein lies the rub for the monopolist. As firms, they want to make profits. If they make profits, they will invite competitors to enter the market. Entry erodes their profits. They want to make profits and would prefer that there were no entry into the market. The only way to retard or eliminate entry is to operate in a market with barriers to market entry.

Barriers to market entry are either man-made or naturally occurring. Natural barriers occur when the production process is such that the market is just not big enough to support more than one firm. You can imagine one firm operating in a market with extremely high set-up costs. As that firm meets demand and the market expands, it experiences a continuously decreasing average cost of production. This would make it difficult for a new entrant to compete with the natural monopolist (assuming that the new firm faces similar set up costs).

Many man-made barriers stem from governmental bodies. Often, access to raw materials, patents, copyright, licensing requirements, and trademarks are given as examples of government imposed barriers. Many states and countries hold monopolies on liquor sales (e.g., Norway, Sweden, Finland, Iceland, Ontario, British Columbia, Pennsylvania, and Virginia).

DISCUSSION AND EXERCISES

1. Is having one seller a good thing or a bad thing?
2. How could a monopoly ever arise in the first place? How does a duopoly arise? An oligopoly? A cartel?
3. If monopoly is a problem, is there any solution? Could anything go wrong with the solution?

Chapter 39

Monopsony Power

Where a **monopoly** is an economy in which there is only one *seller*, a **monopsony** is an economy in which there is only one *buyer*. In a **monopoly**, with only one seller, the *seller* has pricing power. By contrast, in a monopsony, with only one buyer, it is the *buyer* who has pricing power.

Economists predict that in a monopoly, the price will rise *above* competitive levels. When there is only one seller of water, for example, the price of water is likely to be high. Economists predict that in a monopsony, by contrast, the price will fall *below* competitive levels. In the labor market, for example, if only one employer is hiring workers, then the price of labor is likely to be low.

Karl Marx saw the labor market as a monopsony. On his view of the world, there is a "reserve army" of desperate workers who will accept any wage so long as it beats starving. So, as Marx saw it, the supply, or worker side of the labor market is intensely competitive. By contrast, as Marx saw it, there is no competition at all on the demand, or buyer side. On the buyer side, either there is only one employer, or if there are several, they are able to form a cartel, collude, and work together to make sure wages hover near the "starvation wage."

Standard economic analysis tells us that, if competition on the buyer side of the labor market were as intense as competition on the seller side, then wages will rise to a level that matches what a worker's labor is worth. If Henry Ford is trying to break into the market for automobiles, then he goes into the automobile labor market and recruits Chevrolet's best and most underpaid workers by offering them a higher wage to come work for Ford. Chevrolet responds. Realizing that its profitability depends on retaining its most productive workers, Chevrolet tries to retain them by matching Ford's offer. Neither Ford nor Chevrolet wants to offer workers more than they are worth, but ultimately if Ford's workers are worth a lot more than Ford is paying, and if Ford has competitors, then one of Ford's competitors will offer those under-paid workers at least a little bit more to switch employers. So, the economic ideal would be for both buyers and sellers, the two sides of the labor market, to be competitive. It is competition that predictably results in workers being paid approximately what they are worth.

That is the theory. But is the real world like that? It did not look that way to Marx. To Marx, employers had pricing power, while workers had no power other than to accept whatever they were offered. Workers could not shop around in search of a better offer, because the employer cartel was the only game in town. Whatever that employer offered, so long as the offer was better than starving, they had to take it.

DISCUSSION AND EXERCISES

1. Suppose for a moment that Marx was right. Could anything be done? Here are three possible remedies to the imbalance of market power. There may be more than three. Can you think of others?

   A. Workers could join a Union. If all workers belong to a single Union, then the monopsony, the concentrated power of the single buyer of labor is matched by concentrated monopoly power of the single seller of labor, the Union. That doesn't guarantee that workers will be paid what their work is worth, but at least the power is balanced. Further, if a Marxist perspective is wrong, if there is no monopsony, and if in reality the buyer side of the equation is highly competitive, then we have reason to believe that workers are already being paid roughly what they are worth. In that case, concentrating monopoly power on the seller side would not solve a problem.

   B. Legislators could establish a minimum wage. Suppose workers are being paid a starvation wage of $1 per hour but are actually worth $10 per hour. If the Union demands $12 per hour, that won't work, but if the Union demands something in the middle, between one and ten, then somewhere in there is a wage that both sides have reason to accept. Crucially, however, there has to be a gap between what workers are paid and what they are worth, and the minimum wage needs to fit into that gap. That is how the minimum wage can succeed in placing a bottom limit on the monopsony employer's pricing power.

   C. Legislators could aim to make it illegal to have pricing power on the buyer side of the market in the same way that legislators might try to craft "anti-monopoly" legislation that makes it illegal to have pricing power on the seller side. Whether there is an actual problem, and whether the legislation helps to solve the problem will, of course, depend on the details. But the basic idea is that if there can be laws requiring an industry dominant seller to break up, there could also be analogous laws requiring industry dominant buyers of labor to break up.

2. Is having one buyer a good or a bad thing? How could a monopsony arise in the first place?
3. If monopsony is a problem, is there any solution? Could anything go wrong with the solution?
4. Would a minimum wage be a response to a monopoly problem or a monopsony problem? Explain.
5. Suppose we said professional football players should be paid at least $3 per hour. In the world as you know it, what would happen? Who would be affected? Would a problem be solved?
6. Suppose we said high school students who deliver pizza part-time should be paid at least $100 per hour. What would happen? Who would be affected? Would a problem be solved?
7. In general, when would imposing a minimum wage solve a problem? What exactly is the problem that a minimum wage would solve? *See Also: Price Controls: An Experimental Test.*

Chapter 40

International Trade and
Trade Protection

International trade is simply trade across international borders. Trading internationally gives consumers and countries the opportunity to be exposed to new markets and products.

A good or service sold to the global market is called an **export**, and a product bought from the global market is called an **import**. We can use the supply and demand tools we constructed earlier to examine what happens to prices, consumption, production, and surplus when a nation is open or closed to international trade.

We use the term **domestic** to distinguish the home country of concern and **international** or **global** to represent the entire world market. Opening up markets to the world presumably would have some impact on domestic production or consumption. To have no impact, the world price would have to be coincidental with the price that would prevail in the domestic market, but the world price will likely be higher or lower than the domestic price. If the world price is higher than the domestic price (without trade), the home country could become an exporter. If the global price is lower than the domestic price (without trade), consumers in the home country could benefit from lower priced imports. Using figure 40.1, you can see that the lower world price P(NO tariff) allows for more consumption (Qd) but a smaller amount of domestic production (Qs).

When a nation is open to trade, and the world price prevails in the market, the intuition is that the domestic production or consumption is relatively small in comparison to international production or consumption.

Domestic price can differ from world price when there are trade restrictions. A **tariff** is a tax imposed on imported goods or services. Figure 40.1 shows that an imposition of a tariff would raise the domestic price to P(tariff) from P(NO tariff).

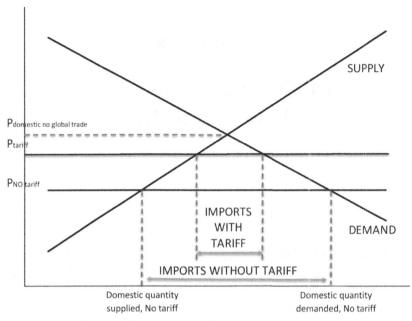

Figure 40.1.   Global price less than domestic price

Protectionism is the placement of legal restrictions on international trade, and includes tariffs, quotas, subsidies, and other bureaucratic barriers. A tariff acts much in the same way as a tax does for domestic goods and services. Remember, an increase in production costs raises the cost of doing business, shifting the supply curve to the left. In this case, the supply curve of foreign imported goods is horizontal indicating that the domestic market is relatively small in comparison to the world market. The tariff merely raises the price of the imported goods by that amount of the tariff P(world + tariff).

DISCUSSION AND EXERCISES

1. We can see from figure 40.2 that tariffs raise the domestic price. How do tariffs affect domestic consumption? How do tariffs affect domestic production? How do they affect surplus? How do they affect the allocation of surplus?
2. Do consumers have a stake on allowing unrestricted imports? Why? Do producers have a stake in protecting domestic markets from imports?

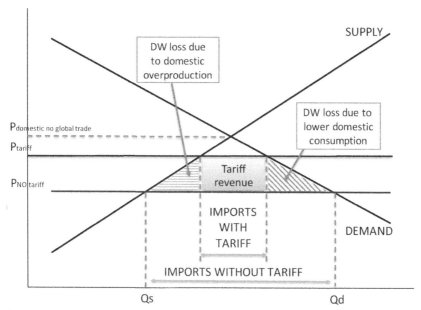

Figure 40.2.   **Revenue generated from a tariff placed on goods**

Why? If there is a conflict of interest between consumers and producers, which group is likely to have more political influence? Why?

3. What are the fundamental differences between domestic and international trade?

Chapter 41

What Should Not Be for Sale

The most important effect of markets isn't that they enable us to sell everything, but that they enable us not to. They make us rich enough that we can afford to say no.

Everyone draws a line. Some things should not be for sale. But how can that be? If it is your kidney, for example, then why can't you sell it?

The answer depends on a distinction between two kinds of rights. First, a regular property right is the sort of thing that you have a right to sell. Second, there is another kind of right that we call an **inalienable right**, which is a kind of property that cannot be bought and sold at all. For example, adult citizens may have a right to vote without having any right to *sell* their vote. Note that for goods that you have a right to sell, the right can still be limited in various ways. For example, adults can own cars, and adults can sell their car if they want to, but they cannot sell their car to a child.

There are things bought and sold every day somewhere in the world that many people think should never be offered for sale, things like sex, weapons, pollution, votes, mercenary services, body parts, and eternal salvation. It may be legal to sell some of these things where you live. In the end, however, there are moral questions, too. Specifically, there are moral questions about what *should* be legal to buy and sell.

Philosopher Debra Satz refers to what she calls "noxious markets," which are markets in things that she believes should not be for sale.[1] Why not? Satz begins with the observation that desperation can make people vulnerable. Desperation can drive people to make bad deals. A person dying of thirst is

---

1. Debra Satz. *Why Some Things Should Not Be for Sale*. (New York: Oxford University Press, 2010).

likely to pay any price for a bottle of water, even if the market price for water is quite low.

Lack of information can also lead people to make bad deals. We have all heard stories of people who have bought cars that turned out to not be in roadworthy condition, just as we have heard stories of people who spent their life savings on houses that turned out to be uninhabitable.

Further, some products are dangerous. Some are addictive. Some transactions could undermine social trust and our institutions of government. Think about buying and selling votes. Think about bribery.

Finally, we have to consider the damage done by blackmail, which is an industry that invests in producing information that customers then pay to keep private. In the case of blackmail, customers would be better off if that market didn't exist in the first place.

Trade is the essence of cooperation. Merchants spend their time making their products maximally useful to their fellow citizens. But part of what makes the system work is that customers are willing and able to walk away in search of a better deal. This formal right to walk away changes everything, both in theory and in historical practice.

To Adam Smith, ending servility was by far the most important effect of markets. If he was right, then we should become uneasy when we find people in situations where they can't *afford* to walk away. At the same time, we realize that in a liberal society, there is such a thing as minding one's own business. We also realize that many of the people we would protect (if we could) are doing the best they can. Taking away a desperate person's best option is one way of proving you care, but people who actually do care look for better answers.

We're all offended by poor taste. You probably know some people who strike you as liking bad music, eating bad food, and so on. Is that a problem? Markets are crucibles in which values take shape. But the same markets that give us the rock band Union Gap (You don't remember Union Gap, but that's the point; their music was not memorable) also give us Mozart.

Not that every consumer likes Mozart, but enough do to bring Mozart into the realm of what is humanly possible. That is, markets for music brought Mozart into the realm of what is commercially possible. Vienna's music authorities did not appreciate Mozart's genius and did nothing to support him, but ultimately Mozart did not need the blessing of the authorities. So long as Mozart had customers willing to pay to hear his music, he was in business.

Finally, markets themselves create our most powerful tools for resisting the intrusion of markets into the intimate aspects of our lives. Noxious markets in child labor, for example, are widespread only in poor countries. Minimum age and minimum wage laws can be used to make children unemployable, but the real objective is not to prevent children from working, but to raise living standards to a point where even the poorest do not need to sell the labor of their children to make ends meet.

Here, then, is the critical lesson. What we want from markets is not for them to empower us to sell everything, but almost the opposite. Part of what is liberating about markets is that they put us in a position of not needing to sell everything in order to survive. Markets have the potential to make us rich enough that *we can afford to say no.*

DISCUSSION AND EXERCISES

1. Recall the story of Cayman Turtle Farm and our previous consideration of the fact that it takes a thriving commercial hub such as Vienna, Florence, London, New York, or Athens to enable someone like Mozart to make a living as an entertainer. There have to be lots of customers with disposable income to spend on the arts. Is Cayman Turtle Farm a related phenomenon, consisting of people who have so much disposable income that they no longer have to worry about marketing a service, and they can instead afford to start a business whose main purpose is to save an endangered species?

2. We have discussed many basic analytical tools in this part of the book: principal-agent problems, externality problems, commons tragedies, monopoly and monopsony problems, and noxious markets. It seems that the task of regulating markets will be profoundly difficult. Is there a way to make this any easier, or is this level of difficulty simply the cost we must pay in order to live in commercial society?

3. Are some markets so noxious that they should be forbidden? If so, what is the principled justification by which this can be accomplished?

Part V

MANAGEMENT OF A COMMERCIAL SOCIETY

Commercial societies, and the economies upon which they are built, are complicated arrangements involving, in many cases, hundreds of millions of people, each with their own goals and aspirations. They do their best to achieve their own ends in a broader context defined by everyone else doing exactly the same thing. Things work for the most part, but there is always friction when people have goals that might conflict with those of others. How can we keep things working well enough to allow people sufficient freedom to pursue their goals, while offering sufficient protection to everyone at the same time?

The answer is that functional institutions and sound policy can make the critical difference in this important task.

Chapter 42

Financial Institutions

Nations often establish rules and guidelines that help to determine the supply and availability of economic currency (money). There are many financial institutions, but the one that oversees most other financial institutions in the United States is the Federal Reserve System.

The Federal Reserve System, commonly known as the "Fed," was created by the Congress in 1913 in an attempt to create a more stable financial and monetary system. As the nation's central bank, the Federal Reserve's responsibilities cover four general areas. Directly quoting from federalreserve.cov:[1]

1. Conducting the nation's monetary policy by influencing money and credit conditions in the economy in pursuit of full employment and stable prices.
2. Supervising and regulating banks and other important financial institutions to ensure the safety and soundness of the nation's banking and financial system and to protect the credit rights of consumers.
3. Maintaining the stability of the financial system and containing systemic risk that may arise in financial markets.
4. Providing financial services to the U.S. government, U.S. financial institutions, and foreign official institutions, and playing a major role in operating and overseeing the nation's payments systems.

Beyond the Fed, there are financial institutions such as banks, credit unions, insurance companies, and investment firms that trade in financial and monetary-related services: deposits, check writing, credit and debit cards, foreign currency exchange, loans, and investments. Financial institutions have two broad types of customers: commercial and retail. Commercial customers

---

1. http://www.federalreserve.gov/faqs/ about_12594.htm

are businesses and other organizations, while retail customers are individuals and households. Financial institutions are heavily regulated by the federal and often state governments in the states in which they operate.

Among the most important financial institutions are stock and commodity exchanges. These "exchanges" are marketplaces that allow for the efficient trading of bonds, shares of stock, which are ownership shares of a company, and commodities such as corn, wheat, silver, and gold. Two large exchanges are the New York Stock Exchange (NYSE) and the Chicago Board of Exchange (CBOE). The CBOE also trades in commodities future prices. If you are a farmer, you can purchase the option to sell corn at a set price during some period of time in the future, such as six or twelve months. On the other hand, a company such as a cereal maker may purchase the option to buy corn in the future at a certain price. Firms or individuals can use this type of trading to lower their risk, and this is especially important when commodities have large price fluctuations.

DISCUSSION AND EXERCISES

1. To learn more about the trading of stocks, bonds, and commodities, visit the websites of the NYSE and the CBOE.
2. Think about the various services banks provide. How many have you used? How many will you use over the next twenty years?
3. If farmers can sell their corn in the future at a specific price determined today, and a cereal manufacturer can purchase corn in the future at a specific price determined today, how do both benefit?

Chapter 43

Fractional Reserve Banking

Money may be the most excellent device ever invented for making it easier for people to trade their services and make each other better off.

Money is categorized by where it originates. Base money, sometimes called "outside money" or "central bank money," is the currency created by the Federal Reserve.

The financial system uses the base money to generate "deposit money," sometimes called "inside money," through a process of fractional reserve banking. Banks, or financial institutions in general, pool together smaller savings and loan them out. Banks receive deposits, they release funds as loans, the loans themselves become deposits, those deposits are loaned out, and the process continues. This progression of deposits and loans through financial intermediaries is another form of money creation. The process of holding back a fraction of bank deposits as reserves and loaning the rest out is called **fractional reserve banking**.

Depositors benefit from leaving their funds in a bank by receiving interest. Banks benefit from accepting deposits because they use those funds for loans, for which they receive higher interest payments. Those loans, in effect, put the deposited money to work by investing in the community.

The reserve requirement is one of the tools that the Federal Reserve has at its disposal (others will be covered in the Monetary Policy section), which enable it to control the quantity of money in circulation.

The **reserve requirement** is the proportion of reserves required to be held and not loaned out by the bank. If the reserve requirement is 5 percent, for example, a bank that receives a $1000 deposit may lend out $950 of that deposit. If the borrower then spends the $950 with her suppliers, and those suppliers deposit that amount, $950, back at a bank, then the bank can treat that new deposit as an additional reserve that enables it to issue another loan for $902.50 ($950 less the 5 percent held as reserves). If suppliers whose products are purchased by that loan deposit the income with a bank, then the bank can issue yet another loan for 95 percent of that, and so on. That may seem a bit magical, but the net result is that the system of fractional reserves enables lending institutions to provide capital for much higher levels of investment, production, and consumption than otherwise would be possible.

DISCUSSION AND EXERCISES

1. What is the relationship between deposits and loans in commercial banks?
2. When considering deposits and loans, how is it that banks are able to make a profit, given that they pay interest to depositors?
3. What is the reserve requirement, and how does it work in practice?

Chapter 44

Measuring Economies

Facts are stubborn things, but statistics are pliable.

—Mark Twain

Economic indicators tell us what the economy is up to, and what direction it is likely to take in the future. They can help people to make plans. Whenever we talk about measures of an economy, it is important to consider what the numbers represent.

We see this when we think about, for example, the goal of student success. Educators want a student's time in school to be a process of growth and learning, but a life well lived means different things to different people. Further, ongoing assessment of a life well lived takes time. So, what are we to measure? When do we measure it? Something as simple as student success quickly gets complicated.

When outcomes occur far in the future or are difficult to measure, we sometimes opt for measuring inputs, things that we believe lead to the outcomes we want. Measuring inputs should work for making decisions about how to allocate resources as long as the relationship between the measured input and the output is direct and stable, but here too there are difficulties.

Returning to student success, let's say we observe that the more kids who graduate from high school, the more our city grows, the happier our citizens are, and the lower our crime rate becomes. We might sensibly decide to incentivize the school system to maximize graduation rates by proposing a new program that pays bonuses to school administrators for each graduating student.

What could go wrong? It depends on what else changes as a result of our intervention. If students are more likely to graduate because they are learning more in school, the new program will succeed. However, the new program could actually undermine the relationship between learning and graduating. The new policy adopts graduation as a proxy for learning, and puts us at risk of "turning the signal into the objective." If we are paying teachers to graduate their students rather than teach them, the effect of our intervention is not that students would learn more, but rather that requirements for graduation could become lax. We often run into problems like this when we measure inputs instead of outputs. So we have to be careful when we measure inputs to avoid creating measures that corrupt the whole system. On the other hand, outputs can be hard to measure. None of this gives us a hard and fast rule beyond the obvious one: we have to be careful and conscientious no matter how we approach these sorts of things. There is no substitute for encouraging everyone involved to keep in mind what their real purpose is, and to avoid getting too wrapped up in any crude measure.

Economy-wide outcomes are referred to as macroeconomic. **Macroeconomics** is the field of economics concerned with large-scale factors such as productivity and productive capacity. Macroeconomic measures are generally the most important indicators to policymakers. Economic activity, employment, and the general level of prices are the three most cited economic indicators. It is important to understand how these measures are created, so we understand the context in which they are used.

DISCUSSION AND EXERCISES

1. Why might we measure inputs instead of outputs? When might measuring inputs be misleading?
2. The example of student success provides a clear discussion of how the difficulty in measuring outcomes yields a policy approach that ultimately undermines the original goal. Can you think of another example of this happening?
3. A "well-lived life" means different things to different people, and can only be assessed over a long period of time. Nonetheless, policy decisions must be made for everyone, and in the here and now. Think about the essential friction brought about by these two observations.

Chapter 45

Gross Domestic Product

Gross Domestic Product (GDP) is a broad measure of economic activity that is commonly used to gauge the economic performance of a whole country or region, and to make international comparisons. More specifically, GDP is the market value of all finished goods and services produced within a country's borders in a specified period of time. This may well be one of the best-named measures in economics. Let's take each part of the definition and match it to the terms in the name:

the market value ← *gross*
of all finished goods and services produced ← *product*
within a country's borders ← *domestic*
in a specific period of time.

GDP, as most often used, is measured on an annual or a quarterly basis.

There are three methods of calculating domestic production. Theoretically, they should all yield the same estimate, but because each measure uses different data sources, the measures do not always coincide. These three approaches are the **expenditure** approach, the output or **production** approach, and the **income** approach. The expenditure approach measures the total sum of all products and services used in developing a finished product for sale. Instead of exclusively measuring input costs that result in economic activity, the production approach estimates the total value of economic output and subtracts costs of intermediate goods that are used in the process. **Intermediate goods** are not final goods and services, but materials and services that are used in the production of something else. The income approach, unlike the other two measures, does not focus on goods and services but what those goods and services created when exchanged in terms of income. It measures GDP by way of totaling domestic incomes earned. Sometimes GDP calculated by the income approach is called gross domestic income.

In terms of the production approach, GDP can be calculated using the following formula:

$$GDP = C + G + I + NX$$

where
C is equal to all private consumption, or consumer spending,
G is the sum of government spending,
I is the sum of all the country's investment,
NX is the nation's total net exports (NX = Exports − Imports).

REAL GDP

We call this sum **Nominal GDP** if it is calculated using current year prices. If GDP is calculated with base year prices, a year that is used as a reference, then we call that value **Real GDP**. If you see GDP numbers being compared year to year, it will likely be real GDP that is being compared. Weighting with base year prices makes for more meaningful year-to-year comparisons. Real GDP can be tracked over long spans of time and can be used in measuring a nation's economic growth. Figure 45.1 shows how Real GDP per capita (in 2012 dollars) has changed in the USA between 1947 and 2018. What could explain this trend?

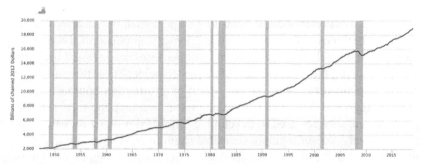

Figure 45.1.   Real growth in U.S. GDP, 1947–2018[1]

---

1. GDP adjusted for inflation using billions of chained 2012 dollars, seasonally adjusted annual rate. Shaded areas indicate U.S. recessions. U.S. Bureau of Economic Analysis, Real Gross Domestic Product [GDPC1], retrieved from FRED, Federal Reserve Bank of St. Louis https://fred.stlouisfed.org/series/GDPC1, accessed on May 5, 2019.

GROSS NATIONAL PRODUCT

Gross National Product (GNP) is a different measure that is sometimes confused with GDP. The difference between the two measures is that GDP sums all production within a country's domestic borders, while GNP sums all production owned by citizens of a country, whether they are inside or outside of that country's borders.

CRITICISMS OF GDP

There a few ways that GDP can be a bit misleading as an indicator of domestic production. For instance, it does not take into account transactions that are not reported to the government. These non-reported activities range from illegal activities to off-the-books barter exchanges between acquaintances. Transfer payments made by the government are also not reported. This means things like social security and various forms of welfare are not included in the calculations. Some activities are not reported because they are not market transactions. Odd jobs around the house are not counted in GDP when done by a homeowner, but are counted if someone is hired to do the work. The sales of used goods are similarly not included.

Criticisms of GDP often stem from the use of GDP as a proxy for the material well-being of a population. There is a strong relationship between productivity and material well-being, so sometimes the readily available figure of GDP is substituted for the more elusive thing to measure: the idea of well-being. Keep in mind that GDP is only a measure of a country's productivity. It does not include data on things like environmental quality, literacy, leisure, or life expectancy.

DISCUSSION AND EXERCISES

1. What are the components of GDP as measured by the expenditure approach? What are some items included in each component?
2. Describe an activity that would be included in GDP but not GNP. Describe an activity that would be included in GNP but not GDP.
3. Can GDP be used to measure well-being? Why?

Chapter 46

Unemployment Rate

The unemployment rate is *not* a measure of the percentage of the population that is out of work. The unemployment rate, as officially measured, is something else: it is a ratio of the number of **unemployed** individuals by all individuals currently in the **labor force**. A person is **unemployed** if he or she is both without work and is actively seeking paid work. The **labor force** is the number of people eligible for work.

The unemployment rate is expressed as a percentage, and is calculated as follows:

$$\text{Unemployment rate} = \frac{\text{Number unemployed}}{\text{Number in labor force}} \times 100$$

For example, if there are ten people in the labor force and one of them is unemployed, then multiplying one-tenth by 100 yields an unemployment rate of ten percent. Knowing the amount of unemployment in an economy can help us gauge the overall health of that economy. Human activity in paid work can be one of the most important resources a country has. The raw number of employed people alone is not helpful, but the number of employed people in relation to a reference population can help us make meaningful comparisons over time. For instance, if we only cite the number of people looking for work, then we don't know whether more people are looking because there is a rising population or because there are fewer jobs. If we look at the number of people looking for work as a percentage of the labor force, which is the number of people eligible for work, we get the useful measure of unemployment rate.

We make one modification to the definition of the unemployment rate by breaking down the labor force into its components of employed workers and unemployed workers.

$$\text{Unemployment rate} = \frac{\text{Number unemployed}}{\text{Number employed} + \text{Number unemployed}} \times 100$$

Notice that the **number unemployed** show up in both the numerator and the denominator of the definition. If the number of unemployed increases more relative to the number of employed, then the top will increase more than the bottom and the resulting ratio will increase, which is exactly what the measure is designed to do.

However, the measure can be misleading. The problem is what it takes to be considered unemployed. Unemployed workers are those who are currently not working but who are willing and able to work for pay, currently available to work, and actively searching for work. Individuals who are actively seeking work must make the effort. If they merely would like to be employed, they are not counted as unemployed. People who disengage from the labor market either by not working or by not actively seeking employment are called **discouraged workers**. Discouraged workers are not counted as unemployed or employed.

If the number of unemployed drops because people are discouraged, and leave the labor market entirely, that can show up as a falling unemployment rate even though the employment situation is worsening. This phenomenon is called the discouraged worker effect.

Some economists cite the labor force participation rate as an alternative indicator of employment. This measure compares the number of people in the labor force with the civilian population. The civilian population in this context refers to people over sixteen who are not in an institution (e.g., prison, or a long-term health care facility) and who are not enlisted in the military.

$$\text{Labor force participation rate} = \frac{\text{Number in labor force}}{\text{Number in population}} \times 100$$

The population includes individuals past retirement age, students, and people too young to work. This measure isn't without its problems. If large numbers of people start retiring because they are rich enough to stop working, the labor force participation rate drops, for example.

The unemployment rate and related measures are conceptually simple to calculate. However, a little investigation into the construction of the measures and the definitions of terms reveal how easily they can be misinterpreted and therefore potentially misused.

DISCUSSION AND EXERCISES

1. What are some reasons that an individual may not be counted in the labor force?
2. What are some changes that could lead to an increase in measured unemployment?
3. Why might we be interested in calculating the unemployment rate?

Chapter 47

Measuring the Price Level

A price level is an overall measurement of the prices of goods and services in an economy at a particular time. This measure allows us to monitor trends and changes that affect prices in general.

Inflation is a sustained increase in the average prices of all goods and services. People care about what their money can buy, but if prices increase over time, faster than income or interest rates, people will have less purchasing power over time. Knowing how prices in general change over time helps us understand if we are living through periods where purchasing power is increasing or decreasing.

CONSUMER PRICE INDEX

It is important to understand that when we measure inflation rate, we are trying to measure a general price trend. We are looking for evidence of a general change in overall prices over time. Therefore, our first task is to measure a general price level.

The consumer price index (CPI) is one way to measure the price level. First, we define a few component parts of CPI.

(1) A base year, *0*, is chosen as a reference year for measuring changes.
(2) A target year, *t*, is chosen for comparison to the base year.
(3) A fixed basket of goods and services is chosen to represent the consumption pattern of a typical consumer relative to the base year.

The CPI for a target year (*t*) is simply the ratio of the cost of the fixed basket in the target year (*t*) over the cost of the basket in base year (0) multiplied by 100. We multiply by 100 to simplify the expression of the CPI.

$$\text{CPI in year t} = \frac{\text{Cost of basket in year t}}{\text{Cost of basket in base year}} \times 100$$

The CPI is constructed so that a CPI of 100 means that, on average, there has not been any sustained, general change in prices from the base year. A CPI of less than 100 means that, on average, prices are lower than the base year. A CPI of more than 100 means that, on average, prices are higher than in the base year. Calculating the CPI is a huge undertaking done by the Bureau of Labor Statistics. The most important part of this measure is the basket of goods and services selected to represent *urban consumer spending*. What is contained in this basket? Rent, food and beverage, apparel, durable items, nondurables, household services, medical, transportation, plus other consumer expenses. Durable items are things made to last—typically three years or more. Examples of durable goods are furniture, consumer electronics, automobiles, and appliances. Nondurables or soft goods are items not designed to last. Paper products, clothing, and shoes are examples of nondurables.

While calculating the CPI, the basket is fixed year to year. The items and the amounts of those items in the basket are represented by each x_i in the formula given next. The subscript i is a label to designate the different items in the basket. You can see that exactly the same items (the xs) appear in the numerator and the denominator of the formula. The only difference between the numerator and the denominator are the year in which the prices are observed. We sometimes say that the basket is "weighted" by the prices in year t. That language reinforces that the basket is fixed and the prices indicate the magnitude of each of the sums in the numerator and the denominator.

$$\text{CPI}_t = \frac{P_1^t x_1 + P_2^t x_2 + P_3^t x_3 +}{P_1^{Base} x_1 + P_2^{Base} x_2 + P_3^{Base} x_3 +} \times 100$$

To demonstrate, we will use the data in table 47.1 to calculate a simple, fictitious price index.

Our fictitious basket is composed of forty coffees, twelve gallons of gas, two t-shirts, and one Internet subscription. Let's say 2008 is our base year and 2016 is our target year. If the items in table 47.1 represent the entire basket, the base year prices, and target year prices, we can use this data to calculate the price index for 2016. First, we calculate the cost of the fixed basket in each year.

Table 47.1. Basket contents and prices of items in basket of goods, 2008 and 2016 prices

Basket	2008 Prices	2016 Prices
Coffee × 40	$1.50	$1.75
Gallon of gas × 12	$4.35	$2.00
T-shirts × 2	$7.00	$6.95
Internet subscription × 1	$35.99	$54.99

Table 47.2. Cost of basket in years 2008 and 2016

Basket	Cost of basket weighted by 2008 prices			Cost of basket weighted by 2016 prices		
40 cups	$P_1^{2008} \bullet x_1$	= $1.50/cup • 40 cup =	$60.00	$P_4^{2016} \bullet x_4$	= $1.75/cup • 40 cup =	$70.00
12 g. gas	$P_2^{2008} \bullet x_2$	= $4.35/gas • 12 gas =	$52.20	$P_2^{2016} \bullet x_2$	= $2.00/gas • 12 gas =	$24.00
2 shirts	$P_3^{2008} \bullet x_3$	= $7.00/shirts • 2 shirts =	$14.00	$P_3^{2016} \bullet x_3$	= $6.95/shirts • 2 shirts =	$13.90
1 net	$P_4^{2008} \bullet x_4$	= $35.99/net • 1 net =	$35.99	$P_4^{2016} \bullet x_4$	= $54.99/net • 1 net =	$54.99
		Sum 2008 = $162.19			Sum 2016 = $162.89	

The base year CPI is always stipulated to equal 100. Using the numbers from table 47.2, we calculate CPI in 2016. Remember, the CPI for the target year is simply the ratio of the cost of the fixed basket in the target year over the cost of the basket in base year multiplied by 100.

$$\text{CPI in year } 2016 = \frac{\$162.89}{\$162.19} \times 100 = 100.43$$

An index of 100.43 is higher than 100 so we know that on average, prices have risen slightly over the time period 2008 to 2016.

CALCULATING INFLATION

An **inflation rate** is a percentage rate of change of a price index. The formula for the **percentage rate of change** is

$$\text{Percentage rate of change} = \frac{\text{Item 1} - \text{Item 2}}{\text{Item 1}} \times 100$$

According to the numbers in the example above, there has been a 0.43 percent increase in prices since the base year. We typically refer to movements as percent changes rather than as changes in index points.

The percentage rate of change of CPI is generally the best measure for adjusting payments to consumers when the intent is to allow consumers to continue to purchase as much at today's prices as they could purchase in an earlier time period.

The CPI is probably the most popular price index constructed by the government. It serves as an important economic indicator and as means of adjusting income payments. Over eighty million people (e.g., social security beneficiaries, people in the military, and Supplemental Nutritional Assistance Program recipients) have incomes indexed to CPI.

GDP DEFLATOR

In economics, the **GDP deflator**, sometimes referred to as an **implicit price deflator**, is a measure of the level of prices of all new, domestically produced final goods, and services in an economy. (Recall that GDP stands for gross domestic product, the total value of all final goods and services produced within that economy during a specified period.)

The GDP deflator measures the ratio of nominal GDP to the real measure of GDP. The formula used to calculate the deflator is:

$$\text{GDP deflator} = \frac{\text{Nominal GDP}}{\text{Real GDP}} \times 100$$

Recall that the nominal GDP of a given year is computed using that year's prices, while the real GDP of that year is computed using the base year's prices. If we rearrange the formula, we can show that dividing the nominal GDP by the GDP deflator and multiplying it by 100 will give the real GDP.

The GDP deflator is not based on a fixed basket of goods and services, like the CPI. The basket changes each year with people's consumption and investment patterns. Specifically, for the GDP deflator, the "basket" in each year is the set of all domestically produced goods, weighted by the market value of the total consumption of each good.

In practice, the difference between the deflator and a price index like the CPI is often relatively small. However, if the best measure of inflation needs to take into consideration a changing basket, there may be reasons to consider a deflator-type measure over a CPI-type measure. Remember, the "best" measure of inflation for a given application depends on the intended use of the data.

DISCUSSION AND EXERCISES

1. What is inflation? Who is inflation most likely to affect?
2. How is inflation measured, and why would we want to measure it?
3. What sorts of things should be included in the CPI? What sorts of things should not be? Why?

Chapter 48

Fiscal Policy

Fiscal means "relating to financial matters." When the word is paired with policy, it always means policy "relating to government revenue and expenditures." Government revenues are typically generated through taxes. So fiscal policy is the means by which a government adjusts its spending levels and tax rates to influence a nation's economy. Governments can purchase goods and services, collect taxes, and transfer payments from some consumers to others.

DEBT, DEFICIT, AND SURPLUS

Governments raise most of their revenue through fees for services, taxes on transactions, and taxes on income. A budget is an approved plan for spending over a period of time, typically a year. When tax revenues exceed spending, the budget is in **surplus**. When government spends more than its revenue in a given year, the budget is in **deficit**. An accumulation of deficits over time is **debt**. It follows that a budget can be in surplus and a country can still be in debt. Current and future tax revenues are used to pay back the debt that has accrued, along with any accumulated interest.

Fiscal policy is said to be tight, or **contractionary**, when the spending plan results in a surplus, and loose, or **expansionary**, when spending is higher than revenues, or results in a deficit. The change in the debt level is the focus of this categorization. Thus, a reduction of the deficit is said to be contractionary fiscal policy, even if the budget is in deficit.

Figure 48.1 shows the federal budget surplus over the period 1965–2018 produced by the Congressional Budget Office of the United States. Notable

238

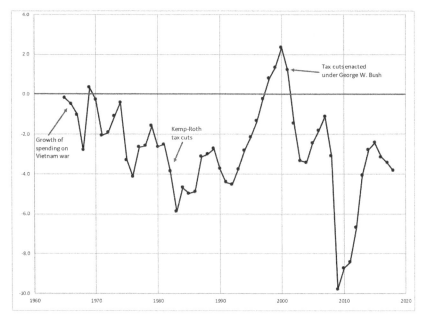

Figure 48.1.   Budget surplus as a percentage of GDP: 1965–2018[1]

on the figure are three large expansionary periods of fiscal policy: the military spending of the Vietnam War, the Kemp-Roth tax cuts of the early 1980s, and the program of tax cuts enacted under George W. Bush.

Aggregate demand is the sum total of the demand for all the goods and services in an economy. It is downward sloping when graphed against the price level. The higher the price level, all other factors remaining constant, the less people will demand. For this discussion, aggregate demand has all the same major components of GDP, that is C, G, I, and NX.

A fiscal expansion, or deficit spending, can occur through increasing spending by government or by consumers (where the latter can be enabled by tax cuts or increased transfer payments). If the government increases its purchases but keeps taxes constant, it increases aggregate demand directly. If the government cuts taxes paid by households, then household disposable income rises, and households have the option of spending more. A rise in spending will, in turn, raise aggregate demand. Suppose government raised taxes paid by households and then spent the money itself. In that case, if $1

---

1. This table was prepared by Cathleen Johnson using Congressional Budget Office data, archived at https://www.cbo.gov/about/products/budget-economic-data#11

spent by the government increased aggregate demand by more than $1, a net stimulus would be the result. If, on the other hand, $1 in government spending increases aggregate demand by less than $1, the result would be the opposite of a net stimulus.

Expansionary policy has an immediate effect. It changes the aggregate demand for goods and services. However, running a deficit also changes the composition of aggregate demand. When the government runs a deficit, it meets some of its expenses by issuing bonds, which means asking for loans. In doing so, the government competes directly with private borrowers. An argument against expansionary policy is that it will raise interest rates, which, in turn, will "crowd out" private investment to some degree. In other words, expansionary policy can reduce the fraction of output composed of private investment (I) in favor of increasing private consumption (C) and government spending (G).

In an open economy, fiscal policy also affects the exchange rate and the **balance of trade**, which is simply the difference between the value of a country's imports and exports over a given period. In the case of a fiscal expansion, the rise in interest rates due to government borrowing attracts foreign investment. The result is that in the short run, U.S. dollars become more expensive relative to foreign currencies. This strong dollar, or currency appreciation, causes imports to be relatively cheap and exports to be relatively more expensive. In the long run, however, another phenomenon can emerge: persistent government deficits can lead outsiders to distrust government assets and can cause a depreciation of the dollar.

As John Maynard Keynes saw it, the first impact of a fiscal expansion is to raise the demand for goods and services. This greater demand (either C or G) leads to increases in both output and prices. If the economy is in recession, with unused unemployed resources, then stimulation will lead mostly to more output without changing prices. However, if the economy is not in a recession, near full employment, stimulation will raise overall prices and have less impact on total output.

The ability of fiscal policy to affect output makes it a potential tool for economic stabilization. As we have discussed, in a recession, the government can expand aggregate demand and therefore put unemployed resources back into the economy. The complementary policy tool that completes the Keynesian theory is that when the economy is too hot and inflation is the problem, the government can run a surplus and help contract the economy. Practicing both expansionary and contractionary policy when needed should create a balanced budget on the whole.

DISCUSSION AND EXERCISES

1. What are the tools that governments use to implement fiscal policy?
2. What are the goals of contractionary fiscal policy on the one hand, and expansionary fiscal policy on the other?
3. What are the dangers of contractionary and expansionary policies, respectively?

Chapter 49

Monetary Policy

Monetary policy is the means through which a government, typically through a central bank, influences a nation's money supply.

Monetary policy decisions influence the amount of credit and money in the U.S. economy. The **Federal Open Market Committee (FOMC),** the monetary policymaking body of the Federal Reserve System, formulates the bulk of the nation's monetary policy. The assigned goals of monetary policy are to (1) maximize employment, (2) stabilize prices, and (3) control long-term interest rates.

The voting members of the FOMC consist of the seven members of the board of governors, the president of the Federal Reserve Bank of New York, and presidents of four other Reserve Banks who serve on a one-year rotating basis. The FOMC meets eight times per year. The Federal Reserve's primary instruments of monetary policy are (1) open market operations, and (2) the interest rate the Fed pays on bank reserves, and (3) reserve requirements.

Before 2008, **open market operations** were the most utilized of the three tools because they are the most flexible. Open market operations consist of Federal Reserve purchases and sales of financial instruments, usually securities issued by the United States.

When the Fed wants to increase reserves, it injects money into the banking system, or buys securities, paying for them by making a deposit to the account maintained at the Fed by the securities dealers' bank. When the Fed wants to reduce reserves, it withdraws money from the banking system, or sells securities, collecting money from those same accounts.

By trading securities, the Fed influences the amount of bank reserves. In a world of scarce reserves, this affects the **federal funds rate**, or the overnight lending rate at which banks borrow reserves from each other. This, in turn, affects the amount that lenders charge private borrowers.

Today the Fed mostly conducts policy by varying the interest rate on reserves. The **interest rate on reserves** is the interest rate that Federal Reserve Banks pay to commercial banks on the account balances they hold at the Fed (the Fed serves as a "bankers' bank"). As a result of "quantitative easing" programs and interest on reserves beginning in 2008, the U.S. banking system currently holds trillions of dollars in excess reserves (reserves above the required level). A higher rate on reserves encourages the banks to hold more excess reserves, which means making fewer loans and thus creating fewer deposits for the public to hold. Other things equal, the result is a contraction in the total supply of money held by the public. A lower rate on reserves has the opposite effect.

Reserve requirements are the portions of deposits that banks may not lend out. The Federal Reserve can change reserve requirements, thus forcing banks to hold more or less in reserve, thereby creating more or less money. Reserve requirements have not been changed in many years, however.

Monetary policy is referred to as being either expansionary or contractionary. An expansionary policy quickens the expansion of the total supply of money in the economy, whereas a contractionary policy slows the expansion of the money supply or even shrinks it.

If the supply of money and credit increases too rapidly over time, the result could be inflation, a decline in the purchasing power of each dollar over goods and services.

Sometimes, in order to dampen the threat of inflation, contractionary monetary policy slows the growth of the money supply. However, slowing the growth of the money supply can temporarily slow economic growth, increase unemployment, and depress borrowing and spending by consumers and businesses. Conversely, expanding the money supply too rapidly runs the risk of creating an unsustainable bulge or bubble in growth together with unwanted inflation.

Real (inflation-adjusted) interest rates matter to individuals and businesses. You can think of real interest rates as a cost of doing business. Interest payments are the cost of using someone else's money for your purposes. High real interest rates may hinder your ability to expand or grow your business, whereas falling real interest rates make business loans more affordable. Expansionary monetary policy may temporarily lower real interest rates, and thus may seem attractive to policy-makers, but it cannot keep them permanently low.

DISCUSSION AND EXERCISES

1. What are the primary goals of monetary policy?
2. What is the difference between expansionary and contractionary monetary policy?
3. How does the Federal Reserve typically conduct monetary policy?

Chapter 50

Public Choice

One of the fundamental insights of liberal political theory is that if human society is to be peaceful and prosperous, then we need the rule of law to hold us accountable for the consequences of our actions. But the people who administer the rule of law are regular human beings with the same issues, desires, and motivations as everyone else. Is there such a thing as a system of government that can work well even if staffed by governors who are not angels?

When it comes to designing the framework of a commercial society, the challenge is to structure the opportunities and rewards of the marketplace in such a way that it pays to pursue an agenda that is agreeable to customers, neighbors, and fellow human beings in general. No one says it is easy. The essential idea of Public Choice theory is that the same challenge presents itself to us when we are trying to structure the opportunities and rewards that go with governance.

The essence of Public Choice theory is the idea that the people who run governments, courts, and legislatures are the same kind of people as those who run businesses or households. Some people want money. Some want power. But anyone who spends a lifetime competing for power wants to use it for something.

James Buchanan won a Nobel Prize in Economics in 1986 for working through the theoretical implications of this insight. Buchanan himself, however, gave credit to his co-author, Gordon Tullock, for the insight that "if there is value to be gained through politics, persons will invest resources in efforts to capture this value."

First, note that Tullock did not say that everyone is selfish. What Tullock said is that if power is valuable, and if we see people competing to acquire power, we know that they have their reasons for competing. How much they are willing to spend competing for the prize will be limited by the value of the prize. If we see candidates spending more and more, that is evidence that the prize is getting bigger.

Second, note that Tullock did not intend this as pessimistic or depressing. He did not say that the process of political competition is especially perverse, or that it favors the worst people. Tullock's simple question was what if political leaders are a lot like everyone else? What if they are neither angels nor devils? What if they are basically normal people, and respond to costs and benefits just like everyone else?

As noted previously, Adam Smith saw that we need legislators to provide a framework of rules so that in the marketplace, we treat each other in civilized ways. The Public Choice insight is that we also want legislators themselves to operate within a civilizing framework of rules. If the people who govern us do not seem to be good people, it is easy to complain that we need to elect better people. At all levels of institutional design, however, the real task is to design a framework that leads imperfect human beings as they are to act in ways that serve the common good.

A crucial insight of realistic political philosophy is that the rules of the game are built and then rebuilt from the inside, by a subset of the players themselves, players who compete, negotiate, and compromise with one another. People can be terrifyingly overconfident in the rightness of their vision. If you are wrong in the marketplace, your trading partners say your offer is not good enough. They walk away, and you go back to the drawing board in search of a better idea. The damage is inherently limited. By contrast, when you have given your life competing for the power to achieve your political vision at the expense of people who do not share it, you will not necessarily care that the people who are paying for your dream do not actually want what you are buying with their money. Nowhere to be found is the kind of discipline that, in the marketplace, makes us pay a price for such overconfidence.

When people acquire the power to rule, and thus to reframe the rules going forward, what stops them from pursuing their agenda at the expense of others? It is a hard question, and there may not be a good answer. What Buchanan thought, and what he credits the Framers of the American Constitution for realizing, is that the constitutional part of constitutional democracy is the part that limits what democratically elected rulers have a right to do. We are not a constitutional democracy unless some things are beyond the reach of majorities. The winning party, for example, does not get to take advantage of its majority status to call for a vote on whether the minority party should permanently lose the right to vote.

Because of the Constitution, legislators have to obey the law of the land just like everyone else. Or at least, that is the theory. No one has ever believed there is any sure-fire way of achieving that goal. It is one of the respects in which adulthood is about coming to terms with an absence of guarantees. The Framers understood this. They believed that eternal vigilance is the price of liberty. They gave us a legislative branch consisting of a Congress with two houses, plus an executive branch headed by the president, plus a judicial branch answerable to the Supreme Court. The aim was to divide power as much as possible without making it ineffective. They divided power further between the federal and state governments, and enshrined freedom of the press in the First Amendment, all of which they hoped would create a rule of law that imposes some constraints on even the highest offices. That is all we can do.

DISCUSSION AND EXERCISES

1. How does Public Choice portray politicians and government workers? What are their motivations?
2. Why might a society wish to limit the actions that a government may take?
3. Public Choice economics applies observations of human behavior in markets to political concerns. Should it? Are politicians motivated by the same sorts of things as everyone else, or are they fundamentally different?

Chapter 51

Corruption[1]

Which social arrangements have a history of fostering progress and prosperity? One answer, following Adam Smith, is that *if* the right framework of rules—plus decent officiating—steers us away from buying and selling monopoly privilege and steers us toward being of service to the people around us, we indeed will be part of the engine that drives human progress and the wealth of nations.

However, to have a rule of law framework within which markets can grow a healthy nation, officials must exercise oversight. Officials not only enforce rules, but must also interpret, amend, and so on. Smith saw this, and perceived a further, chronically tragic reality: namely, this power to oversee markets is what crony capitalists are buying and selling.

Smith's observation changes everything. Imagine concentrated power in the hands of the worst ruler in living memory. Now, assume what you know all too well: namely, concentrated power actually does fall into the hands of people like that. As a preliminary, then, when trying to imagine what would be ideal, we can ask two questions. We can ask, "Ideally, how much power would be wielded by people like *that*?" Or we can ask, "Ideally, how much power would be wielded by ideal rulers?"

Which of these questions about ideals is actually relevant?

The paradigm of corruption consists of officials taking bribes, and thereby treating their fiduciary authority as a service that they have a right to buy and sell for personal gain. Yet, while using public office for private gain is the paradigm of corruption, it is not a definition. Corruption can be a child of greed, to be sure, but also of other vices. For example, seeking to appoint your

---

1. David Schmidtz, "Corruption," *Performance & Progress*, ed. S. Rangan (London: Oxford Press, 2015), pp. 490–464.

brother to be attorney general can cross the line without being an example of greed. (Consider that there is no rule against hiring the best candidate for the job, but what if your brother is the best candidate? A nepotism rule might limit corruption by forbidding you to hire your brother. If no one doubts that Bobby Kennedy is the best candidate for attorney general, that makes a difference to whether appointing him is corrupt, but not to whether appointing him violates the nepotism rule. Again, as we have said, morality is not simply about following rules. Rules cannot handle everything.)

Or, a politician might overlook the crimes of a colleague out of party loyalty, which would count as corrupt regardless of whether it is done for personal gain, and would count as an abuse of responsibility without being an abuse of power.

Needed regulations become more complex over time, in part because new regulations will need to fit into an existing regulatory environment that is itself increasingly complex. As this happens, it becomes increasingly true that the only people who know enough to design, interpret, and apply regulations will be the very people whom the regulations are supposed to regulate. Nowadays, bankers write banking reforms, insurance companies write health insurance reforms, and so on. Such regulators have a history of responding exactly as one would expect, by designing regulations that reduce consumer access to alternative providers.

Adam Smith wondered how stable a community could be in the face of a tendency for its political infrastructure to decay into crony capitalism: mercantilists lobby for subsidies for exporters, protectionists lobby for tariffs or other trade barriers to choke off competition from importers, and monopolists pay kings for a license to be free from competition altogether. Partnerships between big business and big government culminate in big subsidies. These ways of compromising freedom are sold to voters as protecting the middle class, but often their true purpose is to transfer wealth and power from ordinary citizens to well-connected elites. As a result, an ordinary citizen's pivotal relationships are not with free and equal trading partners but with bureaucrats: people whose grip on our community is so tight that we cannot walk away from such terms of engagement as they unilaterally propose. Thus, we reinvent feudalism. We are at the mercy of lords. Corruption makes us less free, not only less wealthy.

So, is there any remedy? Do communities have any tools for limiting the risk of corruption? Again, as Adam Smith understood, we face a conundrum. If our community is to achieve a rule of law, there has to be officiating. We are going to need good referees, and give them the power to take nonconsensual and fraudulent transfers off the table. If we can do that, then players will learn to pursue their interests in mutually advantageous

ways—positive for everyone *involved* in a trade and not a negative for anyone *affected* by it.

But again, we need to give our referees the power to keep the players in
line, and that is a problem, because one of the games that players are playing
is the game of winning elections that give them access to political power.
If we keep trying to create ever more power to control corruption, then the
prize for winning the power game is getting bigger, and the power that we
give the winning candidates to push *our* agenda is also power to push *their*
agenda. And if we create political power worth billions, then the competition
to win control of that power will tend to be won by billionaires. It stands to
reason that the process by which people gain political appointment would
systematically tend, and *increasingly* tend, to select the wrong person for the
job. The truism that power corrupts implies that randomly selected officials
would be corruptible. Yet, the truism is misleadingly optimistic. The realistic worry is worse. Namely, the process of selecting officers is not random.
We *select* for corruption. It is not a randomly selected fox but the most ravenous fox that tends to be willing to pay the most for the job of overseeing
the henhouse. In a democracy, at least we can vote against the most ravenous
fox, but what if the most ravenous fox also is the one who is willing to spend
the most to create the appearance of charisma? What if the most ravenous
fox is also the most adept at convincing voters that voters have nothing to
lose by giving a charismatic leader more power? If the fox can make voters
see politics as a team sport, and can convince voters that the fox is the home
team, then voters will cheer for the fox even as the fox devours them.

Our least concentrated power is our liberty as equal citizens to walk away
from bad deals: the liberty to say no as individuals, that is, to *vote with our
feet*. This is the liberty that we aim above all to protect: the liberty simply to
be a separate person with a right to walk away. This is the liberty that separates liberal from feudal society. An effective right to exit a relationship limits
how corrupt your partner can be.

As mentioned earlier, when we were discussing Adam Smith on progress,
the crucial bottom line regarding the right to walk away is that freedom in
commercial society involves *depending* on many, yet being at the *mercy* of
none.

DISCUSSION AND EXERCISES

1. In a system in which some men govern other men, is it even possible to
   live without corruption? If it isn't, what is the best that can be done?
2. A commercial society brings with it some level of regulation, and the level
   of regulation grows over time. When that happens, people in control come

to use that regulation to benefit some at the expense of others. Is there any way to stop this from happening?

3. Public choice economics cautions us not to expect more from politicians than we would expect from anyone else. But Adam Smith points out that human flourishing increases when we serve each other. Human flourishing has, without question, increased. Have we found a way to expect just enough from politicians, or could we somehow do better?

Part VI

PERSONAL AND BUSINESS FINANCE

Earning money is no guarantee you will be able to live well, or help others live well, later in life. To live well later in life, you need to save and invest wisely. To know how to save and invest wisely, you need to understand the role of financial institutions as well as when to use credit, and how to best save and invest for the future.

There will be crises. In a way, crises are normal. Your house or car will need expensive repairs. You or a loved one may have expensive health issues. You may lose your job. You may start a business that turns out to be a mistake and ends up costing you a lot of money. You don't want to put yourself in a situation where you are always reacting to the most immediate cash crunch instead of saving and investing so as to be prepared for whatever lies ahead. Most obviously, you don't want to wake up someday to find that you have not saved enough for your retirement. You will make financial decisions, and the right answers won't always be obvious. But if you understand the basics, you can face these decisions knowing you did your best to be prepared.

Some of the financial concepts we discuss will pertain more to business. Other concepts pertain more to personal or household finance. However, all of the concepts can be applied to both contexts. They can also be applied to other contexts as well, for instance, how well your local, state, and federal governments are managing financial resources.

Chapter 52

Accounting Basics

Why do we need accounting? Suppose an entrepreneur with a chain of one hundred retail stores in different cities wanted to know how each store was performing. The managers, reporting to the entrepreneur, would use accounting information to help refine and answer this question. In the end, everyone needs to know how to interpret and how far to trust accounting information.

Accounting is regulated by a set of accounting principles and standards which practitioners of accounting, accounting scholars, and governmental bodies establish, using input from various stakeholders such as industry, investors, and other users and beneficiaries of accounting information.

THE LANGUAGE OF BUSINESS

All businesses require assets. Most generate revenue (sales), incur costs, and take on debt. What is left after costs are deducted from revenue (sales) is **profit** or **loss**. **Equity** is what is left after debt is subtracted from assets.

Accounting is often referred to as the language of business. This is because all businesses need to generate economic exchanges with customers (generate sales or revenue), and have economic exchanges with employees and suppliers (payment for these resource inputs). Firms also hopefully generate an excess of revenues over costs: a profit. And, of course, they need assets (inventory, facilities, equipment, and the like). Hence, it is not unusual to hear entrepreneurs and business people discussing things like sales volume, be it from last week or last quarter, profits, and acquisition or disposal of assets. Read the financial press and watch the business news on TV and you will see that the language of business revolves around accounting. We want to help you to better understand this language.

Success in business requires a basic understanding of accounting. Perhaps more importantly, it also can help you as an individual. After all, you can view your household as a small business or micro-economy. Households have revenue in the form of the wages and salaries they earn. They incur costs for food, shelter, clothing, transportation, education, taxes, and other services. Your household also has assets. Think of all of the things you own. Most households also have debt. Debt includes what they owe on credit cards, home mortgages, and automobile loans. Some households also have education loans. Finally, your household has either an excess of assets over debt or the opposite, you owe more than the value of your assets.

ACCOUNTING STATEMENTS

At the outset, we need to mention that accounting statements do not capture all costs, assets, or debts that a firm may incur. You have learned about opportunity costs, and these are not indicated in accounting records. You also may believe that your most valuable resource is the trust you have built up over years of ethical business. But trust is an intangible. It is not explicitly accounted for. Still, a business will lose if it comes to be seen as less trustworthy.

Have you ever said you owe someone a favor? This is a form of debt but is again not recorded. Imagine a fire starts in a commercial building, and one of the janitors on the night shift quickly responds by calling the fire department. As the firefight progresses, the president of the company is found in her office, overcome by smoke. Her life is saved, and she is profoundly grateful to everyone, especially the night shift janitor, but nowhere on the accounting books is her feeling of indebtedness recorded. You need to keep this in mind when you interpret accounting statements and information. Accounting information is useful, but it is never the whole picture.

Records of business transactions are gathered into two major financial statements: the balance sheet and the profit-and-loss statement.

BALANCE SHEET

A balance sheet shows the assets, liabilities, and equity of the business. It is referred to as a balance sheet because the total value of the assets must balance, or equal the liabilities and equity. The basic accounting equation is: $A = L + E$, where A = assets, L = liabilities, and E = equity.

An **asset** is anything that the firm owns. There are two points here.

First, assets are only things that the firm owns. In general, assets can include cash, inventory, supplies, equipment, and buildings. By contrast, employees are crucial to the business, but they are not represented on the balance sheet despite the fact that the business may have made substantial investments in their training. Again, the business may depend on roadways, a legal system, and the marketplace itself, but if the business does not own those things, then it would not represent them on its balance sheets as assets.

Second, there may be debt associated with an asset. For example, the business may own buildings, but it may have borrowed money from a bank to buy those buildings.

A **liability** is what the firm owes to others. "Debt" is also another term used for liability. The entities that are owed could be individuals, suppliers, banks, bondholders, the government (for taxes), or any entity that is owed financial resources. **Equity** represents financial interests the owners (investors) have in the firm. Regardless of what the owners invested in the firm, the value of equity is the assets less the liabilities or debt. If in the extreme case where liabilities or debt is greater than assets, then the firm has a negative equity.

On a proper balance sheet, assets are listed in a particular order defined by how quickly they can be converted to cash. We call this an asset's **liquidity**. The most liquid assets are called **current assets**, which means that they can be converted into cash or cash equivalents within a year. The most liquid asset is cash itself, so cash on hand is usually the first item listed, as you can see from the sample balance sheet (table 52.1). For firms that carry inventory, the next item listed as a current asset would be inventory, because most inventory is held for sale where the sale is expected within a few weeks or months.

Table 52.1. ABC Company balance sheet, year ending December 31, 2015

Assets		Liabilities & equity	
Current assets		Current liabilities	
Cash	$40,000	Accounts payable	$30,000
Inventory	$80,000	Taxes payable	$10,000
Total	$120,000	Bank loan	$20,000
		Total	$60,000
Long-term assets		Long-term liabilities	
Building	$100,000	Mortgage	$50,000
Equipment	$30,000	Bank loan	$30,000
Land	$20,000	Total	$80,000
Total	$150,000	Equity	$130,000
Total assets	$270,000	**Total liabilities & equity**	$270,000

Liabilities, in a similar way, are listed in the order of how soon they need to be repaid. A **current liability** is one that comes due and must be paid within a year.

PROFIT-AND-LOSS STATEMENT

A profit-and-loss statement is a summary for a period of time of all of the sales or revenue of a firm, its expenses, and the resulting profit (or loss). The time period is at the discretion of the firm, but most firms have monthly, quarterly, and annual profit-and-loss statements.

Once again there is a basic equation that captures the profit-and-loss statement. This is:

$$P = S - CGS - SGA - T;$$

where
P = profit or loss,
S = sales or revenue,
CGS = cost of goods and services sold,
SGA = selling and general administrative expenses, and
T = taxes

A sample profit and loss statement is shown in table 52.2. Note, profit is shown before taxes and after taxes.

A balance sheet and a profit-and-loss statement serve different purposes. A balance sheet is meant to show what a company is worth, all things

Table 52.2. ABC Company profit-and-loss statement, year ended December 31, 2015

Total sales	$700,000
Less: Cost of goods sold	$350,000
Gross Profit	$350,000
Less: SGA	
Advertising	$70,000
Salespeople	$80,000
Management salaries	$140,000
Travel	$15,000
Miscellaneous	$10,000
TOTAL SGA	$315,000
Net profit	$35,000
Income Taxes	$12,000
Net profit (after taxes)	$23,000

considered. A profit-and-loss statement, by contrast, is meant to show whether a company is profitable at a given moment. When the two are used together, they help us to assess both whether a company is operating profitably right now, and whether it is headed in the direction of sustained profitability.

CASH FLOW

Here is an important tip: Sometimes the key question is not whether your business is projecting a profit or whether your household net worth is positive. Sometimes, the big question is a question of *when*. The question of when is a question of cash flow. While profit is simply revenue minus cost, the concept of **cash flow** is sensitive to timing. That is, are revenues coming in at the right time? Perhaps your business will be profitable a year from now, but if you do not have the cash flow to cover next month's payroll, then next year's profitability may not save you. If your household net worth is substantial, that is great, but unless you have the cash flow to cover next month's tuition bill, your household net worth is not doing what you need it to do. In short, what matters is cash flow: not only *how much* money you have, but *when*.

DISCUSSION AND EXERCISES

1. Why do firms construct profit-and-loss statements? What information do these statements provide?
2. In what sense, if any, is the language of accounting an exercise in ethical communication?
3. What assets and liabilities would appear on your personal balance sheet? What would improve your position?
4. Compare and contrast the ideas of profit and cash flow.

Chapter 53

Compound Growth

Financial dealings are processes. They happen over time. That means that when we are weighing costs and benefits, we will need to weigh them as they arise and need to be accounted for in particular time periods. Perhaps at some point, you need to repay a $100,000 loan that you took out when you bought a house, but the more relevant question can be, how much of that loan do you need to repay *this month*? On the other side of the ledger, you need to consider how your savings and investments can grow over time if you handle them well.

Many things grow over time. Growth rates are rarely predictable, but growth per se is a common phenomenon. A newborn baby may grow very rapidly at first, then more slowly. A new business venture may grow from a small first-year sales volume to a very large sales volume in subsequent years. Walmart, a nearly sixty-year-old enterprise, started as a small store of less than 20,000 square feet in rural Arkansas with less than $1 million in annual sales. Today, Walmart is a $450 billion global enterprise, with nearly 5000 stores in over a dozen countries.

An explanation of compound growth begins with definitions. You need to understand the time value of money, which is how much a dollar today is worth in the future, and how much a dollar received in the future is worth today.

The **future value** (FV) is how much something today will be in value at a specified later time. In our example, this will be how much you will owe in ten years from now. The **present value** (PV) is the starting value that will grow over time. In this case, it is the loan you take on today. Suppose you borrow $40,000 for your college expenses. We need to know how much you will owe when it is time to repay that loan, so we need to know the interest rate. The **interest rate** (i) on the loan is similar to a growth rate, since it is the rate at which the debt will grow. In our case, we use an annual interest or growth factor of 8 percent.

The information we just described can be put into the following formula:

$$FV = PV(1 + i)^n$$
$$FV = 40,000(1 + 0.08)^{10}$$
$$FV = 40,000(2.1589)$$
$$FV = \$86,356$$

Thus, at the end of ten years, you will owe $86,356. If you cannot make this payment when the loan comes due, you may need to take out another loan where you make monthly payments to pay this debt. Of course, this new loan will have its own interest rate and duration.

LONG THINKING AND GROWTH

Consider the preceding example with a bit more detail. You enter college at eighteen and graduate at twenty-two. Your loan is due when you are thirty-two. But when the time comes, you are not in a good position to repay, so you take out another ten-year loan, again with a lump sum due at the end when you are forty-two. At age forty-two, your first child is getting ready to go to college, and you have other expenses and you think, "I will be in a better position to pay off this loan when I am fifty-two," so again you take another ten-year lump sum loan. In all of these situations, the loan continues at 8 percent annual interest. How much will you owe at age fifty-two? The $86,356 that was due when you were thirty-two needs to be multiplied by the growth factor of 2.1589 (see earlier), and when this is done, you owe $186,434. Then you take out another loan, and this $186,434 needs to be multiplied by the growth factor of 2.1589, and the result is $402,492. Unfortunately, at age fifty-two you have an unpleasant surprise of your partner dying unexpectedly, and with that the loss of your partner's income. You feel lucky because your house has appreciated in value considerably, and even better, it is almost paid off. You know in ten more years, you can collect social security, and you also have some retirement savings. You also feel lucky, because someone is willing to lend you the $402,492 in return for a lien on your house in case you default. Again the interest rate is 8 percent. The amount you will owe in ten years when you are sixty-two years old is $868,940, not far away from $1 million. Stated alternatively, your $40,000 college loan taken out a bit more than forty years ago is now a shockingly large amount. It looks like you will need to delay retirement. Keep in mind, you are not the only one who can borrow money and get yourself into the situation like this. For instance, the federal government has an accumulated financial debt of roughly $22 trillion as of early 2019.[1] This amount generally keeps growing because the government keeps borrowing (as in the case given earlier) to pay off past debt, all the while running up ever more debt.

The government on occasion will issue zero-coupon bonds. These are bonds that do not pay interest to the bondholder every month, quarter, or year, but at the end of the duration of the bond. This is similar to the situation above where you borrowed a set amount today and paid no interest and let it accumulate (grow) for a set period of time. As an example, if you purchased a $10,000, thirty-year, 8 percent, zero-coupon bond from the federal government how much would it pay you in thirty years? The answer using the earlier given formula is:

$$FV = 10,000(1 + 0.08)^{30}$$
$$FV = 10,000(10.0627)$$
$$FV = \$100,627$$

EXTREMELY LONG-TERM THINKING AND GROWTH

In the aforementioned example, you learned about how compounding of interest (a form of growth) on a debt can result in very large future obligations, especially if that obligation is a long time in the future, and if the interest rate is high. We can use the same formula that was used for debt to look at savings and investment.

A very small amount of money, when invested for an extremely long time, even at a low rate of growth, results in an extraordinary amount of money in the future. When we talk about an extremely long time, we will use 1000 years. You will likely not be around in 1000 years, but set that aside for the moment. Perhaps you are of a mind that this investment could be earmarked for some cause (perhaps your university, city, or church) to be paid in 1000 years.

The question we would like to raise is this: If you invested $1 today (something most everyone could do) and it could gain (grow) 2 percent per year (adjusted for inflation) how much would it be worth in 1000 years? The correct answer is here:

$1 invested today at 2 percent interest for 1000 years

$$FV = \$1(1 + 0.02)^{1000}$$
$$FV = \$398,264,652$$

Now assume that you are a wise investor, and you think others will manage the money wisely after you die. Thus, you surely think you

---

1. www.treasurydirect.gov

could earn 2.1 percent per year over 1000 years. Will this make much of a difference? The answer is a resounding yes. Very small differences in growth over a very long time have extraordinary results. The computations are here.

$1 invested today at 2.1 percent interest for 1000 years

$$FV = \$1(1 + 0.021)^{1000}$$
$$FV = \$1,061,065,239$$

Most people are shocked to learn that if they invested $1 today at 2.1 percent for 1000 years, their descendants or beneficiaries would have $1 billion in 1000 years.

PRESENT VALUE

If you understand how to compute future value, you have the basis for understanding present value. **Present value** is the worth today of money received in the future. The future can be any period of time, be it a year, decade, or twenty-five years. Businesses often compute the present value of various projects or investments in new market offerings, asking, for example, suppose we expect a new product to generate net income of a million dollars per year for at least ten years. The question is, what is that product worth right now? How much should we be willing to pay right now for that expected return?

Present value is, however, more than a business concept. It is also a concept you can use to manage your household or your individual investments. One part of managing your individual investments may be deciding how much to invest in your education. In the United States, you have free access to public education through grade 12. Part of your decision to invest in education should be focused on lifetime income, and how lifetime income is affected by education level. Before that, you need to consider the present value (PV) formula. Begin with the future value (FV) equation and show how PV can be derived from that formula.

$$FV = PV (1 + i)^n$$
$$PV = FV/(1 + i)^n$$

Say that although you plan to work for at least forty years, you want to see what the present value of your education would be worth for your first ten years after graduation.

Here, i is not technically the interest rate, but what you would want as a return on an amount of money you had today to invest. You might consider it your opportunity cost of money. In business, it is often referred to as the cost of capital. What could you do with this money today, other than invest in education, and what type of return would it pay you? Assume a 5 percent return or cost of capital.

As mentioned above, you could extend the increased earnings to a longer time horizon, maybe even forty years. We are trying to keep this example simple.

The answer, using the preceding formula, is:

$$PV = \$40,000/(1.05)^1 + \$40,000/(1.05)^2 + \$40,000/(1.05)^3 + \$40,000/(1.05)^4 + \$40,000/(1.05)^5 + \$40,000/(1.05)^6 + \$40,000/(1.05)^7 + \$40,000/(1.05)^8 + \$40,000/(1.05)^9 + \$40,000/(1.05)^{10}$$

$$PV = \$40,000/1.05 + \$40,000/1.1025 + \$40,000/1.1576 + \$40,000/1.2155 + \$40,000/1.2763 + \$40,000/1.3401 + \$40,000/1.4071 + \$40,000/1.4775 + \$40,000/1.5513 + \$40,000/1.6289$$

$$PV = \$39,216 + \$36,281 + \$34,554 + \$32,908 + \$31,341 + \$29,849 + \$28,427 + \$27,073 + \$25,785 + \$24,556$$

$$PV = \$309,990$$

Thus, today the economic value of your college education, with ten years of increased earnings would be $309,990. If you computed this for the entire forty years, the answer would be well over $1 million.[2] You can use the preceding formula to put in different assumptions, assumptions about your annual increased earnings, the number of years of increased earnings, and your cost of capital or cost of money. You can also use this formula to help you decide how much you might be willing to invest today in your education. This amount should be less than the present value of that investment. Usually, it is considerably less. We hope you will customize this application to your situation.

DISCUSSION AND EXERCISES

1. Suppose as a result of education you earned an additional $20,000 per year for ten years and $50,000 per year for the following ten years. How much would it be worth today? What assumptions do you need to make to answer this question?

---

2. https://www.newyorkfed.org/medialibrary/media/research/current_issues/ci20-3.pdf

2. How might you live differently knowing about the present and future value of money? What sorts of decisions that you make would be impacted knowing these things?
3. What questions would you ask if you were trying to decide whether you should borrow money to attend college?

Chapter 54

Saving, Borrowing, and Investing

As an individual or head of household, you will often use the services of a bank. Almost everyone has a checking account or a credit or debit card, and we use banks for any number of other things too. Banks are so convenient that we tend to take them for granted, but we really shouldn't. They are the backbone of commercial society. You can find a bank usually within a few miles of your home, and ATMs (automatic teller machines) can be found in many high-traffic areas, such as supermarkets, gasoline service stations, and even on street corners.

SAVING

Banks also are a common place where people save money for their future needs. One can easily open a savings account that pays interest or purchase a **certificate of deposit** (CD). CDs are a way to save money over different lengths of time, usually from ninety days to five years, and they usually pay a fixed interest rate, typically higher than a standard savings account pays. They usually can be purchased in $500 or $1000 increments. If you purchased a five-year $1000 CD and it paid 3 percent annual interest, the amount you would receive in five years would be

$1000(1.03)^5$ or ($1000 × 1.1593) or $1159.30.

If you are in the market to purchase a CD, be sure to shop around for a competitive interest rate; also examine closely the terms of the CD, specifically if there are any penalties for early withdrawal. In most cases, if you withdraw early the interest rate diverts to a lower rate, so you should be comfortable doing without the money you deposit for the length of time you agreed to leave your money in the certificate.

If you are going to do well in life, you need a retirement savings plan. Part of your plan can include the required payments you make, as well as those your employer makes, to the U.S. social security program. That will not provide you with the income you will want to have upon retirement, though. Many firms have additional retirement programs, where employers and employees contribute each payroll period to the employee's retirement savings or investment account. If your employer has a matching program, try to take advantage of it to the extent possible. For instance, if your employer will match your contributions up to 7 percent of your salary, then you could get 14 percent of your salary each pay period contributed to your retirement savings or investment account. These funds would then grow tax-free until you retire and withdraw funds. In many cases you can decide how to invest your funds, including the purchase of shares of stock in any number of companies or mutual funds. It may also include purchasing debt instruments such as debt issued by the U.S. Treasury or various corporations in the form of bonds. These topics are discussed later.

BORROWING

Banks are a common source of loans to individuals and households. You can use loans to help you purchase an automobile, buy a home, and so on. Perhaps most relevant to you right now, you can use loans to cover the costs of a college education. Loans have to be paid back at some point, of course, and you have to pay interest on the amount you borrow, but loans can be taken for different lengths of time, and at different interest rates. Generally, loans over a longer time period require a higher interest rate. You will want to shop for a competitive rate, especially if the loan is a thirty-year home mortgage! Over the term of a thirty-year mortgage, you will pay a large amount of cumulative interest, so consider a fifteen-year mortgage instead. If you opt for the latter, your monthly payments will be higher but you will pay off the loan in half the time, and you will save a lot of money that you otherwise would have paid as interest on the money you borrowed. You will likely take out many loans over the course of your life, and you should understand the terms under which you borrow before you sign anything.

How do banks decide who will get a loan? Banks loan money to individuals and businesses, but it is important to remember why the banks make loans in the first place. Banks loan money that customers have deposited into their savings accounts. Banks charge more interest on loans than they pay on deposits. This is how they stay in business. It is imperative, then, that banks only loan money to people and businesses that will repay them on time. When a loan is considered, the bank looks at what are often referred to as the 3 Cs of lending: capacity, collateral, and character.

Capacity is the ability of the borrower to make the required payments, monthly or otherwise, to pay off the loan. When an individual borrows, the bank will often consider that person's credit score.[1] A credit score is an index that takes into account your past and current credit-related behavior, and your ability to repay a loan. The most commonly used score is known as a FICO score. This is a number that ranges between 300 and 850, and is a popular scoring system that most banks use to assess the relative risk involved with making loans. The higher a person's score, the less risky that person is to the bank. This matters in terms of whether a person will even be offered a loan in the first place, but it matters on another level too: people with lower credit scores represent higher risk to the bank, and the bank makes up for this risk by charging those people higher interest rates. So, while you will want to pay your bills on time in order to be a good person, you have another motivation too.

The second C is **collateral**. Whether you have collateral is another thing that banks take into account when they decide whether to lend money to you. Collateral is an asset you can pledge that makes it safer for the bank to lend you money. If you obtain a loan for a car, the bank is likely to put a lien on the title of that car, which gives them the right to repossess the car if you don't make the payments. In this case, you are minimizing the risk that the bank is taking when it issues you a car loan. You do this by offering the car itself as collateral to secure the loan. There will be times when collateral is unavailable, as is the case with student loans. For this type of loan, you may need a cosigner, someone who agrees to assume your payments if you fail to make them. This is why parents are often involved with their children's student loans, and why they are typically very nervous about the process. By cosigning, they agree to make the payments if the person who took out the loan doesn't.

Finally, borrowers are examined for their **character**. Character is hard to judge, but it includes such things as your overall trustworthiness, reliability, and reputation. Some aspects of character can be picked up in your credit score, such as evidence that you have a history of being reliable in making payments on loans or credit cards. Banks can also check things like arrest records, child support payment histories, and other public databases when assessing your character.

A note of caution: your reputation is important. When you take out a loan, your reputation will be at stake. If you miss payments, that will become part of your reputation. It will signal to lenders that you have a history of

---

1. http://www.myfico.com/CreditEducation/WhatsInYourScore.aspx

borrowing more than you can afford to repay, which will make it harder for you to get a loan in the future.

Student Loans

College is expensive; in some cases, very expensive. You might not be able to afford to pay for college as you go, which means you will need to find some other way. For most people, this means taking out loans to cover the cost. These are then paid back in the future when you can benefit from your education in the form of higher wages. College, when approached this way, is thus an investment. The first thing you need to ask yourself is if it is worth it. To answer this question, you will need to know two things: what college costs, and what your anticipated salary will be given what you choose to study. These are complicated things that you will need to research fully when the time comes, but there are couple of things that you should know before you even look into college. First, the average college degree in the United States costs roughly $250,000 to complete. Second, the average college-bound high school student would command a salary of roughly $25,000 per year in the workforce. The $100,000 of foregone salary is part of the $250,000 average total cost of a college education.

Student loans come in several varieties, but the most important thing you need to understand is that they are real debts which must be paid back. If you took out student loans to cover the entire $250,000 average cost of a college education, your monthly payments (assuming 6.8 percent interest) would be a little more than $2877 a month. For ten years. After ten years, you would have paid back $345,240 on that loan. It will be up to you to decide if you can afford that level of debt. You might decide to borrow less, saving money by living at home, going to community college for two years, or by going to a less expensive state school. If you "only" borrowed $100,000, your payments would be $1150 a month for ten years. At the end of ten years, you would have paid back $138,000 for that loan. Is a student loan a good investment? You will have to figure that out. Whatever your answer, you should probably not skip class too often. And whatever your answer, you should also know this: students loans are not dischargeable in bankruptcy, which we will cover later.

Automobile Loans

Auto loans are also very popular with young people. Once you have the responsibility of a job, you have to get to work. Often, this means buying your own car. The average new car in the United States costs over $36,000, while the average used car costs over $19,000.[2] Whichever way you go, a car is a big expense. And this is just the purchase price. You will also have to factor in the cost of ownership, which includes things like gas, repairs, registration costs, and insurance. The interest rates for automobile loans vary dramatically, and are very much linked to your credit score. People with good or great credit get loans at much lower rates.[3] People with excellent credit scores, between 740 and 850, get auto loans at 3.2 percent interest on average. People with average credit, with scores from 680 to 739, get 4.5 percent interest, on average. People with poor credit scores, 680 and below, get auto loans from 6.5 to 12.9 percent interest, on average. On a $20,000 auto loan, the difference between excellent and poor credit can be over $5500. There are real costs to having poor credit.

Mortgages

For most people, a mortgage will be the biggest loan they ever take. The median cost of a home in the United States is $200,000. That's a lot of money, but this only tells part of the story. There are some markets in the United States that are much more expensive. The median home price in San Jose, California, for example, is over a million dollars. Most people will be closer to the national median, but the point to remember here is that your choices will go a long way toward determining the quality of your financial life in years to come.

When do you borrow money to purchase a home? The answer to this question is different for everyone, but there are a few common elements that you should be aware of. At the simplest level, you need a place to live. You can (and likely will) rent for some time. Buying a home should not enter your thoughts until you are pretty sure that you will not be moving any time soon. Once you know that you will be staying long enough for it to make sense to buy a home, you then have to have saved enough for a down payment. A down payment is typically 20 percent of the total home price. Another thing to consider? The 36 percent rule. Almost all financial advisors will tell you that no more than 36 percent of your gross income should go to pay for debt. And this is all debt combined. If you have student loans and a car loan, this will leave less for you to spend on a house.

So if you want to buy the median house in the United States, which costs $200,000, you will want to have 20 percent of that total for a down payment. This means saving $40,000. You will have to finance the remaining

2. https://roadloans.com/blog/average-car-price
3. https://www.carsdirect.com/auto-loans/what-credit-score-do-you-need-for-an-auto-loan

$160,000 with a mortgage, which at 4.5 percent will cost you $811 a month for 30 years. You will end up paying $291,960 for that $100,000, so it might be in your interest to look into that 15 year mortgage after all.

But look at what has happened here. If you have $1150 in student loan payments, and a $400 car payment, and an $800 mortgage, you are paying out $2350 a month in debt payments alone. The average household income in the United States is about $4500. You would be over 50 percent of your gross household income in debt payments, but every financial advisor you meet will tell you that you need to keep that under 36 percent. And we haven't even considered other forms of debt yet, things like credit card debt.

Credit Cards

We typically don't think of credit cards as loans, but that is exactly what they are. Unlike debit cards, which draw money directly from your bank account, credit cards allow you to spend money that you might not have. A credit card is a loan that a financial institution gives you every month. The bank that issues your credit card decides how much credit you should have, typically by considering your FICO score along with your income. People typically get low credit limits at first, but they tend to increase over time with good financial behavior.

Like all loans, credit card debt has to be repaid with interest. Banks make money on loans and outstanding credit card balances. Hence, they will want you to borrow more as long as you remain credit worthy, but to consumers who use credit cards, interest charges are an expensive trap. The best advice is not to use your credit card at all unless you have a solid plan for paying off the balance before the interest charges can accumulate, because credit card interest rates are among the highest interest rates you will ever pay on borrowed money. The average interest rate on credit cards in the United States is over 15 percent. Many are over 20 percent. And people with very little credit history, people like you, get assessed the highest rates of all.

The long and the short of it is that you should be very judicious in the amount of debt that you take on. When you have loans to repay, and you often will, you should first pay off the loans with the highest interest rates. These will typically be your credit cards. Again, you have to understand that credit cards are not free money. On the contrary, they are typically the most expensive money you can borrow. They are what we might call "a dangerous servant and a terrible master." They are a valuable convenience, but don't let them tempt you to live beyond your means.

Bankruptcy

Some people do, of course, live beyond their means. Sometimes this is a matter of simple irresponsibility, but oftentimes it is a matter of changing circumstances. At any given point in time, we all make assumptions about our future financial health. You wouldn't take out a big mortgage, for example, if you didn't have a stable source of income. But mortgages typically last for 30 years, whereas the median length of time U.S. workers have worked for their present employers is just over four and a half years. There will be times when things don't go well. Medical emergencies, the deaths of family members, and economy-wide concerns well beyond the control of any individual can get in the way. What are people to do when they realize that paying their debts has gone from routine to impossible?

There was a time when people like this were sent to debtors' prison. Thankfully, that time is a matter of history rather than an ongoing practical concern. We have had bankruptcy laws in the United States since 1800, but what we now consider to be bankruptcy emerged in the middle of the nineteenth century as a way to allow people a humane and dignified way to restructure debts they can no longer pay, and remain productive members of society. Some debts are wiped clean, while others are restructured to allow repayment over longer periods of time without penalty. Sometimes property used as collateral is repossessed. Whatever the details, when people go through a bankruptcy process, it will hurt their ability to borrow money in the future. But they are able to start again, which is the important part. One thing to remember, though: student loans are not dischargeable in bankruptcy. That debt will always remain, which is ever more reason to act with great care when taking out student loans.

INVESTING

You may decide that you want to have more than savings and CDs at a bank, or perhaps you want to seek some higher returns, and are willing to take on more risk to get them. More risk is often necessary, because banks are federally insured, and thus your savings and CDs are relatively free from risk. If the bank were to go bankrupt, your savings and CDs would be safe. This kind of safety can only be purchased by trading off big returns.

Equity Instruments

There are many options for investing for higher expected rates of return than you get in your savings. Investing in stocks is the most common. Many companies are publicly traded, and that means that people can purchase shares of stock in the company. This means that shareholders are part own-ers of the company in which they hold shares of stock. Some of the stocks widely held by individuals in the United States include Apple, Coca-Cola, Walmart, and General Electric. While these companies are among the most well-known, there are thousands of publicly traded companies you can purchase shares in.

Stocks that are publicly traded have a price, which is determined by vari-ous holders of stock selling their stock at varying prices and different buyers paying varying prices. Thus, the supply of shares of stock and the demand for those shares act together to determine the price of a share of stock at any particular time when the stock market is open and trades occur. In short, it is a market like any other.

When you invest in a particular stock, you may look at financial ratios such as those we discussed previously. You might also look at the growth in the company or broader industry over the last few years, both in terms of sales and profit. However, it is never easy to decide how much you should be willing to pay for a stock. Remember, when you buy a share of stock in a particular company, you are buying a share that some other investor is selling at that price. Do you know something that the seller doesn't? (In some sense, this sort of trade is just like any other mutually beneficial trade, insofar as a seller prefers to give up the risk of owning that stock while a seller prefers to take on the risk. If the stock price continues to rise, it is easy to imagine that both buyer and seller are happy to have made the trade. However, we admit that when people are buying and selling just for the sake of an item's anticipated resale value, the trading does begin to look a bit like simple gambling, where one person wins only if other players lose.)

Investors in stocks often consider the earnings per share (EPS). EPS is determined by taking the most recent annual net profit after taxes, and dividing that by the number of shares of stock outstanding. For instance, if a company had a net profit after taxes of $5,000,000 and had one mil-lion shares outstanding then it would have $5 EPS ($5,000,000/1,000,000). From this, you can calculate the price to earnings ratio (P/E). The P/E is the price per share of stock divided by the EPS. If in the prior example, the price of a share of stock was $60 and its EPS was $5 then its P/E would be 12 ($60/$5).

Essentially, EPS is a number that answers the question: How much do I have to pay for a share of stock for each dollar of earnings it generates? Stocks with a high P/E (price to earnings ratio) are more costly, but that is not to say they are not a good investment. Generally, P/Es range from 8 to 20, however, some firms have a P/E below this range while others significantly higher.

Debt Instruments

Two types of popularly traded debt instruments are bonds, notes, and bills issued by the U.S. Treasury and corporate bonds.

The U.S. Treasury issues a variety of debt instruments that allows the U.S. government to borrow money from individual and other investors. Many of these investors in U.S. debt are foreigners. U.S. Treasury debt has a **maturity date**. A maturity date is a specified date when the principal and all remaining interest is due to be repaid. Maturity for U.S. Treasury bonds is thirty years. The U.S. Treasury also issues Treasury Bills and Notes. Treasury Bills are short-term debt instruments that mature in less than 365 days. The maturities are usually four weeks, thirteen weeks, twenty-six weeks, and fifty-two weeks. Treasury Notes usually mature in two years, three years, five years, seven years, and ten years. A Treasury bill, note, or bond is usually issued in $100 increments and can be purchased through an investment firm or directly from the Treasury.

When the Treasury issues new debt, it uses an auction. The auction sets the interest rate. The interest rate on U.S. government debt is viewed as very low risk because a default on the debt would essentially require the U.S. government to go bankrupt or collapse. A key advantage of U.S. Treasury debt obligations is that there is an active resale market. For instance, if you purchased a thirty-year bond, and then need to sell it seven years later, you will be able to do so. Of course, there is no guarantee you will be able to sell it for what you paid; that would depend on market conditions (that is, supply and demand). The point, though, is that you would be able to sell your asset relatively quickly if you wanted to. The person who buys the bond then becomes the person to whom the Treasury will owe the principal plus any remaining interest on the bond's maturity date (which in the example at hand is now twenty-three years down the line, because we are supposing that you bought the 30-year bond seven years ago).

Corporations often need to borrow for long term. When they do, they turn to the bond market. Corporate bonds vary in length but usually are between ten and thirty years. When a new issue of corporate bonds is made, it is usually auctioned off, and thus the financial markets set the price of the bond and hence the interest rate. For instance, a firm may issue bonds with a face value of $1000 that pay 6 percent interest, but as a result of the auction, the bonds may trade at $975, meaning the effective interest rate is greater than 6 percent, or the bond may trade for $1025 which would mean the effective interest rate is less than 6 percent.

People may invest in bonds because they pay a higher yield than a similar maturity U.S. Treasury debt instrument. Bonds also provide a regular stream of income reflected in the payment of interest (often monthly or quarterly).

They also allow the protection of principal, because at maturity, the face value of the bond is paid to the bondholder.

Corporate bonds are often rated for their quality. A high rating would pay a lower yield and vice versa. When investors purchase a portfolio of corporate bonds, they can better manage their investing risk. The portfolio may represent firms in different industries, of varying credit quality, and of varying maturities.

As with U.S. Treasury debt obligations, it is relatively easy to sell bonds in publicly traded companies. Thus, if you find you cannot wait for the bond to mature, you can sell it and hope to get what you paid for it, but you may receive less, or maybe more, than what you paid.

DISCUSSION AND EXERCISES

1. Why might a person borrow and invest money at the same time?
2. Some investments are inherently riskier than others. A savings account at a bank is insured by the federal government, but money invested in stocks is always at risk. What considerations must go into deciding what to invest in?
3. What does the ability to borrow money do for us? As a thought experiment, imagine what life would be like if borrowing money were impossible.

Chapter 55

Marketing Fundamentals

Markets work without marketing, but customers have to be able to find what they are looking for. Effective marketing can help with that.

> The best marketing doesn't feel like marketing.
>
> —Tom Fishburne

MARKETING DEFINED

Marketing is the practice of serving customer needs by developing, supplying, packaging, and pricing an offering in ways that help customers understand and appreciate a product's value, possibly even enhancing its value in the process. Some common marketing activities that you might observe in daily life include market analysis and research, transportation of goods, warehousing or storage of goods, wholesaling, retailing, merchandising, assortment building, packaging, advertising, personal selling, trade shows, warranties, branding, and credit and financing of purchases.

Utilities from Marketing

In most markets, buyers exchange money for services offered by sellers. The price reflects how much buyers are willing to give in exchange for the market offering.

A seller can offer to provide a particular service at a given price, but whether the offering is worth that price to a particular buyer is something that only the buyer can decide.

Four Kinds of Product Utility

1. **Form utility** refers to getting the product to buyers in a form that is useful to them. Both a CD and a cassette are ways of recording a concert, but neither is of any use to potential customers if they don't have the equipment to play them.
2. **Time utility** refers to getting the product to buyers at a time that is useful to them. People might be happy to pay a lot of money to attend a concert in the evening or during the weekend, but a show on Wednesday at 2 pm will not draw nearly as many people due to the inconvenient time.
3. **Place utility** refers to getting the product to buyers at a location that is useful to them. People might be willing to pay a lot for tickets to a show across town, but if the show is happening a hundred miles away, that's a problem. A more convenient place saves customers time and money.
4. Finally, **possession utility** refers to making it easier for buyers to take possession of the product. Delivering concert tickets to a customer's door is one example; making tickets available online is another. But perhaps the best example is allowing customers to pay by credit card, which brings a level of convenience that was previously unheard of.

MARKETING AND DEMAND

Because marketing helps to provide these utilities, it can influence customer preferences. What would the demand for housing be like if buyers had to make 360 monthly payments before they could take possession of a house? The possession utility created by the institution of mortgage lending makes all the difference in the world in terms of what customers can afford.

Or consider what we normally imagine when we think of advertising: creating a unique and appealing brand image. If you consider a typical demand curve, you can see that as price rises, the quantity demanded falls. But effective marketing can shift the demand curve to the right, so that buyers demand more at any given price. Effective marketing can make the demand curve steeper as well, so that demand does not fall as quickly when the price rises.

MARKETING AND SUPPLY

To a firm, effective marketing is a lot like inventing a more effective transportation network; it allows the firm to reach a larger customer base. If the firm's marginal cost of production declines as it deals in larger quantities, then selling the product can be profitable at a lower price.

Effective marketing can make a market work better in another way too. As firms develop their brand awareness and customer loyalty, the cost of retaining customers declines. In fact, the cost of finding and motivating a new customer can be several times the cost of retaining an existing customer. In short, high-quality marketing efforts that develop customer relations can result, in the long run, in customers being able to find better services at lower prices.

Because marketing efforts can expand demand and lower production cost at the margin, it can positively impact net revenues. Of course, some firms spend too much on marketing, which reduces profit.

MARKETING SHOULD BE USEFUL

The idea of marketing inevitably calls to mind high-pressure advertising and manipulative sales tactics. But people who work in marketing are agents of the seller, and sellers have to be able to trust the marketing people to do the best they can to sell the product.

This raises strategic questions, and ethical questions too. Why should buyers believe anything that an advertiser says? People who work in sales are agents of the seller, and buyers know that, but that means that people who work in sales have to be able to give buyers a reason to trust what they say. Sales people have to be able to say, "I work for salary, not for commission. I don't get paid extra if you decide to buy, so I'm just here to help." Or, sales people have to be able to say, "You can try this out yourself, or you can read the reviews, so you can have independent evidence that what I'm telling you is true." Or perhaps they need to be able to say, "My employer has a reputation that she spent years building, one satisfied customer at a time. You can trust me when I tell you that she doesn't want you to buy something that is not right for you." The bottom line is that sales and marketing people are agents of the seller, but both ethics and a long-term profit incentive give sellers reasons to encourage the marketing people to find ways to become agents of the buyer as well.

If marketing is doing its job, potential customers should value the marketing and perhaps even be willing to pay for it. It should be a service they find useful and that offers value. Examples might be advertising that is informative, and that can be trusted to help the potential customer to make good decisions. In business-to-business selling, some of the best salespeople practice consultative selling. They serve as a trusted consultant would in advising the potential buyer. These salespeople may, in fact, recommend a competitor's product if they believe it is the best solution for the customer. In the process, an honest sales force can serve as a seller's early warning system, because sales people are sometimes the first to realize that the seller's product is not good enough, and therefore, that the seller needs to improve the product or be left behind. Sounding that early warning takes honesty and courage—in a word, integrity—but it is not contrary to self-interest.

DISCUSSION AND EXERCISES

1. Why do firms engage in marketing? What are the benefits of successful marketing?
2. Does marketing benefit consumers? Explain your answer.
3. Is marketing an exercise in ethical behavior? How so, or how not?

Chapter 56

Insurance

If you don't want to take the risk of loss, you can insure against it through the purchase of insurance. In some cases, insurance is even legally required.

Think about all of the bad things that could happen to you, things like your car being stolen or wrecked or your house burning down or losing your job and not being able to pay your credit card bill or car payment. You might be surprised to learn that others may be willing to take on this risk. However, they will want to be paid for assuming this risk. Firms that take on this risk in return for payment are referred to as insurers, and you will have a lot to do with them in the years to come.

WHY YOU MAY NEED INSURANCE

Insurance is a form of risk management. If you cannot afford the financial consequences of an event like those described earlier, you may decide that it is worth a relatively small payment to allow you to transfer the risk. All kinds of things are insured by all kinds of people, rich and non-rich alike. No matter what is being insured, though, insurance is the transfer of risk from one party, usually an individual or a business, to another, usually a business.

Insurance carriers assess risk by a variety of characteristics of the person or property being insured. Young drivers, for example, are riskier than older drivers. This is why it costs more for a young person to buy auto insurance than it costs an older person. Once a person has accidents, or gets speeding tickets, that person's rates will also go up. Why? Because that person is a greater risk, and greater risk costs more money. On the other side of the coin, most insurance carriers give a good student discount, because students who do well academically are lower risk drivers. If you live in certain cities where the risk of auto theft is higher, the cost of insurance is higher. Certain types of cars are more costly to repair; they cost more to insure. The same sorts of things are also true for health insurance. Younger people pay less; smokers pay more.

Insurance carriers factor in various risk factors, which means that the more you fit these factors, the riskier your situation is, and the more you will benefit from insurance. You need to consider the cost of both insuring and not insuring, knowing that bad things sometimes happen. You need to consider possible outcomes and potential costs, all the while with an eye on your financial well-being. You may also need insurance because you have debt, or a lien on an asset. When there is debt or a lien, the holder of the debt or lien may require you to have insurance. This is because you are not the only person at risk. Since most people borrow money to purchase a car or a house, auto, home, and even mortgage, insurance may be required as a condition of the loan.

Insurance is a big business. Since there is generally a high need for insurance, there is usually competition for your insurance business. Premiums can vary significantly for the same amount of coverage. It is up to you as a consumer to shop around. And price isn't the only thing that matters. Be sure to check on the reputation of the insurer. Does the insurer make timely and fair payments on claims? Is the insurer financially healthy? Does it have adequate financial reserves to pay claims?

Some people decide they can self-insure. This is where they set aside money each month into a savings or other account to offset any terrible things that may occur. The problem with self-insurance is that terrible things are not spread evenly over time or a population. A tornado might destroy both your house and your car on the same day. You could lose your job a week later (because the tornado also destroyed your employer's factory). Consequently, self-insurance is a high-risk option. One way to balance the risk would be to buy insurance policies that cost less because they have high "deductibles." For example, if you have car insurance that protects your car but has a $1000 **deductible**, that means that if your car is badly damaged, you pay the first $1000 and your insurer covers the rest. By increasing the deductible, or amount you are responsible for in the event of a loss, you are in effect taking on more of the risk, but doing so can lower insurance premiums significantly. It is a tradeoff.

TYPES OF INSURANCE

There are many types of insurance. Some of the more common kinds include automotive insurance (including for trucks or motorcycles), house or property insurance, life insurance, health insurance, burial insurance, credit insurance, and renters' insurance. While there are many kinds of insurance, they all accomplish the same thing: they transfer risk in exchange for money. How much risk you will want to transfer to a company in the form of insurance will vary given the details of your life. When you are young and just starting out, you will likely need less than when you are older, more established, and have more to lose. You will have to reassess your insurance needs continuously as you go through life, so there are no hard and fast rules, only details that change over time.

DISCUSSION AND EXERCISES

1. What should you insure? *When* should you insure?
2. Describe the components of a typical insurance policy.
3. How does self-insurance differ from insurance policies you might purchase? What are the pros and cons of each?

Chapter 57

Break-Even Analysis

When does a course of action become profitable? Knowing when an activity becomes profitable can help with short-term goals and long-term investment strategies. The **break-even point** represents the sales amount—in either unit or revenue terms—that is required to cover total costs. All costs, whether **fixed** or **variable**, need to be considered in determining the break-even point. As a narrowly accounting concept, break-even analysis uses accounting costs only, but later we discuss a broader understanding of break-even analysis that takes other economic costs (specifically opportunity cost) into account when we apply it to long run decisions.

VARIABLE AND FIXED COSTS

There are many ways to classify costs. Here are two broad types:

(1) **Variable costs** rise in direct proportion to unit sales or some other measure of activity (we will assume a linear relationship). For example, your payroll may be 15 percent of each sales dollar (for employees who work on commission), or your advertising could be 3 percent of each sales dollar. Or each unit of a manufactured product may require inputs of $5 in materials and labor.

(2) On the other hand, your **fixed costs** are those that have to be paid regardless of sales volume. This could be for your rent and the insurance on your building, or management salaries paid monthly regardless of sales volume.

BREAK-EVEN QUANTITY

In this simple example, we will assume the business sells only one product at a price (p), and the quantity sold is (q). We use (f) for fixed costs and (vc) for variable costs per unit sold of the product. Assume also that the amount produced per period is equal to the amount sold.

We can now show a profit (π) equation that is sales (price per unit multiplied by number of units sold) minus total cost (variable cost per unit, multiplied by number of units sold, plus fixed cost). More formally this is:

$$\pi = (p \times q) - [(vc \times q) + f]$$

where:
π = *net profit*
p = *price*
q = *quantity*
vc = *variable cost per unit*
f = *fixed cost*

The break-even point is the point at which output is positive and profits are zero.

$$0 = (p \times q) - [(vc \times q) + - f]$$

The break-even point is also where the sales revenue of the firm ($p \times q$) is equal to the total costs ($vc \times q + f$). Thus, we have

$$p \times q = (vc \times q) + f.$$

We continue to solve for the break-even quantity:

$$p \times q - vc \times q = f$$
$$q(p - vc) = f$$
$$q = f/(p - vc)$$

We find the break-even quantity is total fixed cost divided by the difference between price and variable cost. Intuitively, we know that price must be at least as high as variable cost. But now we know that that difference must be large enough to cover all of fixed costs.

A slight manipulation of the last equation tells us that to break-even, average fixed costs must equal the difference in price and variable cost.

$(f/q = p - vc)$

Let us further illustrate with an example. A business has annual fixed costs of $60,000 and variable costs of $20 per unit sold. It has a price per unit of $50. How many units does it need to sell to break even? The answer is:

$Q = \$60,000/(\$50 - \$20)$
$Q = \$60,000/\$30$
$Q = 2000$

The firm needs to sell 2000 units to break even. The value of price less variable cost per unit (p–vc) is often called the **contribution margin**. Up to the break-even point, each unit of sales contributes $30 to cover fixed costs. Once fixed costs are covered (i.e., once you break even), then each additional unit of sales generates the contribution margin as profit.

You can use the break-even formula to examine how different price levels will influence break-even. For instance, with a price of $60 per unit, the break-even would be:

$Q = \$60,000/(\$60 - \$20)$
$Q = \$60,000/\$40$
$Q = 1500$

You need to keep in mind that break-even analysis tells you nothing about whether there is a demand for your product at different prices. What you have learned about supply and demand will provide those sorts of insights. You do not want to get into the situation where you look at the cost structure above and decide to simply set a price of $1020 per unit, because with that price you would only need to sell sixty units of your product: $60,000($1020 − $20) = 60. The question becomes would anyone, let alone sixty people, pay $1020 for your product? In short, you cannot ignore demand when establishing your price.

ADDITIONAL USES OF BREAK-EVEN ANALYSIS

Break-even analysis can be used to help make other business or household decisions. For example, if you are running a business, and your sales manager comes to you and wants to hire an additional salesperson, you have a decision to make. The annual cost of this salesperson, including salary, fringe benefits, and travel costs, are estimated at \$80,000. The product you sell is priced at \$300, and the variable costs are \$200. How much additional product do you need to sell to break even on this added expense? The answer is: \$80,000/(\$300-\$200) or \$80,000/100 or 800 more units would need to be sold to break even on hiring a new salesperson.

Households can also use break-even analysis. We often confront major purchase decisions, such as the purchase of a new car or the installation of a new heating and cooling system. When making this kind of decision, you may want to know the payback of purchasing a more efficient car or heating and cooling system. Consider a \$7000 purchase of a new heating and cooling system. Currently, your average monthly energy bills are \$300 per month and with the new system, the average bill is projected to fall to \$160. How long would it take to break even on this investment? You will be spending \$140 (projected) less per month on your energy bill. That means that it will take 50 months for those savings to repay your initial investment of \$7000. Does that make the initial investment worthwhile? You have to decide, but you might say it is a good investment in the long run. In this case, the long run means 50 months. That is to say, you will break even in 50 months. If you project that the new system will be saving you \$140 per month for ten years, then you are better off (in the long run) making the investment.

DISCUSSION AND EXERCISES

1. Why is break-even analysis important for businesses?
2. How can break-even analysis help in making household decisions?
3. What are the relevant things that break-even analysis *cannot* help to clarify?

Chapter 58

Budgeting

A budget is a useful tool for controlling expenses and debt, and for developing the habit of saving and investing for your future. Everyone can benefit from a budget, and virtually everyone can save and invest for the future.

Households, like businesses, can quickly find themselves in a negative cash flow situation without careful planning. At its heart, a budget is a planning tool. It is a plan to decide today what to do in the future with your expected future income, savings, and expenses.

Because plans are based on expectations, they seldom represent what will, in fact, occur. When you have a budget, though, your income, savings, and expenses are more likely to be what you expect or plan. In fact, a good budget plan includes a contingency for unexpected things that may arise. Since unpleasant surprises can and often do occur, it is important to save and investment for what some call a rainy day.

A rainy day is a time that does not go according to plan: you may have an expensive health crisis, or you may need a new car. If you own a house, the unexpected is just around the corner: sooner or later, you will need to replace your roof, your water heater, and so on.

HOUSEHOLD BUDGET TEMPLATE

All budgets have two major elements: sources of income and uses of income. Usually, income comes from jobs, but it may come from other sources as well, sources like investment income. Some households have a single income, but more often, there are two or more people in the household working. In some situations, a person may hold a full-time and a part-time job.

The uses of income are varied, but primarily include savings, debt payments, utilities, insurances, and household expenses.

As you can see in the budget template below, a budget needs to include every category of expenditure that you have. When you notice that you have spent money on an uncategorized expense, you should revise your budget. Your budget can be monthly, annual, or for any other amount of time you think is appropriate. Your budgeted income should include your after-tax take-home pay and any other money that comes in regularly. Your debt obligations should include all of the debt that you have to make payments on. Beware: debt easily can run as high of 50% or more of your monthly or annual budget. Finally, you should treat savings as you would any other monthly payment, an account into which you put money on a regular basis. If it is useful, you can use an electronic spreadsheet. This can make it easier to revise the budget as new information comes in (Table 58.1).

Always examine each budget period for the actual income and expenses you incur in relation to your projected budget. Where are you overspending? Are you not saving enough? You should have sufficient savings for major contingencies such as the loss of job. Ideally, you will be able to save enough to have at least 6 months of savings in hand to cover your expenses through a time when you have no income. On an annual or more frequent basis, take time to ask yourself: what if I had to cut expenditures 20 percent? What would I cut? Why not cut that expense right now?

Pay particular attention to the interest rate on any mortgage, home equity loan, auto loan, and credit card debt. Usually, the credit card debt has the highest interest cost, and you should avoid just making minimal monthly payments because by the time you pay off the debt, you would have paid several times what you borrowed. Pay off your highest interest obligations first.

The real lesson of budgeting is that there is simply no magic to the process. Money comes in, and money goes out. How you deal with those simple facts will go a long way toward determining how happy you will be, but it is hard work that requires self-discipline. The usual question remains: What kind of life do you want to have?

BUSINESS BUDGET TEMPLATE

A business budget helps you to know what to expect in terms of sales revenue.

A budget for a business is more difficult to develop primarily because the sources of sales revenue are unpredictable. When a member of a household has a job, that person usually receives some fixed wage or salary and unless the person gets fired or quits, the income is fairly reliable. This is not the case for businesses because every sales transaction with a potential customer is uncertain. Perhaps your customer finds a better offer from a competitor, or

Table 58.1. Household budget worksheet

	Monthly	Annual	Comments
INCOME (Take Home)			
Individual #1			
Individual #2			
Other sources			
Total income			
Savings			
Debt obligations			
Mortgage/rent			
Car payment			
Home equity loan			
Real estate taxes			
Credit card payments			
Student loan			
Other debt			
Total debt payments			
Utilities			
Electricity/energy			
Phone			
Internet			
Water and sewer			
Other			
Total utilities			
Insurances			
House/apartment			
Automobile(s)			
Health			
Life			
Service warranty plans			
Total insurances			
Household expenses			
Groceries			
Eating out			
Entertainment			
Household supplies			
Child care			
Clothing			
Auto maintenance/gas			
Gifts			
Charity			
Out of pocket medical			
Subscriptions			
Vacation			
Contingency fund			
Total household expenses			
Total income			
Total savings, debt payments, utilities, insurances, household expenses			
Shortfall			
Additional savings			

can no longer afford your market offering. Customers may just decide to cut back on consumption and save more.

A business budget template is provided. You will note that there are three columns: plan, actual, and actual minus plan. The latter is a control tool. When actual sales revenue is greater than planned, it means sales are higher than planned. Usually, when sales go up so do at least some variable expenses. The key is to look to the bottom line or net profit (after taxes), because if sales have an unexpected rise, but the bottom line is less than planned, then expenses are not being well controlled. Of course, another reason may be that the business cut price on its market offering.

You may also want to review the section on break-even analysis because it provides useful information on how to determine if an expense is variable or fixed. Also in the break-even section, we learned that sales revenue is calculated as price per unit multiplied by the quantity sold. Often a business sells multiple products, and thus you can break down your sales estimate by each product.

Net operating profit is the profit from the normal course of business. Some businesses, however, have unrelated income or expenses. Perhaps they have some extra land they lease, or extra office or warehouse space they rent (Table 58.2). Unrelated expenses may also occur, such as those expenses related to the extra office and warehouse space.

Table 58.2. Business budget template

Revenue & expense categories	Plan (estimated)	Actual	Actual minus plan
Sales revenue			
Expenses			
Cost of goods or services sold			
Gross profit			
SGA			
Non-management personnel			
Management personnel			
Fringe benefits on personnel			
Advertising and promotion			
Equipment rentals			
Legal services			
Rent or occupancy			
Interest expense			
Travel and entertainment			
Communications			
Depreciation			
Other			
Total SGA			
Net operating profit (before taxes)			
Taxes			
Net profit (after taxes)			

SUNK COST

Sunk cost is another concept that is relevant to financial decision making at home and at work.

When deciding what to do next, you compare costs and benefits of your various options. But the cost of the decision you are about to make and the cost of decisions already made in the past are different things. It normally would be a mistake to treat them the same way.

For example, suppose you own a house and now you want to sell because you are moving to another city. Suppose you are offered $200,000 for your house. How would you decide whether to accept the offer? Suppose $200,000 is less than you paid for the house a few years ago. Is that a reason to reject the offer? If you decline the offer because it is less than you paid a few years ago, then you are focused on a sunk cost. Someone who cares about you might say, "You can't think about it that way. You need to sell the house, so the only question that matters is: are you better off having the house, or having $200,000? If you are better off having $200,000, then take the offer. If you are better off having the house, then decline the offer. Either way, what you paid a few years ago is ancient history, and has no bearing on the task of identifying your best option right now."

Costs that have already been paid and cannot be recovered are called **sunk costs**. In general, thinking about sunk costs will not help you decide what to do next.

DISCUSSION AND EXERCISES

1. What information would you need to construct a personal budget?
2. What kinds of decisions could a budget help you make? How would it help in these cases?
3. What are the differences between a personal budget and a business budget?

Chapter 59

Financial Management

Financial statements and accounting data present a real opportunity to make smarter decisions when it comes to your investing opportunities, whether as a business person or a private individual.

FINANCIAL STATEMENT RATIOS

Financial ratio analysis, when done properly, can provide a lot of information and strategic insight into a business, both to assess current performance and to suggest directions for change. Financial ratio analysis is based on the information in accounting statements which reflect economic transactions.

The mechanics of preparing a profit-and-loss statement and balance sheet can be time-consuming, since even a small firm has many transactions to record. But entrepreneurs and business managers can understand their balance sheets and profit-and-loss statements relatively easily by computing various financial ratios. These ratios give insights into how well the business is performing from a financial perspective.

BALANCE SHEET RATIOS

There are two primary financial ratios derived from the balance sheet. These are the **current ratio**, and the **financial leverage ratio**.

The **current ratio** is equal to current assets divided by current liabilities. Remember, these categories include the most liquid assets and the most pressing liabilities. It is always desirable that this ratio is above 1.0, and some firms strive for it to be closer to 2.0. If the ratio is 1.0, it tells us that the firm will have sufficient financial resources over a year to pay its debt or liability obligations that come due in a year. When the ratio is 2, it means that the business has $2 in current assets to support every $1 of liability or debt due within a year. This would give it a large safety margin in paying its financial obligations. Consequently, firms with higher current ratios are more liquid, and thus are less likely to default on their financial obligations.

Financial leverage is the ratio of total assets divided by equity. When a firm has no liabilities (debt), then its financial leverage is 1.0 because all the assets are accounted for as equity. Stated alternatively, for each $1 of equity, the firm has $1 of assets. A financial leverage of 1.0 means the firm is not financially leveraged at all, or it does not use debt to finance assets.

When a firm has a financial leverage ratio of 2.0, it means that $1 of equity results in $2 in assets. In this situation, the firm is financially leveraged. Recall the basic accounting equation where assets equal liabilities plus equity (A = L + E). If $1 of equity results in $2 of assets, then liabilities must be $1. A firm with financial leverage of 2.0 would thus have 50 percent equity and 50 percent liabilities on its balance sheet. Essentially, this informs us that the business owns 50 percent of its assets, and the other 50 percent is financed by debt or liabilities. Most firms in the United States will have a financial leverage of between 1.5 and 3.0. As financial leverage rises, the firm is in a riskier position. This is because a highly leveraged firm needs to make regular large payments on its liabilities and debt. Failure to do so could result in bankruptcy.

PROFIT-AND-LOSS STATEMENT RATIOS

Two common financial ratios computed from the profit-and-loss statement are the **gross profit margin**, and the **net profit margin**.

Taking the revenue of the firm, and subtracting the CGS equals **gross profit**. When this gross profit is divided by sales, it results in what is known as the **gross profit margin**. The gross profit margin is the percent of each dollar of revenue left after paying the cost of producing goods, or providing services. For instance, if a firm has sales of $100,000, and a cost of producing goods or providing services of $60,000, then it has a gross profit of $40,000 ($100,000 − $60,000) or a gross margin of 40 percent ($40,000/$100,000).

Net Profit is equal to sales or revenue minus cost of production, service, and administration (CGS and SGA, as per the chapter on Accounting Basics). The **net profit margin** is net profit divided by sales or revenue.

If a firm has a net profit of $5000 and sales or revenue of $100,000, then its net profit margin is 5 percent ($5000/$100,000). Incidentally, this is the net profit margin before taxes. Taxes must be paid, and are an additional cost of doing business.

Net profit after taxes is as the name implies: net profit minus taxes. The **net after tax profit margin** is obtained by dividing net profit after taxes by total sales or revenue. In the preceding example, if the firm has $2000 in taxes, then its net profit is $3000 ($5000 in net profit less $2000 in taxes). The net profit margin (after taxes) is thus $3000 divided by $100,000 or 3 percent. In the United States, it is not uncommon for businesses to pay between 30 percent and 40 percent combined in local, state, and federal income taxes. Of course, businesses not only pay taxes. They also create jobs, and their employees also pay taxes. Many firms collect sales taxes for the government as well. It is easy to understand why governments seem eager to attract businesses and entrepreneurs to their communities.

THE DUPONT MODEL

The DuPont Model of financial performance is one popular method of combining critical information in the balance sheet and the profit-and-loss statement. The DuPont Model is also often referred to as the strategic profit model. The DuPont model is composed of five financial ratios, two of which have already been defined: the **net profit margin (after taxes)** and the **financial leverage ratio**. The other three ratios are defined below.

Asset turnover is a measure of how productively a firm is using its assets. This ratio takes one key item from the profit-and-loss statement (sales or revenue), and one key item from the balance sheet (total assets). Asset turnover is computed as total sales or revenue divided by total assets. If for example, a firm has $100,000 in sales and $25,000 in assets, then its asset turnover is 4.0. This means that for each dollar of assets, the firm generates $4 in sales or revenue. Firms generally strive for high asset turnover.

Return on assets takes the net profit (after taxes) from the profit and loss statement, and divides it into the total assets from the balance sheet. A firm with $25,000 in total assets and $3000 in net profits (after taxes) would have a return on assets (ROA) of $3000/$25000 or 12 percent. For each dollar of assets, the firm earns 12 cents in profit (after taxes).

Return on equity, also known as ROE, is computed by taking net profit (after taxes) and dividing it by the total equity (as shown on the balance sheet). Consider a firm with $3000 in net profit after taxes and $12,500 in equity. It would have a ROE of $3000/$12,500 or 24 percent.

LINKING THE RATIOS

The five financial ratios that comprise the DuPont or strategic profit model include net profit margin (after taxes), asset turnover, ROA, financial leverage, and ROE. We will show that when the net profit margin (after taxes) is multiplied by asset turnover, the result is ROA. When ROA is multiplied by financial leverage, the result is ROE. For example, a firm with a net profit margin (after taxes) of 3 percent, and an asset turnover of 4.0, will have a ROA of 12 percent (3 percent × 4.0). This ROA, when multiplied by a financial leverage of 2.0, will yield a ROE of 24 percent (12 percent × 2.0).

The DuPont model also informs us that three types of managers are needed. However, one or two people could perform all of the duties required. Often, a single entrepreneur needs to perform all these functions First, **margin managers** are responsible for helping the firm maintain adequate gross and net profit margins. This involves focusing on both revenue generation and expense management. Second, **asset managers** are responsible for helping the firm achieve appropriate levels of asset productivity. This involves focusing on having a mix of assets that is effective in generating sales. Finally, **debt managers** are responsible for making sure the firm properly utilizes debt, and does not take on excessive debt. Both current liabilities and longer-term obligations need to be managed.

The DuPont model also suggests that the primary financial objective should be ROE, or how much profit is generated in relation to the equity invested by owners of the firm. Firms should strive for high-performance results that are often thought of as being in the top 25 percent of their industry in terms of ROE.

Finally, the model shows that there are alternative strategic paths to ROE. Some firms may operate on a low net profit margin but have relatively high asset turnover and modest financial leverage. Other firms may have a high net profit margin, low asset productivity, and high financial leverage. For example, consider two examples of possible pathways to a 24 percent ROE; one firm could have a 3 percent net profit margin, asset turnover of 4.0, and financial leverage of 2.0 (3 percent × 4.0 × 2.0 = 24 percent), whereas another firm could have a 1 percent net profit margin, an asset turnover of 6.0, and financial leverage of 4.0 (1 percent × 6.0 × 4.0 = 24 percent).

DISCUSSION AND EXERCISES

1. Draw a figure to represent the DuPont model.
2. The U.S. Securities and Exchange Commission (SEC) regulates the financial securities of publicly held and traded corporations. All of these corporations are required to regularly file audited financial statements with the SEC regularly. To learn more about how to search for and use filings with the SEC, you should take the EDGAR Tutorial (www.sec.gov). Once you are comfortable with how to use EDGAR, download the financial

statements for a corporation that might be of interest to you. Apply your learning and compute the five financial ratios for the DuPont Model.

3. What can you learn from a firm's profit margin?
4. What does return on equity measure? Why is this important?

Part VII

INNOVATION AND ENTREPRENEURSHIP

Innovation and entrepreneurship are deeply related concepts in commercial society. Indeed, they are inextricably linked. Ideas are the beginnings of great entrepreneurial ventures, but they are only the beginnings. Innovation has to be operationalized, and entrepreneurs are pivotal in both identifying new possibilities and in bringing those possibilities, ultimately, to market.

Chapter 60

Knowledge Discovery

> The whole [scientific] process resembles biological evolution. A problem
> is like an ecological niche, and a theory is like a gene or a species which
> is being tested for viability in that niche.
>
> —David Deutsch

Physicist David Deutsch once remarked, "The whole [scientific] process resembles biological evolution . . . . A problem is like an ecological niche, and a theory is like a gene or a species which is being tested for viability in that niche." Similarly, an opportunity is a market niche, and an offering is like a gene or species that is being tested for viability in the market niche.

The entrepreneur is thus not unlike a scientist in this sense. Both advance knowledge. Markets and science advance society in fundamentally the same way. They enable the failure of theories and the hypotheses that drive those theories, thus advancing human knowledge.

THE ENTREPRENEUR AS A SCIENTIST

Both the scientist and entrepreneur begin by questioning the world around them. Their questions often come from an acute ability to observe the world. The entrepreneur may question why customers are not buying a firm's offering, or why they have switched to a competitor. Or they may observe that individuals do not have a solution to a common problem. The entrepreneur then develops a theory that explains what he has observed. Of course, most entrepreneurs do not think in terms of developing a theory, but they do something very similar if not essentially identical to the scientist. They develop an explanation for what they observe. These explanations are often of the "if A, then B" variety. These often take the form of "if I develop a product with these attributes, then customers will purchase that product." Entrepreneurs then test their hypotheses, not in the laboratory, but in the marketplace. They may do a test market or pursue full-scale commercialization, but in either case, they gather empirical data, which they then analyze to either confirm or refute their hypothesis. Regardless of whether the hypothesis is confirmed or rejected, the level of knowledge in society increases. As a result of this test, we know what works and what doesn't. If something does not work, the entrepreneur modifies his theory and makes another offering to be tested in the crucible of market reality.

HOW HUMANS LEARN

You may argue that not everyone needs to be a scientist or an entrepreneur to advance knowledge. Learning occurs throughout life by all of us, and as we grow older, we become more knowledgeable. Of course, we know that some of us become more knowledgeable than others, just as we also know that some scientists make more discoveries, and some entrepreneurs are better than others at seeing and providing what people want and need.

In a market economy, most individuals have many market offerings and need to choose among them. Generally, neither consumers nor producers are forced or told what choices to make in the market. Predictably, there are institutions that are put in place in society that may restrict or take some choice away from actors. Sales of tobacco, firearms, and liquor are forbidden to minors, for example. Generally speaking, though, markets are quite free and open, and it is because of this openness that people learn how to serve each other better. Of course, some businesses learn more quickly than others, just as some businesspeople and entrepreneurs learn more quickly than their peers. In every instance, those who learn quickest become more knowledgeable, and they are the ones best able to succeed in a market economy.

DISCUSSION AND EXERCISE

How are entrepreneurs like scientists? What is the role of the market?

Chapter 61

It Takes More Than Ideas

To succeed as an entrepreneur, it takes more than ideas and more than an invention; it takes innovation that changes how people do things. The best entrepreneurs see possibilities for novel market offerings that others do not see. It is not hard to find people who see how products could be better. We all do that. The entrepreneur is the one who acts on such ideas.

Ideas, especially novel ideas, are the beginnings of potentially great entrepreneurial ventures. Nonetheless, even the best idea is worth little or nothing until translated into an invention. This is the point at which most potential entrepreneurs fail. Ideas are not enough. To make people better off, ideas have to be brought to market.

Inventing is a crucial step along the way from idea to reality. An invention could be a tangible thing or a new piece of software or website. Regardless, every invention should be thought of in terms of the service it will provide to potential users. This focus on service to the user, early in the process, can aid in the design process, which may involve developing, testing, and evaluating a series of prototypes.

If you are an inventor, you may obtain a patent to protect your intellectual property. Note, however, you cannot go to the U.S. patent office and obtain a patent on an idea. What you need is an engineering or design drawing and a detailed description of the process to make the invention. To obtain a patent, your design needs to be novel, and not violate other people's intellectual property. Of course, you do not have to patent your invention. You may try to keep it secret, or you may believe society is better off if you don't patent but instead let others freely copy your design or take key pieces and try to improve upon it.

Thousands of devices are invented each year. Many are awarded patents. As of June 1995, a U.S. registered patent has a twenty-year life, which gives the inventor exclusive rights to its use. The inventor can then decide to enter the market with the invention. An inventor can enter the market by selling a component (the invention), or an integrated systems solution. An inventor of an artificial knee could sell it to knee surgeons as a component of the service that surgeons provide. Alternatively, an inventor could sell a knee replacement system consisting of the knee, plus the tools for inserting and aligning the knee. This could be coupled with a five-year warranty backed by an insurance policy to cover knee replacement if needed. The inventor could also license the technology in the patent. This would grant another party a right to use the technology for a fee.

Another option is to neither go to market nor license. A surprising number of patents are never used.

If the inventor or entrepreneur takes the invention to market, through sale or licensing, and it is adopted by customers, then an innovation has occurred. Innovations are determined in the crucible of market reality. Stated alternatively, if the invention is not adopted, there is no innovation. When acceptance is strong, it attracts competitors, often with superior offerings. The entrepreneur cannot sit and rest on the success of an innovation, because these successes are always short-lived in a dynamic and rapidly changing world.

TYPES OF INNOVATION

It is useful to categorize the types of innovation. However, let us first note that many firms set aside part of their annual budget for research and development (R&D). In most industries, a few small percentage of sales is spent on R&D, but in some industries such as pharmaceuticals and semiconductors, it could be as high as from 10–20 percent of every sales dollar. In brief, R&D is, and will continue to be, a big business. There is also R&D at major research universities around the world, and from this new business firms emerge.

Most innovations are incremental. They make small changes in a market offering, and consequently have minimal impact on how people live. Examples of this could include a change in the formulation of a laundry detergent to improve its cleaning ability, or a change in a cereal to improve its nutritional value. We often see incremental innovations on a continuous basis such as with the annual models of new automobiles. Most companies participate in *incremental* innovation.

Another, riskier type of innovation is radical or *disruptive* innovation. It is discontinuous, and not what people expected or predicted. These innovations are the big surprises that disrupt an industry. Notable examples are the steam engine, telephone, automobile, and personal computer. They disrupt because they change how people live. The disrupter is not necessarily the person with the idea or even the invention; it is the person who successfully brings the idea to market.

DISCUSSION AND EXERCISES

1. Learn more about the process of patenting at the U.S. Patent Office website (http://www.uspto.gov).
2. Discuss the morality of disruptive innovations. Suppose you are expecting to make a perfectly good living making horseshoes, or buggy whips, only to see your life plan ruined by the invention of the "horseless carriage." Perhaps you learned the craft from your parents, and expected to pass that craft to your children. You expected that life would go on in the same way, and now your dream is shattered. You and all the other buggy whip makers all need to find another way. It is easy for someone to say your comfort zone does not define the moral limits of progress. But you have a response, which is to say that you never said the world owes you a living. You spent a lifetime becoming a master craftsman in a kind of career that has suddenly become a thing of the past. Your mind and your hands hold a world of expertise, and for your lifetime of commitment to excellence to suddenly seem worthless—well, it hurts. What is a society to do? It seems obviously wrong to hold back progress, but it also seems wrong to simply leave formerly skilled workers with nothing to do.
3. How should those disrupted workers respond? What, if anything, should communities do to enable disrupted workers to get back on their feet, and renew their faith in their own ability to contribute to their communities in dignified and productive ways? Suppose you were a mayor or a minister or a teacher in a small town whose main employer was a manufacturer of key punch cards, or something that suddenly has no customers and closes down. For that matter, what if you were an inventor, considering the idea of buying that otherwise abandoned factory and putting it to some other use? What would be the right thing to do?

Chapter 62

What Innovation Looks Like

Innovation is not a predictable and linear process, but rather is irregular and surprising. There are many moving parts and unseen factors in any attempt to innovate. Innovation is unpredictable and risky.

If you want to play it safe, then you had better not pursue innovation. Innovation is about designing the future, which is inherently unpredictable. It is unpredictable, in part, because as the innovator is designing new ways of doing things, so are other people. Increasingly the playing field for innovation is global, which makes it even more uncertain.

PLANNING FOR INNOVATION

Unpredictability does not mean that organizations or entrepreneurs should not have an innovation plan. Many organizations use a stage gate model, which is a model of multiple stages, where at the end of each stage, a hypothetical gate is opened that allows movement to the next stage.

THE SIX STEPS IN THE STAGE GATE MODEL

Identification of needs or problems. An innovation should solve a problem. Often inventors get heavily involved in making a new device without asking themselves what the job to be done by the new device, and what need it addresses. Employees, suppliers, and customers can be a source of ideas for new market offerings.

Research. Often there is no existing solution to a problem because more knowledge needs to be developed. The knowledge can be about the natural world or the social world.

Development. At this stage, a working prototype of the device or offering needs to be developed. This is the stage where the firm or individual considers obtaining a patent.

Commercialization. To find out whether an invention is useful, it almost always needs to be commercialized. Commercialization involves taking the new offering to market. This requires four primary decisions: final product form and packaging, distribution or marketing, promotion, and pricing. It is also important at this stage to identify the target market for the offering. At this stage, the firm tries to estimate sales revenue as well as production and distribution/marketing cost.

Diffusion and adoption. After the commercialization, the market offering begins to diffuse as more and more buyers adopt.

Evaluation of results. Evaluation typically involves comparing expected sales and costs, and consequently profit and loss, to actual results.

As stated earlier, innovation is not predictable. For instance, in the research phase, new knowledge may trigger ideas for solving other problems and needs. Or, as the offering is adopted, the firm may find out that the purchasers are not in the intended target market, and thus may need to adjust its marketing strategy. The evaluation of results may even trigger a redesign of the offering, or a change in the price.

Innovation is inherently risky. A company may evaluate one hundred ideas to get one that it judges worth moving to the research stage. Ideas may also fail as they move through development to commercialization. Most new product launches, even after extensive and costly research and development, fail because they are not sufficiently diffused and adopted to be economically viable.

TWO RESPONSES TO A CHANGING WORLD

You are entering an uncertain world. Over the next several decades, the human species will experience an unprecedented level of innovation and change. Many industries will be disrupted. Some will disappear altogether. To whom will your knowledge, skills, and capabilities be of service? If you are like most people, your best answer to that question will change several times over the course of your life.

Exploitation. One option may be to exploit what you know, along with your skills and capabilities. You reason that no matter how the world around you changes, if you are good at what you do, there will always be a demand for your services. The world will surprise you, but you will survive.

Firms facing the forces of change may decide that they have a well-recognized brand, established marketing channels, and a loyal customer base. Thus, getting even better at what they do best will assure them success. In the process, they may make incremental or continuous innovations that help to drive down cost or expand revenue. It sounds like a safe strategy.

Exploration. A second option is to become an explorer. This is where you go beyond what you know, and beyond your current skills, learn about new things, and develop new skills. Predictably, because the world is filled with surprises and uncertainty, you are not quite sure where to focus your new learning and skill development. Consequently, to lower your risk, you make multiple investments in different areas of knowledge and skill development. Take a moment: What are some of your options right now?

Exploration is also a common option. Many experts will tell firms to stick to their core competencies, to the things they are already good at. In many situations, though, that may be bad advice. It is not unusual for firms to explore, and often they can do this by hiring people with different knowledge and different skill sets. At other times they may make a small acquisition that exposes the larger firm to a newly emerging industry.

Entrepreneurs are known for exploring new avenues. Entrepreneurs may become bored, and decide to sell or put someone else in charge so they can explore new areas. Most entrepreneurs are inherently curious, and thus thrive on learning new things. New learning often leads to perspectives and insights that can stimulate a great entrepreneurial idea.

THE AMBIDEXTROUS OPTION

In an uncertain world, it is hard to know whether to exploit or explore. A third option is to do both. An ambidextrous individual, entrepreneur, or firm continues to exploit and refine existing knowledge and skills but also explores by investing in new knowledge and skills.

The more turbulent the world in which you operate, the more you would choose to put exploration ahead of exploitation. In more stable worlds, you would put exploitation ahead of exploration. In *our* world, though, an ambidextrous approach will help to balance competing potential risks and rewards.

DISCUSSION AND EXERCISES

1. How can you know whether developing new skills is the right approach as opposed to sticking with your strengths?
2. Assess the relative merits of exploitation and exploration in your own life right now.
3. What are the relative strengths of the ambidextrous approach? Its weaknesses?

Chapter 63

Entry, Exit, and the Role of Profit

The short and long run are conceptual time periods. They will be different intervals of time depending on the business or industry in question.

In the **long run**, there are no fixed factors of production. In other words, every factor is variable. For example, there are no binding contracts, no set suppliers, no production capacities of a specific factory. There are no constraints on changing the output level by changing the capital stock, workforce, or even entering or exiting an industry.

The long run contrasts with the **short run**, in which some factors are variable and others are fixed. In the short run, a firm may be constrained from entering or exiting an industry. An example of a short-run question decision would be something like, "Given the size of my factory and the prevailing price in the market for my product, how much should I produce?"

When there are no barriers to enter or exit a market, firms will enter when profits are positive and exit when profits are negative. When profits lead firms to enter the market, prices will fall, eroding profits in the industry. Under these conditions, higher cost, less efficient firms will typically be the first to exit, because they will be the first to start losing money as prices fall.

Depending on a firm's cost of production and market price for its product, it will either make an economic profit, break-even, or make a negative economic profit. Economic profit is simply a firm's revenue minus its cost (that is, opportunity cost plus explicit monetary cost). This is subtly different from accounting profit, which is a firm's revenue minus only monetary costs. Economic profit is a more nuanced measure that takes into account a fuller understanding of the cost of doing business.

If a new cost-saving technology is discovered, a firm can produce more at lower costs. At current prices, this will allow it to enjoy higher economic profits than it earned before the cost savings. Should the firm switch over to the new technology? Other things equal, the switch promises to be profitable in the long run. What about the short run?

In the long run, positive economic profits are the signal to potential entrants that operating in that particular market is a productive use of resources. Entry will shift the market demand curve to the right and cause the price to fall. A falling price will cause profits to decrease for firms participating in that market. Entry will persist and prices will fall until no firm is making positive economic profits.

If the most profitable firms in an industry are breaking even with **economic profits of zero**, there is no further incentive to enter that market. There is also no long-run incentive to exit the industry, because zero economic profits imply that the opportunity cost of staying in the market is taken into consideration.

If a firm is making **negative economic profits**, it will exit the market in the long run. However, it may continue to produce in the short run. Simply put, if the firm is better off operating at a loss than shutting down, it will stay in business until it has an opportunity to exit. If the firm shuts down in the short run, it will have certain fixed expenses that it will still need to pay. These are commonly known as fixed costs (FC). By shutting down, the firm saves the expenses that vary directly with production. These are commonly referred to as variable costs (VC). Remember, when a firm shuts down, it also loses the revenue it was collecting from customers through sales.

By comparing the outcomes of shutting down (output = 0) and continuing to operate (output = x), a firm, in the short run, can make the best decision.

Profit (output = 0) = − FC
Profit (output = x) = Revenue − FC − VC

The firm will take the action with the higher profit. It will shut down if output = 0 yields a higher profit.

− FC > Revenue − FC − VC
or, VC > Revenue

If the firm cannot cover its variable cost, it will shut down. However, if a firm's revenue is higher than its variable cost, that means it can cover all of its variable cost, plus some of its fixed costs if it stays in business. That is better than taking a loss of all the fixed costs.

DISCUSSION AND EXERCISES

1. In economic terms, what distinguishes the short run from the long run?
2. What are some examples of sunk costs? Should these costs influence your future decisions?
3. How does profit influence a firm's decision to enter or exit a market?
4. What is meant by zero economic profit? Is zero economic profit desirable or undesirable? For whom?

Chapter 64

Creative Destruction

Disruptive innovators blow away outdated methods of production in what economist Joseph Schumpeter called a perpetual gale of creative destruction. Journalists and other social commentators report on the "funerals" of old-fashioned jobs. The standard example is the buggy-whip manufacturers who went out of business as automobiles overtook the horse and buggy. There is never any shortage of companies that fail to adjust to changing times. When the farm became mechanized over hundred years ago, it was a common fear that the farm workers being displaced would not have jobs. Particular jobs in farming were undoubtedly lost, but other jobs were created. Journalists and social commentators rarely talk about those new jobs. New jobs are not much of a story, so they become "unseen benefits" of a sort, analogous to the unseen costs that we discussed earlier.

Today, we see similar anxieties regarding robotic factories. Will robots displace workers? Of course! At the micro level, we can indeed see the loss of direct factory production jobs. But the larger or macro view shows a growth in jobs. Jobs in software design, maintenance and repair, computers, and the growth of jobs related to supporting higher levels of sales revenue brought about by lower cost production are the largely unseen benefits of the shift in these markets. Few people now mourn the loss of Blockbuster Video. Streaming services like Netflix, Hulu, and Amazon Prime made video stores obsolete.

Creative destruction is the process by which innovation disrupts markets and industries, and where the new methods drive out old ones. This driving out of the old is the heart of the dynamics of commercial society.

In figure 64.1, we illustrate the process of creative destruction. It is driven by disruptive innovation, which is the child of the entrepreneur.

The process of creative destruction can be viewed as a wave. A disruptive innovation starts small then builds to a larger wave, finally crashing down as another wave begins to take its place. The process never ends.

Disruptive innovation results in the dislodging of dominant practices. In turn, this results in skills and jobs becoming outmoded, complete with the loss of jobs. Predictably, this makes room for new skills and new jobs. We then witness related industries being impacted, and finally the proliferation of new dominant practices.

For example, consider the invention of the automobile around the beginning of the twentieth century. In the United States, the automobile replaced the horse-drawn carriage, and was initially called the "horseless carriage." Before this, the "horsepower" that powered the movement of wagons had

Figure 64.1.   Stimulus-response learning

literally been supplied by horses: untold thousands of horses in every city, needing to be fed and cared for (and cleaned up after) by untold thousands of workers. With the emergence of the automobile, all these thousands of workers had to develop new skills in new industries, including (of course) car manufacturing. Tires, batteries, and spark plugs all needed to become industries unto themselves, in service of the automobile. Further, automobiles were expensive and dangerous, so we created more jobs in finance and insurance. The automobile also required highways, gas stations, and repair shops. All of this resulted in new institutions and even a new culture. What we now call "suburbia" is a child of the automobile, as it became possible to plan lives around homes many miles from our places of work. And none of this even begins to address the many wonderful things that drive-through windows have brought into our lives. Incredibly, the computer is now emerging as a technology that will change how we live even more than the automobile did. Already, for many of us, computer technology has made it possible for our place of business to have no specific physical location. Our work can be simply "in the cloud" as they say.

THE ENTREPRENEUR

The wheel of creative destruction shows where the entrepreneur's agency is brought to bear on markets, and this happens in two separate steps. The most important, of course, is in providing the disruptive innovation itself, which is what starts the process in the first place. This leads to some effects: dominant practices are dislodged, and outmoded skills and jobs are lost. But then, the entrepreneur's agency is felt yet again, this time as new skills and jobs are gained. This, in turn, leads to still more effects. Other industries are impacted, and new dominant practices proliferate. And just when you think everything is settled and all is well, the whole process begins again. All of this is driven by the entrepreneur.

Entrepreneurs take upon themselves risks that others run away from. When they create something novel and integrate all of the resources needed to offer it to others, they are taking a risk. There are no guarantees. They often get up early and stay up late, worrying about how to meet payroll, cover household expenses, secure loans, convince investors, and learn and deal with applicable laws and regulations, all the while anticipating that no matter how good their product is, it is just a matter of time before the competition dreams up something better. Sometimes they have terrifyingly bad days. It goes with the territory.

DISCUSSION AND EXERCISES

1. What is created in the process of creative destruction? What is destroyed?
2. What are some examples of creative destruction that you have observed? What have been the consequences?
3. Is innovation always disruptive?

Chapter 65

Entrepreneurs as Resource Integrators

While the forces that entrepreneurs unleash result in creative destruction, entrepreneurs are themselves resource integrators at heart. They take on risk to explore what lies beyond the resources that prospective customers currently possess. Entrepreneurs aim to access and integrate resources that will enable them to offer customers a new and valuable service.

Entrepreneurs always seem to be a hot topic in the popular press, and even in everyday conversation. When we hear the word "entrepreneur," we typically think of people like Henry Ford, the founder of the Ford Motor Company; Sam Walton, the founder of Walmart; Oprah Winfrey; Steve Jobs and Stephen Wozniak, co-founders of Apple; Coco Chanel; or Martha Stewart. But most entrepreneurs are not famous, and they are everywhere. Ordinary entrepreneurs are the engines of economic growth.

Not all businesspeople are entrepreneurs. What separates them? Here is a handy list of characteristics:

- Entrepreneurs identify opportunities to serve the needs of others.
- Entrepreneurs are on the lookout for new ideas and new resources, and new uses for old ones.
- Entrepreneurs ask how they might access and integrate all of the resources needed to be able to offer customers a service that customers will value.
- Entrepreneurs take on risk that often others are not willing or able to assume.

These are the characteristics of the entrepreneur. Any business enterprise can have an entrepreneurial orientation or spirit. Entrepreneurial firms: (1) regularly explore new opportunities to better serve customers, (2) are open minded regarding the nature of resources and how to obtain them, (3) identify

ways to integrate resources in creative ways to produce or operate more effectively, and, (4) acknowledge and accept risks associated with the preceding.

A business that avoids this kind of risk would be characterized as more
conservatively operated. A business that embraces the risk/reward equation
that goes with investing in new ideas is, to that extent, an entrepreneurial
enterprise. Conservative firms react to opportunities; entrepreneurial firms
create opportunities. An entrepreneurial firm is more proactive than reactive.

We say these things in order to describe entrepreneurship, not glorify it.
Risk management is an ongoing key to successful business. Obviously, there
is a time and place for a more conservative approach.

TWO FUNCTIONS OF THE ENTREPRENEUR

An entrepreneur has two functions. Performing these functions successfully
benefits others (including employees, suppliers, customers, and the government) along with the entrepreneur.

First, entrepreneurs innovate. Innovations are new ways of doing something. Sometimes innovations are intangible, like when someone creates a
new process such as saving time and money by shipping an entire intact truck
instead of boxed merchandise.

Second, entrepreneurs create customers. People become customers when
entrepreneurs make a compelling value proposition.

CONFRONTING RISK

Entrepreneurs, as we suggested, accept risk. To innovate and to create customers requires thinking about the customer as a potential beneficiary. It also
requires overcoming resource constraints along with knowledge, skill, and
technological limitations. There is a real risk of failure at every step. Often,
entrepreneurs fail initially, then find a way to survive and carry on.

To give a small but important example of an innovation in developing tools
for managing risk, traders in Amsterdam invented calls and puts in the early
seventeenth century. A **call** is an option to buy, and a **put** is an option to sell
a stock or commodity at a specified price. In other words, suppose you own
shares in a company where the shares are valued at $75. You might give your
agent a standing order to buy more shares in the company if the price falls
to $50, and perhaps also to sell your shares in the company if the price ever
rises to $100. The conditional order to buy at $50 is a **call**, and the conditional
order to sell at $100 is a **put**. Calls and puts give traders tools for managing
investment risk in general and market volatility in particular.

An entrepreneur is a resource integrator. Inventions and innovations are combinations of existing resources. Things that today we take for granted, such as the wheel, eyeglasses, or the bicycle, took a long time to develop and represented many rounds of combining and recombining resources in clever ways that ultimately resulted in an innovation that offered significant benefits to people. This process is sometimes called combinatorial innovation. An innovation is an integration of existing resources. The automobile can be integrated with a restaurant to create a drive-through window for ordering and paying for breakfast. Or the automobile can be integrated with remote sensors and geo-positioning software to create a driverless car. The list is limited, in the end, only by human creativity.

DISCUSSION AND EXERCISES

1. What does it mean to "integrate resources"?
2. How does an entrepreneurial firm differ from a conservative firm?
3. What are the primary functions of an entrepreneur? How does the entrepreneur accomplish these functions?

Chapter 66

Entrepreneurship as a Process

Entrepreneurs—the ones who last—tend not to be reckless. The risks they take are calculated. Going in, they want to make sure that they will be able to handle the downside, and they want to make sure that the likely upside is worth the risk. All entrepreneurs deal with incomplete information about customers, technologies, and other external factors. They never know for sure how potential customers will respond to new possibilities, or whether the cost of delivering a promising new technology will drop far enough to make the new technology commercially viable.

Consider why there is so much risk and uncertainty in an entrepreneur's world in the first place. Chess is a simple game. There are only a handful of rules, and they are well defined. Even so, the game involves more than one player. That alone makes the game of chess a radically uncertain domain. Now imagine that there are millions of other players, and imagine that some of the squares on the board are so far away that the best you can do is look them up on a map. Imagine further that the rules are somewhat loose, and there is nothing to stop the more entrepreneurial players from inventing new ways of moving around the board. Science can study this world and identify all kinds of interesting patterns, but it will never be able to make this world highly predictable. It will never tell you something as straightforward as, for example, what the exact price of oil will be a week from now. However, the science and the logic of economics can tell you some things. Economic logic can tell you that if you increase the money supply, prices will rise, all other things being equal, just as the cost of borrowing money will rise, other things being equal. But it cannot tell you that other things will, in fact, be equal. As each entrepreneur commits resources and makes his or her next move, thousands or millions of others are doing likewise. Thus, the market system is inherently dynamic and uncertain. Economics cannot be an exact science, nor should we expect it to be. The world in which entrepreneurs live is predictable in many ways, but even so, every day brings relevant and sometimes costly surprises.

Next, we can identify, describe, and explain the seven separate and distinct steps of the entrepreneurial process. Please note that although we describe seven sequential steps, entrepreneurs go back and forth among the steps, often skipping steps to return to them later. In short, the steps are an integrated set that comprises a whole. The first three of the seven begin with the entrepreneur asking three important questions.

1. ***Who are we?*** This question can place realistic bounds on the space that the entrepreneur explores for invention and innovation. If I am a young person in Kansas City with passionate interests in food and dining, that can help me sort out what sort of entrepreneurial life I want. I might think that curing breast cancer is far more important than opening another restaurant in Kansas City, but that does not mean that I am in any position to help cure breast cancer. Who I am and what I can do are often more relevant than abstract questions about what it would be good for someone to do.
2. ***What do we know?*** This question puts realistic bounds on the space you explore for invention and innovation. Generally, you will make fewer mistakes and take less risk in areas where you are skilled and knowledgeable. If you grew up in Kansas City and your parents ran a restaurant, then what you already know about the city becomes a major resource for you.
3. ***Whom do we know?*** Answering this question helps to determine the extent to which the entrepreneur can draw upon family, friends, acquaintances, and other social connections to get access to resources. These resources could be financial assistance, knowledge and expertise, potential employees, or suppliers. Successful entrepreneurs are especially successful at using their networks to bring together resources in order to lower risk.

Through the process of answering these three important questions, who we are, what we know, and whom we know, the entrepreneur begins to restrict the areas or spaces where he or she may pursue an entrepreneurial endeavor. When taken together, these three questions give us a sense of what we can do, what we, in particular, are in a position to accomplish, and what we, in particular, have to offer to our community.

4. ***Interactions with other people.*** Once you know what you want to do, you will want help. In fact, one of the key resources the entrepreneur integrates with other resources is people. Interacting with others may allow you to raise initial financial resources, or test the validity of your idea with potential customers and suppliers. In many communities, there are angel investor clubs where groups of individuals with prior entrepreneurial and investing experience come together to network and provide expertise and financial support to promising entrepreneurial ventures. Angel investor clubs are an excellent way to interact with people who may help you with your venture.

Interacting with others also allows you to expand your network. The people you know may not have the necessary expertise or connections, but they may know people who do.

Many entrepreneurs need some space and connections, and thus may seek an **incubator**. An incubator is a facility where entrepreneurs temporarily reside along with other entrepreneurs and advisors to develop their business plans and proofs of concept. A **proof of concept** is a demonstration that there is a viable market and demand for your proposed offering. Many communities have incubators that charge little or no rent for a limited time.

5. ***Stakeholder commitments.*** Entrepreneurs make commitments to stakeholders as they go. You may take on a partner and thus agree to particular terms of ownership or shared responsibility. You may recruit and hire employees. You probably need banking or financial services, leading to a whole category of commitments. Similarly, you may commit to various suppliers and distributors (who help take your offering to market). Deciding to locate your business in a particular community is a commitment to that community.

6. ***New means.*** To an entrepreneur, it always seems that "if there is a will, there is a way." There are always pathways or means to achieve goals. The world is complex, of course, so there will always be uncertainty and risk. However, as entrepreneurs interact and make stakeholder commitments, they discover new means. For example, an investor may see a better way to go to market or know a less expensive supplier. An employee may see a different engineering solution. An alert entrepreneur is always listening and learning something new.

7. ***New goals.*** When new possibilities emerge, new opportunities can emerge along with them. New tools expand the realm of possibility. Thus, when we discover better ways to approach an old goal, those new tools and capabilities can prompt us to develop more ambitious goals too. Finding a better way to do something we want to do can leave us with better things to do.

Perhaps the entrepreneur has the goal of being the most efficient and thus lowest cost provider of a service. Over time, he or she may discover new pathways to achieve that goal. In the process, though, an entrepreneur may find that potential customers care less about low price and more about finding a high-quality solution to their problem. With this new knowledge, the entrepreneur may shift away from efficiency and toward effectiveness, thereby better satisfying the customer.

DISCUSSION AND EXERCISES

1. How do the first three questions an entrepreneur asks help to define his efforts?
2. How do the remaining four steps help to focus an entrepreneur's activity?
3. How do entrepreneurs mitigate risk?

Chapter 67

Creating Markets

What exactly is a market? In a way, this is a hard question, because people use the word in different ways. However, one key point is that a market is not exactly a thing. A market is a process. In any marketplace, the main thing that you observe is a process of people buying and selling. You see people offering, negotiating, and ultimately, deciding. If all goes well, there is an offer, then there is uptake, and a deal has been made.

Behind all this, a marketplace at its best involves people respecting each other in a particular way. Specifically, the idea of offer and uptake—of buying and selling—presupposes that people have a right to say no and walk away. Services transfer only if buyer and seller each consent. When people relate only by consent, they are treating each other as self-owners. Respecting persons—treating them as persons—starts with respecting their right to say no. If you want your business to succeed, you need to make people feel safe doing business with you. It all starts with making them understand that you will respect their right to say no, no matter what.

Note that the freedom of choice we are talking about is bilateral. Both buyer and seller have a right to walk away if what they are being offered is not good enough. The bilateral right to say no enables people (as buyers) to look for something better to buy, and motivates people (as sellers) to look for something better to sell.

In a standard market transaction between informed adults, anything and everything can go wrong, but usually the deal-making works out pretty well. Typically people go home without major regret about having bought or sold something. More often than not, when we venture to marketplaces as we experience them in the real world, we find what we are looking for, and at a price we are willing to pay. Admittedly, sometimes we are disappointed. We fail to find what we are looking for and come home empty-handed. Or we make a deal but decide in retrospect that the product is not what we thought it was, and that we should not have bought it after all.

More oddly, sometimes the greater disappointment is that we learn in retrospect that we could have gotten a better deal. Why is that odd? Because that kind of disappointment consists in finding not that the marketplace had *less* to offer than we expected, but that it had more. We learn our lesson, chalk it up to experience, and go back to market resolving to do better, not because product was not worth what we paid but because we now know that the market was offering something even better.

Blockbuster Video was a spectacularly successful business for a time. Now Blockbuster is gone and no one misses it. Blockbuster was not able to lobby, legislate, or otherwise protect itself from market forces. It was not able to make streaming illegal (on the pretext that streaming would come at the cost of thousands of American jobs or damage the fabric of American culture). Perhaps Blockbuster did not even try to protect itself in that reprehensible way. In any case, as it actually happened, the gale of creative destruction that is the marketplace was able to find better use for resources otherwise wasted on an obsolete product.

In a nutshell, the essence of markets at their observable best, and the exact reason why markets are places where societies make progress, is (1) customers can sort out best options, and (2) providers of bad products lack the option of blocking access to better options.

At their observable worst, by contrast, markets are captured by crony capitalists (or crony unions). We sometimes observe companies and products that are heavily subsidized, massively expensive, and obsolete—protected from international competition that would otherwise blow them away on the field of product price and quality. At their best, markets leave it to customers to sort out the merits of services offered by companies such as Blockbuster Video. We don't let industry regulators decide that Blockbuster Video is too big to fail. Decisions like that are too important to be left to regulators. It is actual paying customers who have the right and responsibility to make decisions like that.

Notice that the market is a process of constant change.Ask yourself, was there a market for internal combustion automobiles in 1890, televisions in 1920, artificial hips and knees in 1960, personal computers in 1970, the computer mouse in 1980, the Internet in 1990, the smartphone in 2000? All of these markets were created and probably none of them will last forever.

CREATING VALUE

It is tempting to view entrepreneurs as creators of value. They invent, integrate, develop a service, and create customers. Undoubtedly, the entrepreneur is a key contributor to the creation of value. However, because entrepreneurs draw upon different types of resources and many of these are created or developed by others, it is reasonable to see value as co-created, with the entrepreneur as the primary resource integrator.

A common belief is that value resides in tangible objects, but value is actually similar to resources in that it is a function of human appraisal. Imagine that you are at an art museum at which you and a friend are viewing a painting. After viewing the painting, you and your friend discuss the experience, only to find that you loved the painting, but your friend hated it. From a material or tangible standpoint, we know that you and your friend were looking at the same work of art. If we asked what you would pay for the painting, you might be willing to pay $10,000, while your friend would rather destroy it than own it. Recall our earlier discussion of subjective value.

A firm or seller cannot provide the potential customer with value; they can only make a value proposition. A value proposition is a promise of some benefit associated with a market offering. Firms and sellers, however, compete, and the potential customer is confronted with a sea of competing value propositions. Firms must compete in providing a relatively more attractive or appealing value proposition. There are several types of value that might be emphasized in a value proposition.

VALUE EXPLORED

There are at least four types of value that a firm can emphasize in its value proposition. These are value in exchange, value in use, value in context, and value in achievement.

Value in Exchange. Perhaps the most popular type of value that is emphasized in a value proposition is simply the price of the market offering. Price is the value in exchange, or the amount of money that a buyer gives up to acquire a market offering. In the United States, you have probably observed that price advertising is very common, but it is hard to successfully compete successfully on price alone. This is because it is often easy for competitors to copy your value proposition if it is heavily focused on price.

Value in Use. Few individuals obtain value at the point of trade or transaction, where they pay immediately or with credit. What most people receive value from is in the use of a market offering. Perhaps you have acquired a new SUV that can easily seat your family of four, and also transport your dog and plenty of other things if need be. The SUV company probably will likely advertise and promote this vehicle showing how convenient it is to use on a daily basis.

Thus part of the utility being promised is flexibility of use.

Value in Context. The use of market offerings always has a contextual nature. Think of context as the other actors and resources that are associated with the use of market offering. Many firms, when they advertise and promote their value proposition for their market offering, will emphasize certain contexts that may have special appeal. For example, if their target market is middle-aged families with children, they may show the SUV loaded with family members and their dog going on a camping trip. Thus, the focus is on use value, but in a specific context.

Value in Achievement. People acquire goods and other market offerings to do a job. Getting that job done is often the focus of promotion and advertising. In focusing on value in achievement, it is common to look for the higher order needs to be filled. The value achieved is never about what the firm makes in the factory. It is about how people feel a sense of achievement from the use of the market offering. For cosmetics, it may be achieving hope; for a motorcycle, it may be the achievement of personal freedom; and for a fine dining experience, it may be the achievement of deeply connecting with family or friends.

PRICING FLEXIBILITY

When there is high value to the customer, you can charge a higher price. Price is determined in part by demand, that is, what the customer is willing to pay. Hopefully this covers your costs. Customers couldn't care less about your costs, of course. What they care about is the value they obtain from your market offering. A seller's pricing flexibility is determined by the difference between the seller's cost and the value to his or her customer. Ideally, sellers want to create an offering with a lot of pricing flexibility.

Marketing can enhance a value proposition. By building a brand image, a firm can differentiate itself from competitors. Branding of this nature protects a seller to some degree from price competition, and provides more pricing flexibility. If value propositions are effective, customers obtain value not only from a tangible product, but from an extended product that embodies many intangibles.

DISCUSSION AND EXERCISES

1. What are the four kinds of value? How are they different?
2. How are markets fixed? How are they not fixed? What can an entrepreneur do with this information?
3. How is value co-created?

Chapter 68

Competitive Advantage: The Dynamics of Remaining Viable

Firms are known to compete along two dimensions: being more efficient (lower relative resource costs), and being more effective (relatively more appealing value propositions). For each dimension, a firm can be in three states: advantage, parity, and disadvantage. The interaction of three states across both dimensions results in nine states represented in the competitive advantage matrix below.

There are three states of competitive disadvantage. These are shown in the upper left corner of the matrix. Similarly, there are three states of competitive advantage, shown in the lower right corner. A situation of neither advantage nor disadvantage occurs in the middle of the matrix, where the firm is at parity on relative resource costs and appealing value proposition. The lower left corner (low relative appeal of value proposition and low relative resource cost) is uncertain in terms of advantage or disadvantage, and the upper right corner (high relative appeal of value proposition and high relative resource cost) is also unclear regarding advantage or disadvantage.

Firms that find themselves in the lower left area of the matrix need drastic strategic and operational revival; they need to both improve their cost position and their value proposition. If they fail to do so, they will fail in a competitive market. Firms in the upper right area of the matrix are in a sort of ideal or nirvana situation but need to protect that position because others will try to advance their own competitive advantage. Firms that learn fast and apply this learning and knowledge will be better able to maintain their competitive advantage (Figure 68.1).

		LOWER	PARITY	HIGHER
Relative resource cost	HIGHER	C.Dis	C.Dis	?
	PARITY	C.Dis	parity	C.Adv
	LOWER	?	C.Adv	C.Adv
		Relative Value Proposition		

Figure 68.1. The competitive advantage matrix (Shelby D. Hunt)[1]

DISCUSSION AND EXERCISES

1. What is competitive advantage? What does it entail?
2. What should entrepreneurs consider to determine whether their products have competitive advantages or disadvantages?
3. What does it mean for a firm to be in parity with other firms? Can such a firm be successful?

---

1. Shelby D. Hunt. "Market Segmentation Strategy, Competitive Advantage, and Public Policy," *Australasian Marketing Journal* 12 (2004): 7–25.

Chapter 69

The Big Errors

Surviving as a business in a dynamically competitive environment requires that the firm continuously innovate. As we reviewed earlier, this innovation can be focused on developing a relatively more appealing value proposition and developing an advantage in relative resource cost. As entrepreneurs strive to innovate, they tend to make three major errors.

FAILED VALUE PROPOSITION

Often, the value proposition that a firm develops is not in tune with what customers want. A firm can think too much about what it does best within the firm, and too little about how its market offering enables customers to achieve things they could not otherwise achieve. A good value proposition creates a sort of glue that binds the customer to the firm's offering. Some experts refer to this as customer engagement. A compelling value proposition invites engagement from the customer.

TIME TO MARKET

Firms typically face a lot of competition. This means that competitors are always trying to innovate and outsmart each other with a more appealing value proposition or lower relative resource cost. Here is the problem: some firms work too hard to develop the perfect new market offering. In striving for perfection, they take too long to get to market with their innovation. In fact, in some firms, the accountants unnecessarily slow down the process and may often kill new venture projects so they never get to market. Increasingly, firms need to respond quickly and learn continuously how to improve without becoming obsessed with perfection.

TECHNOLOGY FOCUS

Some firms focus on customers. Some focus on technology: on how new technologies can dramatically improve a market offering. There can be a tendency to over-engineer the product to enable it to do too many things that customers may neither need nor want. Engineers need to learn to be customer focused. Engineers can also understand how customers use products and understand that customers can be a valuable source of new product ideas.

DISCUSSION AND EXERCISES

1. What are some of the pitfalls an entrepreneur must avoid to be successful?
2. Why might successful firms continue to innovate?
3. Why do many firms lose sight of their own customers as they bring products to market?

Chapter 70

The Entrepreneur and Self-Assessment

Some entrepreneurs may appear to be arrogant, but consistently successful entrepreneurs are not over-confident, and they are not self-absorbed. They understand the basic value proposition. That is, they are political animals, so they understand that being successful in life involves building a place for themselves in a community of other political animals. They want something from other people. A big part of what they want is *to be wanted*. They want other people to know and appreciate what they do to be of service. They want other people to be aware of what they do to make sure that their community is better off with them than without them.

YOU HAVE A LOT TO LIVE FOR

We often hear older and wiser people saying things like "you have your whole life ahead of you" or "you have so much to live for." These clichés are meant to be reassuring, of course, but it can be irritating to have to nod your head as if this is some great insight. You know that they are just trying to help. You know perfectly well that there is an important grain of truth in the clichés, too, but you already know that having a lot to live for does not come easy. To have a lot to live for is to have a purpose, and having a purpose is an achievement. It is not the sort of thing you can take for granted.

You have seen people blow it, and you know that could happen to anyone. You know that the life of a pure consumer is not a way of having a lot to live for. You know people who have every imaginable consumer good. Some of them seem pretty happy, and in a way, they should be. But you also know that some of them are miserable, living empty lives.

Some people do better than that. Some people are not only rich. They also have outlandish otherworldly talent as entertainers. They are treated as idols. What they do on a stage or a football field inspires millions. It sounds glorious. Then you read that they committed suicide, or died of an unbelievably careless drug overdose. Wealth, even when combined with fame, is not enough. Not even close. Evidently, it does not even guarantee the most basic self-respect.

What else does it take? What are you really looking for? We know this is not an easy question. We know because we are all in the same boat.

What does it take for you to be able to get up in the morning wanting to give thanks for the fact that you have this day—this incredible gift of one more day of not-to-be-wasted life on this earth? What does it take for you to know in your bones that this is *your* day?

We told you that there would be a test. You will be taking that test every day for the rest of your life. But as we said at the beginning, we like your chances.

DISCUSSION AND EXERCISES

1. What kind of enterprise would you like to work for? Why?
2. What kind of enterprise might you like to be in charge of some day? Why?
3. What will you remember as your finest hour? What will the people around you remember?
4. What is the best thing about you, right now? What will be the best thing about you twenty, thirty, forty years from now? Advice: Do not be humble about this! If you don't see a seed of greatness somewhere inside you, look harder. That seed may not look like an oak tree yet, but it's in there somewhere.

Index

About the Authors

Cathleen Johnson is an experimental economist. She works in three main areas: behavioral aspects of investment and social norms, implementation of large research projects and research teams, and teaching economics through the use of laboratory experiments. For her Ph.D. in economics (Virginia Tech, 2000), she combined work from the areas of game theory and graph theory to develop models of social networks, norms and social capital. Her experimental work focuses on applications of network theory to models of network formation and in-depth work on time preferences, risk aversion and interaction and exchange and literacy.

She has designed and implemented several large-scale, innovative field studies that examined individual investment in post-secondary education in Canada. This work led her to develop experimental instruments for measuring inter-temporal and risk preferences, developing state of the art adaptive and graphical techniques. She also used lab-in-the-field experimental methods to measure inter-personal preferences, and time and risk preferences among Houston high school students and Mexican villagers.

She has developed a large body of experimental protocols for teaching economic concepts, designs experiments for policy makers, and has run the Office of Economic Education at the University of Arizona. She also serves on the board of Arizona's Council for Economic Education.

She has published in economic journals such as *Games and Economic Behavior, Journal of Risk and Uncertainty,* and *Journal of Economic Behavior and Organization.*

Robert Lusch (1949–2017) was Professor of Marketing, Pamela and James Muzzy Chair in Entrepreneurship, and Executive Director of the McGuire Center for Entrepreneurship at the University of Arizona. He formerly served as Dean of the College of Business Administration at the University of Oklahoma and at the M.J. Neely School of Business at Texas Christian University. Professor Lusch was an active scholar in the field of marketing strategy, services marketing, and marketing theory. He was editor of the oldest scholarly journal in marketing, the *Journal of Marketing*. He authored or coauthored 20 books and over 150 articles, including (with Steve Vargo), *Service-Dominant Logic: Premises, Prospects and Promises*. The National Association of Accountants awarded him the Lybrand's Bronze Medal for contributions to accounting literature. The Academy of Marketing Science awarded him its Distinguished Marketing Educator Award. The American Marketing Association gave him its IOSIG Lifetime Achievement Award, its Sheth Foundation Award for contributions to marketing literature, its Irwin/ McGraw-Hill Distinguished Marketing Educator Award, and its Harold Maynard Award (twice, in 1997 and 2005) for contributions to marketing theory. The Marketing Management Association has honored him with an award for Creative Career Contributions in Marketing.

David Schmidtz (http://davidschmidtz.com) is Kendrick Professor of Philosophy and Eller Chair of Service-Dominant Logic in the McGuire Center for Entrepreneurship at the University of Arizona. He is the founder of the Department of Political Economy & Moral Science, Professor of Economics by courtesy, and founding Director of the Center for Philosophy of Freedom. In his field of political philosophy, the University of Arizona has been ranked as the #1 program in the world since 2011. He also is editor in chief of *Social Philosophy & Policy*, which by subscriber base is the largest philosophy journal in the English-speaking world. His published works have so far been reprinted 97 times, in 13 languages, and are featured on hundreds of college syllabi around the world.

Made in the USA
Las Vegas, NV
21 August 2023

76409473R00208